Veterans of
Iraq and Afghanistan

Personal Accounts of
22 Americans Who Served

HARRY SPILLER

McFarland & Company, Inc., Publishers
Jefferson, North Carolina, and London

LIBRARY OF CONGRESS CATALOGUING-IN-PUBLICATION DATA

Spiller, Harry, 1945–
    Veterans of Iraq and Afghanistan : personal accounts of 22
Americans who served / Harry Spiller.
        p.   cm.
        Includes index.

    ISBN 978-0-7864-4869-2
    softcover : acid free paper ∞

    1. Iraq War, 2003–2011—Personal narratives, American.
    2. Afghan War, 2001– —Personal narratives, American.
    3. United States—Armed Forces—Biography.   4. Soldiers—
    United States—Biography.   I. Title.
    DS79.766.A1S65 2014
    956.7044'30922—dc23   2013037438

BRITISH LIBRARY CATALOGUING DATA ARE AVAILABLE

On the cover: The police mentor team Iron Horse in Helmand
Province, Afghanistan, 2009, from left: two unidentified Afghan
Civil Order Police Officers, SFC Thomas Verdorn, SPC Jeffery
Daily, SPC Daniel Baker, SSG Robert McGuire, Cpl. Benjamin
Chapman, Sgt. Robert Mocoby, Sgt. Dustin Cade, SPC Pete Oye
and dog Kimmy, SSG Randy Thacker, SPC Brent Corzine, Sgt.
Ryan Norman, ANCOP Major Noddler, Interpreter Vodka, SFC
Edward Sadler, Interpreter Shotgun, and an unidentified Afghan
Civil Order Police Officer (courtesy Daniel Baker)

Manufactured in the United States of America

McFarland & Company, Inc., Publishers
  Box 611, Jefferson, North Carolina 28640
  www.mcfarlandpub.com

For Tara

Acknowledgments

I would like to thank all the Afghanistan and Iraq veterans who shared their stories for this book. I would like also to thank Jenifer Wilkins for her typing assistance with the voice recorder, and always a special thanks to Candice Lahr of CATASBOOKS@ YAHOO.COM for her editorial assistance.

Table of Contents

Introduction

In retaliation for the September 11, 2001, attack on the United States, U.S. Armed Forces began air attacks against Al Qaeda and Taliban military camps and bases in Afghanistan. On October 19, the first combat troop paratroopers were dropped in that country.

On March 19, 2003, American and British forces began the invasion of Iraq. The U.S. government called the conflict "Operation Iraqi Freedom." There are several basic reasons for the war. First, there was lingering tension and hostility from the Gulf War of 1991 in which Iraqi occupation troops were forced out of Kuwait. Second, the Iraqi government agreed to surrender or destroy several types of weapons, including SCUD missiles and various weapons of mass destruction. Third, there were two "no fly zones" established over northern and southern Iraq for the protection of Iraqi minority groups who were in opposition to the Saddam Hussein government. Allied planes patrolled these areas, and over the years Iraqi air defense forces fired missiles and other weapons at the allied planes, mostly American and British, in unsuccessful attempts to shoot them down. Fourth, following the attacks on the United States on September 11, 2001, President George W. Bush implied an Iraqi connection with Al-Qaeda using the potential threat of Saddam supplying weapons of mass destruction (WMDs) to terrorists attacking the United States.

On March 19, 2003, at 5:34 A.M., U.S. Stealth bombers and Tomahawk cruise missiles struck leading targets in and around the Iraqi capital, Baghdad, to begin the second major war between the United States–led coalition and Saddam Hussein's Iraq. Soon thereafter, air attacks began against Iraqi targets in southern Iraq, followed by missile attacks from Iraq toward U.S. military positions in the Kuwaiti desert.

On the first full day of the war, March 20, U.S. and British ground forces advanced into southern Iraq, entering the port city of Umm Qasr, near the major Iraqi city of Basra, while a second wave of air attacks hit Baghdad. Resistance from the Iraqi militia known as the Saddam Fedayeen caused several casualties to U.S. and British troops.

By March 23, Coalition forces had seized H-2 and H-3, airfields in western Iraq, and controlled parts of Umm Qasr, Basra, and Nasiriyah. Forces had advanced to within 100 miles of Baghdad and forced a crossing of the Euphrates River at Nasiriyah, where Iraqi forces put up a stiff fight. In northern Iraq, the U.S. launched an attack with 40 to 50 cruise missiles on forces of two Islamist parties opposed to the pro-U.S. Patriotic Union of Kurdistan. Also on March 23, U.S. forces began airlifting troops into Kurdish-controlled northern Iraq.

On March 27 fierce fighting erupted in the city of Samawah, where U.S. forces were faced by approximately 1,500 Iraqi irregulars at a vital bridge over the Euphrates River. U.S. forces took control of the bridge and continued the advance to Baghdad. In northern Iraq, approximately 2,000 paratroopers of the U.S Army's 173rd Airborne Brigade parachuted onto an airfield in order to open a northern front against the Iraqi forces.

On March 29, the 10th day of the war, U.S forces had advanced as far north as Karbala, where major battles took place with Iraqi forces. Bombing raids on Baghdad and other Iraqi cities continued, as did Iraqi attempts to hit Kuwaiti-based targets with surface to surface missiles. The first suicide bombing on Coalition forces took place, killing four American troops at Najaf.

From March 30 until May 1, 2003, the Coalition forces continued the advance. They reached the outskirts of Saddam International Airport on April 3. U.S. armored forces entered Baghdad and conducted a large raid. By April 9, U.S. forces were in control of Baghdad. A small crowd of Iraqi citizens cheered as U.S. Marines helped them tear down a statue of Saddam in the center of the city. The speed of the victory astounded the Arab world.

The victory was followed by looting as well as destruction brought by Coalition bombings. The Baghdad museum and other institutions were looted of priceless archeological finds, and Mosul University was trashed by looters. It became evident that the U.S. had allowed large quantities of explosives and nuclear materials to disappear from sites. Several thousand tons of explosives disappeared from an Al Qaeda base and presumably fell into the hands of Iraqi resistance. Resistance to the U.S. occupation grew. Angry crowds gathered and chanted "No to Saddam. No to Bush" and other such slogans. The crowds were incited by Sunni and Shia imams who told them that the war was being waged to protect Israel.

By April 22, the situation had calmed sufficiently to allow a huge traditional pilgrimage of Shiite Muslims to their shrine in Karbala. This was the first such pilgrimage on foot allowed in many years. The pilgrims were grateful for their freedom and cursed Saddam, but not many connected their newfound freedom with gratitude for the U.S.

Critics of the war continued to point out that no definitive evidence of weapons of mass destruction, the reason for the war, had been found at all. U.S. teams continued to search for evidence of WMDs, finding clues and promising leads. Several reports determined that there were no WMDs in Iraq and probably had been none before the war. Intelligence suggested that Iraq had been purchasing aluminum tubes and other materials for a nuclear weapons program and was intent on creating an atomic bomb. It turned out that the intelligence was based on forgeries and inventions of detectors, and may have been improvised by U.S. government officials anxious to find a rationale for invading Iraq.

U.S. and British forces did uncover evidence of the brutality and corruption of Saddam Hussein's regime, including mass graves for thousands of political prisoners and huge stashes of cash amounting to hundreds of millions of dollars. Intelligence documents implicated Russian and German intelligence in aiding and abetting Saddam. Subsequently, these charges proved to be unfounded, but many other politicians and businessmen were shown to have created bribes from the Saddam regime in the form of oil coupons.

France and Germany, formerly outspoken and bitter critics of the war, initially hurried to align themselves with the United States in the hope of participating in lucrative postwar reconstruction contracts, but were disappointed when the U.S. and the provisional Iraqi ruling council announced that no bids for reconstruction would be given to France or Germany. Europe again distanced itself from the war when it became apparent that the U.S. would not succeed in restoring order quickly in Iraq, and President Jacques Chirac of France continued to insist that the war and U.S. occupation were illegal.

Some of Iraq's Muslim neighbors, in particular Syria, were quite bitter at the U.S. victory. President Bashar al-Assad of Syria said the Arab people would resist the Iraqi occupation. The Pentagon reported that Syria sent busloads of Arab fighters, including Palestinians, returning Iraqis, Egyptians and others into Iraq. Syria denied these allegations, but the U.S. captured many non–Iraqi fighters in Iraq and determined they were coming from Syria.

On May 1, 2003, President Bush declared the war over. The U.S. had still not succeeded in installing an interim government, despite two meetings held for this purpose. Some services were restored in the destroyed cities of Iraq, but numerous people remained destitute. In Fallujah, anti–U.S. riots broke out and marines were forced to fire on crowds on different occasions, resulting in about twenty civilian deaths.

In June, the U.S. announced that, because of internal rivalries, it was giving up on the plan to have Iraq form a provisional government and would instead appoint a government. This interim government began in July, but bombing and sabotage continued, and reconstruction work lagged behind forecasts. U.S. morale was increased when Saddam's son Uday and Qusay were killed in a shootout with U.S. troops, but Saddam remained at large throughout the summer, despite a huge monetary reward for information leading to his capture. A number of videotapes supposedly made by Saddam were aired. An explosion in the Shia holy city of Najaf killed an important Shiite religious leader and over ninety other worshippers. Another explosion at a UN compound killed twenty more. Not a day passed without some act of violence against U.S. troops or Iraqis who supported them or were opposed to the Saddam regime. The Coalition failed to find any evidence of weapons of mass destruction, and in August 2003, evidence emerged that the U.S. and British officials had distorted intelligence estimates to help make a case that there were WMDs still in Iraq.

UN Security Resolution 1511, on Iraq, recognized the legitimacy of the Coalition-appointed interim government, while calling for a timetable for Iraqi self-government. The Coalition announced that Iraq self-government would be achieved in June 2004, though the Coalition forces would remain in Iraq.

On December 13, 2003, U.S. forces captured Saddam Hussein alive in a small underground hideout. No shots were fired during the capture. Saddam had grown long hair and a beard. Provisional-government officials promised that Saddam would be tried for crimes against the Iraqi people. He was finally tried, convicted and executed.

From that time the war continued until December 18, 2011, when the last combat troops were withdrawn from Iraq. However, the war has continued in Afghanistan. Over this period many men and women have served in combat in Afghanistan and Iraq. The purpose of this book is to reveal their experiences as military combat personnel in country. This book contains twenty-two accounts of men and women who have fought in the Afghanistan/Iraq war. The information about their experiences came from taped interviews, written questionnaires, official military documents, or documents the interviewees gave me between 2009 and 2012. These stories are real, they are compelling, and they give a true picture of life as a combat veteran in the Afghanistan/Iraq War.

CHAPTER 1

Sergeant Lindsay Griffith

Army National Guard: 88M Transport

IRAQ • OCTOBER 2004–OCTOBER 2005

We were mobilized in August 2004 and went to Fort McGuire for two months of training — different battle drills and classes on the Iraq culture. Then we deployed in October 2004 and when we got to Iraq they told us to forget everything that they had taught us because by the time we got there battle tactics had changed.

Our missions were to transport all kinds of equipment all over Iraq to different units. We also transported trash, but I could never understand why they would make us risk our lives to get rid of trash, but we would get a mission which would consist of about twenty army people and then we would get TCNs [third-country nationals] from Egypt and Pakistan and other countries considered as our allies and they would go with us. We would have them drive trucks also, so we would have army and TCNs driving in the convoys. It was a challenge because most of them could not speak English. We would have to learn how to use our hands to communicate with them which was difficult because they used different hand language too. They usually drove three trucks to our one.

We would usually go pick up our load at one of the ports and then haul it into Kuwait, then into Iraq. The missions would last anywhere from a week to three weeks, depending on where the battles were going on or where we were going.

We got hit during the convoys. There were a lot of roadside bombs that went off. We had a lot of damage to trucks. There was one mission we went on to Karma. We went there and were almost back to camp about five or ten miles out of camp and an IED [improvised explosive device] went off and the two trucks directly behind me got hit. The guy in the truck directly behind me got hit in the chest. We stopped and I ran back to the truck. When I got into the truck you could see where the shrapnel had gone through the engine and through the entire truck. They are powerful explosives. I don't know how they are made, but they are full of shrapnel. An insurgent will be watching and somehow they will take a cell phone and have it coordinated to where they can call the bomb and it goes off.

We lost a girl in our unit and she had actually taken my mission. I was supposed to go and she begged to go. Because when you're sitting back at the camp there is nothing to do. It was February and she was in the truck with another guy and they were running a mission. She got hit by an IED. A few minutes before she got hit she had been the driver and had switched with the other soldier she was with. The bomb went off and hit the passenger side. She was gone instantly. She took the direct hit from the bomb. It took the other soldier's foot off. It is scary as hell how close it was to having been me, but I believe everything happens for a reason. I think that when it is your time it is your time regardless of where you are.

I never got hit. You didn't have to worry about that in Kuwait. Once in a while they would find a bomb on the base, but very rarely would they go off. I can only remember once that one did and nobody was hurt. But there were camps in Iraq where we stayed that would get hit. We got mortared a lot. One night we were staying outside at a camp about 20 miles from Baghdad and we were mortared. We counted 14 mortar rounds that came in on us. I also was fired at by small arms fire. We were outside this camp at about two in the morning waiting to get in and we started getting small arms fire. No one was hit though.

There are a few guys in the army that want to give girls a hard time. There have been cases of rape, not in my unit, but in other units there have been cases of rape. There are some guys that are going to say stuff they shouldn't to us, but I learned to handle myself real well. The TCNs that we ran with I had a hard time with. There were several that tried to come up and touch me and put their hands on me and want me to have sex with them. They obviously have no respect for women and they admit it. There was one guy that came up to me and started rubbing my leg. We had just got done with the mission and back to the camp. I was sitting in the truck and reading. I had the door open and had my feet propped up minding my own business and this guy comes up and starts rubbing my leg. I said, "Hey, what are you doing?" He starts making some hand gestures and I said, "I am reading a book, what do you mean?" And after about ten times trying to communicate with him he points to my crotch and then his. He wanted to have sex.

There are a few men that think women shouldn't be in the military and they give you more of a hard time and more extra duty just to see if we can handle it. Then there were the guys who thought we couldn't do anything so they tried to do everything for us. I didn't like that either. Then it seemed that the males always had everything right there for them. Like the showers, they were always right by where the men slept. The females had to walk to get to their showers.

I don't think we should be there. In 2005, we set out to get a new government established and stable. I'm not going to say it is stable, but it is there. They are going to have to learn to function on their own and all they are doing is killing each other. We are just in the middle. I don't see how us staying there and getting troops killed is going to help. There have always been religious wars in that area.

I wasn't involved in training the Iraqi soldiers, but don't think it is a good idea to teach them everything we know. They just run around and use it against us. We would train the Iraqis and then hand over the main checkpoints on the roads. Some of the checkpoints would be our soldiers and Iraqis and some would be just them. The insurgents took over a checkpoint that the Iraqis were guarding without a shot. The Iraqis had plenty of men to protect the checkpoint, but the insurgents just took it over. The Iraqis just let them do it. They were on the insurgents' side.

The living conditions we had were horrible. The temperature was 130 degrees with 100 degrees of humidity. You walked outside and were immediately drenched. It wasn't just the humidity. Your clothes would just stick to you. There were lots of sandstorms. All the camps I was at had a Burger King and Pizza Hut. Most of the living quarters were tents.

When I came back it had an effect on me. I had anxiety. When I would hear loud noises it would scare the shit out of me. I have had a lot of anger. Every time I see a foreigner I get pissed off even though I know I'm in the States and have nothing to worry about. But I am still angry. I had appointments with a doctor for about six months after I came back. It helped a lot. I mean a lot. Everyone needs to see a doctor for a month or two when they have been there. It is going to affect some people more than others, but it is always going to affect everyone to some degree.

I know God was watching over me. I can probably count seven or eight times that IEDs went off either directly behind my truck or a couple of seconds after I passed them. I mean I had so many bombs blow up close and I never got hurt once. There were some close calls that I almost shit my pants. I am just glad to be home now and safe.

CHAPTER 2

Corporal Jesse R. Hines

U.S. Marine Corps: 2nd Battalion, Fox Company, 1st Platoon, 8th Marines

IRAQ • MARCH 22, 2003–MAY 9, 2003

I arrived in Kuwait on March 22, 2003. We departed on CH-46 helicopters and landed in the middle of nowhere. They dropped us off and there was nothing anywhere. Engineers had just started to bulldoze big mounds of dirt for protection. There was nobody around. It was a long time before I was face to face with any Arab people. The only people we saw were the people that helped us out at the chow hall. They helped us set up tents and the whole time we were in Kuwait we were in tent city. There were just rows and rows of tents. What we were doing was getting adjusted and training to learn Arabic, learning urban patrolling, and working on our procedures such as taking down houses during fire missions and various training exercises for infantry. A lot of PT [physical training], which helped us get ready for the battlefields we would be fighting in.

We loaded up all our extra gear and rode out in trucks. We rode all day. The first night we stayed in Kuwait and the next morning we were in Iraq. It took another days' drive into Iraq. All the time that we drove, it was through [a] desert area, no cities or anything. We slept next to our vehicles at night. We would get out and set up a defensive position in the middle of nowhere.

I will always remember the first night we were firing off a Patriot missile and it was the first time I had ever seen one. I was impressed with how cool it looked. Lighting up the sky it was real live shit I was looking at. Then I started to realize why these missiles were going off. They intercepted missiles in the air. Then I realized that we were having missiles fired at us and I didn't think it was so cool anymore.

The third day we got in the trucks and started out again. Our orders were to bypass Basra and relieve our buddies unit, 1st Battalion, 2nd Marines, in Basra on the southern bridge of the Euphrates River. It was the morning of March 23, 2003, and we were parked right outside the city and we were waiting to receive orders to go in. 1st Battalion had just recently been ambushed. They went straight through the city instead of going around it and were hit. They got separated from the trucks in front of them when they were ambushed. They were getting hit pretty hard. The rest of their unit abandoned the bridge and went in to help them out. When they did we took over the bridge. We were the lead company in the battalion and my platoon was the lead for the formation. I was one or two trucks behind the head of the formation. As we were driving in we saw a lot of enemy tanks and trucks burning. None of our tanks were burning, but some of the trucks and convoys were being hit. We could see forty-six helicopters flying out casualties. I thought, "This is what I wanted," and realized it was the real deal.

We stopped about five hundred yards from the bridge and dismounted. We were supposed to clear everything from our position to the bridge. For the first five minutes we weren't even getting fired at. It was the first time that we had heard rounds being fired other than at a rifle range. We were in high intensity. All we were supposed to do was to get on line and move forward, but for several minutes it was nothing but chaos. We were trying to move forward with no communications and finally we loaded back up into the trucks and moved to the bridge and got it together.

The whole time I was in the truck moving toward the bridge all I could think of was my dad. He was in a truck in Vietnam and was shot in the arm. That just kept running through my mind. We got out of the trucks when we got to the bridge and the truck was facing the bridge parallel with it. I set my guys in position and gave them sectors of fire. I told them to hold fast and that I would be back with orders. I went back to my lieutenant and the word was we were going to sit in position for the night. Nothing happened that night.

The next morning we moved our position from the left side of the road to the right side. We started receiving fire, heavy fire. All at once I had to take a shit. I thought, "If I don't, I am going to shit my pants." The staff sergeant came running by me and I stopped him and said, "I got to take a shit." He looked at me and said, "What you want from me?" I grabbed a roll of shit paper and ran behind one of the trucks. I took off my uniform and dumped with rounds being fired over my head. I finished and returned to my position. Shortly after that the shooting stopped.

We moved our platoon closer to the bridge and we covered the right front area from the bridge. We found a dirt mound or put our packs in front of us for protection. There was a little house inside our perimeter. There was a hospital about one hundred yards in front of me. It was fenced in and had sandbag bunkers on top of it. Me and several other leaders were going to check the hospital out, but then decided not to. There were people going to and from the back side of the hospital. It all seemed okay and we let it go for the day.

The next day I was standing behind my men on the perimeter talking to them and all of a sudden there is this explosion about thirty yards out in front of me. It really startled me and I thought, "What the hell was that?" Then the first squad of our platoon, which was on perimeter near the riverfront, started getting hit hard from a houseboat across the river. Then a second explosion hit about twenty yards in front of us. A third shell went off about fifteen yards out and I moved my guys down to the first squad to help them against the houseboat.

The only people left on my side of the road now was myself and a machine gun unit. I took off running and told them to get out of their position and go to the other side of the road. There was fighting going on the other side, but no shelling. Just as we got across the road a shell went off exactly where the machine gun position had been. As we were going down the other side of the road a shell went off in the middle of the road. It knocked us down and we rolled and got up. One of the guys in front of me looked at me and looked like he had seen a ghost. We took positions on the right end of the perimeter and shortly after that the firing stopped.

After it was over I started smoking cigarettes one after the other. Then slowly I started coming down from the high. It was the best feeling I ever had in my life. As I look back at it now I liked every bit of the intensity. I wanted more. My captain came by and I was chain smoking. He asked how I was doing and I told him fine. He said keep up the good work, I was doing a fine job.

Not five minutes after the attack was over, the captain comes up and says we are going to go get the hospital. We had gotten shot at from the hospital a little, but not much. I was with the breach team. First squad was the assault team with third squad in reserve. I was in the front headed toward the hospital and heard over the radio, "Hines, get the fuck over there." I start off in my medal of honor run and rounds start going off. There was a perfect spot in front of the hospital to set up, and I set my men in and we started firing at the hospital. I didn't see any enemy, but we kept firing while our demo guys were rigging up some explosives to blow a hole in the fence. They set the explosives and came running back, saying fire in the hole. I will never

Cpl. Jesse Hines with children near Fallujah, Iraq, in 2003 (Jesse Hines).

forget it. Everybody quit firing and put their heads down for several seconds and everything went silent. Then suddenly the explosives went off, but it didn't blow a big enough hole. One of the demo guys says, "That won't happen again," and brings up a lot of C-4 and blew a big hole.

We get into the compound and then the hospital. One of the guys shot the metal door with a rifle grenade. The grenade didn't knock out the door, but the shrapnel from the grenade blows back and hits him in the eye. We finally get the door open and start clearing the hospital. We had to take every corner not knowing if there would be an Iraqi soldier. We cleared room by room and flushed five Iraqi soldiers out the back of the hospital. Gulf Company killed them all.

We took the hospital and found jail cells in it. It had large numbers of gas masks and an armory. Torture rooms with beds and frames with car batteries hooked to the frames. We went to the top of the building and the staff sergeant took the Iraqi flag down and gave it to me.

Then we set up a defensive position in the hospital and the small buildings outside the hospital. We had a couple of machine guns sitting out. We started eating and suddenly an AK round came through the building and zipped by. Nothing else happened, but it was scary. We sat there for a couple of hours and then the lieutenant colonel came and congratulated us and then withdrew us from our positions and sent us back to the original positions we were in. I don't know why he done that, but the next day people went back into the hospital and we had to take the hospital again. We took it without any problem the next time.

After that we pushed our defense further out past the hospital and we had several houses inside our perimeter which we took control of. Then we get the word to dig in and bed down. We stayed there for two weeks and ran combat patrols around the villages in front of us. We didn't engage much after that.

Our use of force was, if we got shot at then you shoot at them. Then it went from that to any adult carrying a weapon. Then to any kid with a rifle and then down to anybody in the area because we had loudspeakers blaring out Arabic, telling them to get out of the area. Before we took the hospital we were still getting shots from the hospital. I can remember this one guy trying to make a run from the hospital to the road. For the first time I fired my rifle. During the whole time we were under attack I had never fired my rifle because I was directing my platoon. I had everyone set in and I saw this guy and I put my rifle to my shoulder, and right before I did I thought, this is the first time I was going to put my rifle to my shoulder and I was looking above my sights and that's when you get that moment. That's when you find out if you can pull the trigger or not. The one big test that any rifleman wants to know is if they have it in them. You'll never know unless you are put in a situation. Lucky that happened to me at a moment where life and death wasn't put directly in front of me. It took me about five seconds to deal with it then I executed. I aimed in and fired about seven or eight rounds. I don't know if I hit him. I never saw his body after I shot.

CHAPTER 3

Corporal Neal Brown

U.S. Marine Corps: Caat Platoon, 3rd Battalion, 4th Marines

IRAQ • FEBRUARY 11, 2002–FEBRUARY 11, 2006

March 19 the war broke out. We crossed over into Basra and I watched south point hill getting lit up. We took the left flank while the British troops and the 1st Army took the highway. A little way down the road we began to take tank fire from the enemy. The tanks were just dug in and used like artillery by the Iraqis. Corporal Drake, my toe gunner, fired a TOW missile and hit one of the tanks. Two other TOW gunners fired, but because they were so far away missed the tanks. Corporal Drake began firing again and hit another tank. We were going for a third kill when some Cobra helicopters wanted to have some fun and started strafing the tanks. The Cobras took out the rest of the tanks and it made us mad. When they were done they flew over us and fired a flare to let us know they had taken them out. We were giving them the finger.

The next couple of days we just kept moving forward. We really didn't start getting into anything until April 1. On April 1, we went to one city and did a flanking movement for one of the units as we went in. We came under machine gun fire from antitank weapons. We found ourselves on one road and stopped because the other units were still under fire. We found that there were bunkers all up and down the road we were on and they had been abandoned. If the Iraqi soldiers had stayed there they would probably have wiped us out. We finally moved down the road and saw our first American dead. It was Corporal Edmonds. He was a sniper. We were supposed to meet up with

Cpl. Neal Brown with recovered weapons from insurgents near Fallujah, Iraq, in 2003 (Neal Brown).

Colonel McCoy, and as we were moving toward him they began to receive fire from the palm grove. They began suppressing fire. They took out most of the enemy, but the sergeant major saw another enemy soldier. He told Edmonds to see if he could take him out. As Edmonds raised up to fire he was killed. When we entered Nasiriyah we did a flanking movement and received some small arms fire, but we received more mortar rounds than anything. Then we hit the Yellow River crossing, which was the river that crossed into Baghdad.

We crossed the bridge and then we blew the bridge. We fought for two days and then my platoon was ordered to try to outflank the resistance. We were going through this palm grove and we immediately started receiving fire from the grove and from across the river. They were hitting us with small arms fire, RPGs, mortar rounds and antiaircraft guns. We started engaging the enemy inside the palm grove. Our vehicles were still moving beside us so we had to get out of the palm grove. When we did we found ourselves

Insurgent cache discovered by Cpl. Brown's unit near Fallujah, Iraq, in 2003 (Neal Brown).

surrounded by a big wall. We were trying to find a way out. I saw this hole over by where the bridge was blown and I told Corporal Drake that I saw an engineer bulldozer and that I was going to get it. He told me to wait until he told the platoon leader that I was going. I started running for the dozer and Corporal Drake caught up with me. The entire time we were running we were under fire from the palm grove. We finally got to the dozer and we could hear rounds bouncing off the bulldozer. It sounded like popcorn popping when it hits metal. We couldn't get the driver's attention so we climbed up on it. We could see tracers zipping by the whole time. We finally got the driver's attention and we told him we had men in the palm grove and we needed to knock down the wall. He followed us down and he knocked out the wall. Not five minutes after we got the last man out, artillery rounds hit right where the platoon had been. They said it was enemy fire, but I believe it was friendly fire. If we hadn't knocked the wall down we would have lost a lot of marines.

After three days of fighting we headed for West City, or what is known as Saddam City. We got in a firefight as soon as we got to the edge of the city. Today they would be called insurgents, but they were called the Republican Guard then. The fight didn't last long so we continued on into Baghdad. We thought that the fight in Baghdad would be like trying to take Stalingrad, but there wasn't much of a fight. We had a few firefights here and there, but that was all. Then when the fighting was over we pulled down the statue of Saddam.

During the second tour we went to Hedeta. Our main job was to train Iraqis to be police officers and soldiers. When they were done we would let them go home. About two months after we got there we went on a patrol one night. Karbala sets on a hill in a valley with a river going through it. My buddy Rose goes down a circle road and we started hearing RPGs [rocket-propelled grenades] and small arms fire. We started returning fire, and after we ceased fire we walked up to the area and started turning over bodies — at least the ones that were still intact enough to turn them over — and the insurgents were the police officers we had trained. They had turned around and ambushed us. You can't trust anybody over there. When we went back the second time, Iraqis could carry weapons again. If you saw an Iraqi carrying a gun you could do nothing about it unless they fired at you. They could wave it at you or aim it at you, but you could do nothing. They had to fire at you first. It is so stressful over there because of that.

A couple of days after that ambush we were near the fuel station, which was not even a mile from the police station. We saw an Iraqi police officer

Weapons discovered by Cpl. Brown in Fallujah, Iraq, in 2003 (Neal Brown).

and at the time we didn't realize it, but he was carrying a jacket and a prayer mat, all of it in a bundle. We didn't think too much of it at the time. My staff sergeant told me to take the high ground. I took it and I saw the same Iraqi cop coming from the opposite direction [...] and the bundle was gone. Then all of a sudden we started receiving machine gun fire. I was behind a small rock and I could hear the rounds pinging against the rock so I knew they had a fix on me. I ran and managed to get into a ditch, which was better cover. Then we started firing back and lighting up everything in the area.

After the firing stopped I used my 240 Golf, a special scope I carried, and could see the insurgents running. I ran to the captain and told him that we needed to go to the left after them, they were running in that direction, but he wouldn't listen to me and we went down to the position where they had been firing from. We found an RPG launching tube and six belts of ammo. We didn't find any bodies, but we had hit one of them because we found blood. We figured it was someone who was working with the police department.

About two weeks later we got a hit on a guy we called Big Red. He was a big Iraqi guy with red hair. We thought he was the one that had been carrying the prayer mat. We went and got the guy and his family was so pissed off they started fighting us. We pointed our guns at them and told them to leave us alone. We took him back and interrogated him. Then we had an interrogation team that interrogated him. They told us later he wasn't the one, but we knew it was him because we had a picture of him. After we took him back that day we knew we were going to get shot up that day. It was just in the air. Just before we got to his house, when we took him back we started seeing people running. It was dusk, but you could still see them running. We got to the house and dropped him off and I called back to headquarters and told them people were running all over the place and I thought we were going to get hit with something. A couple minutes later we started receiving machine gun fire, small arms fire, and RPG rounds. Everything went wrong. My machine gunners gun jammed on him, my weapon jammed on me, and our radios went out. I was calling for help because we were getting hit real hard, but still couldn't get the radios to work. We ran to my vehicle, which had been hit several times, and made it to the top of a hill. When we got there we realized we had a vehicle missing. We finally got the radios working and got in touch with the missing truck. The driver had gotten in and when he came under fire had driven into the fire and toward the city. He got turned around and started toward our position. The truck was receiving heavy fire and we returned fire until the truck got to our position. Right after that they cease-fired. We rallied up and made sure none of our men were hit. We went back to the city. When we got there we beat the shit out of any man on the streets that was of age and went into their homes looking for weapons. We went through the entire town. We didn't find any insurgents, but we did find a lot of ammo. We found some rockets too. It was just starting to get daylight by now and we went back to camp, got more men, and came back to town. That's when I found a weapons stash. They had gone back to their house and dumped all their weapons in a stash. There were two wounded men in the house and we got them and were taking them in. My staff sergeant wanted to give the people in the house food because there were so many children and we didn't like it a bit. I told the staff sergeant, "Hell no! I'm not giving them any food, they are the ones who shot at us last night if you recall." The staff sergeant told me I was being cruel and told me to go back and do rear security.

I was all pissed off and one of my buddies comes by to keep me company. I kept kicking the ground and then looking through my scope every once in a while to make sure no one was trying to sneak up on us. Then as I was walking around kicking at the ground, I noticed a square hole, like in the ground. I told my buddy, "That looks weird don't you think?" My buddy thought that they had buried a family member. I said they bury stuff around here all the time. We started moving rock and we found a blanket with plastic wrapped around it. We moved it and started digging some more and found another blanket. We pulled it up and we found five AK-47's with rounds in them. We called the staff sergeant over and showed him. I told him, "You want to give them food, and here is the weapons they stashed after shooting at us last night. Do you still want to give them food?" He said no and told us to get the food and put it back in the truck. We did and also got an AK-47 he had given this old man in the house. Then we continued the search. We found propaganda like DVDs and films showing how they blow us up. We found two big bags of powder, bayonets, and more ammunition. Then we went to all five houses nearby and we found stuff in all five of them — weapons, mortar rounds, antiaircraft rounds. They had them hid in their shitter holes in the houses. It sure changed the staff sergeant's mind about giving them food again.

About a month after that we get a call to go into Fallujah. Once we got there the first thing we had to deal with was a riot. We get to the location and I was looking for people with guns. Before I see anything two guys beside me get hit. The crowd began to break up and we never did see anyone with guns. There were hundreds of people. Once the crowd broke up we returned to camp.

After being in camp for about four days Colonel McCoy gave us a big morale speech. The next day we moved into Fallujah. My platoon stayed on the train track and covered the roadways. That was when I saw my first kid

IED discovered in the road outside Baghdad, Iraq, in 2003 by Cpl. Brown's unit (Neal Brown).

holding an AK-47. When I saw him he froze and I froze. I couldn't believe it. The gun was bigger than him. Finally, I put a burst into him and he dropped. The fight got so bad that our captain declared 2200 hours happy hour. Anyone out after 2200 hours, man, woman, or child, we were to shoot. An old man came out of a house and I let him go because I thought he was just an old man. Then I was ordered to shot him. I shot him in the head three times and he just kept coming. The insurgents chewed a root called qat that made them high and they felt like superman. We believed he was on it.

The insurgents started hiding behind people. We started taking small arms fire. I spotted a guy with a radio. I told the lieutenant and he told me to fire on him. I had a Mark-19, which is an automatic grenade launcher, and I fired a burst and was waiting for the round to hit so I could adjust my aim. The insurgent called out two little kids so he could hide behind them. Then they opened up on us with mortar rounds. They went over our heads and hit behind us. The lieutenant ordered me to shoot at the insurgent. I unloaded all 48 rounds I had and hoped it didn't hit the kids, but it did and also took out the building behind them. It really got to me.

During the battle we saw our first ambulance run. They would come over and pick up the bodies. It was a mess during the first battle. Fallujah was a real bad area and for some reason they made us pull back. It pissed us off because we were halfway through the city. I mean we are in the middle of the city and the politicians want to pull us out.

Of course, the second time we went in it was real bloody and more marines got killed. We were told we did a better job the second time, but I don't know about that. At night we would call in the C-131 gunships. The insurgents thought they were sneaky at night because they didn't think we could see them, but we had night vision thermo capability. We would let them get in as close as we could and then we would call a C-131 and give their position. We would tell them we wanted to see some fireworks and they would start firing. You could see one of them raise a AK-47, then they would get hit. The round would light up like a spotlight on a person and all at once you would see a flash and the person was just disintegrated. We didn't even shoot sometimes, we would let the gunship have some fun. We thought it was funny just watching them get blown up.

We did have some close calls, though, because we had some snipers come in. We heard there was a sniper from Syria, he was well known and had killed a lot of marines. We dumped everything on them—fifty-caliber machine guns, TOW missiles, Mark 19s, and even dumped what we called shake-and-

Land mine discovered by Cpl. Brown in Baghdad, Iraq, in 2003 (Neal Brown).

bakes, which is sulfur rounds, and also HE rounds which is high explosive rounds. We fired flares and when they would hit the ground they would turn green. The enemy thought we were using chemical warfare on them and they would run out of the buildings. We would just light them up.

The insurgents brought up a couple of tanks and were shooting at everything. One of my buddies threw a couple of charges at the tanks. After he leveled the tanks they kept shooting. I talked to a couple of Vietnam vets and they said they are almost like Viet Cong. They just don't die and when they do die you can't find the bodies.

Found out they had tunnels and we had to clear a couple of them. It scared the shit out of me because my uncle had told me about clearing tunnels. Thank god we never found anything other than bandages, blood trails, and empty magazines.

When we finally ended the battle there were so many bodies they had to come in and load them by trucks. It smelled so bad, I can't even describe it. When you first smell it it makes you sick, but then you start getting used to it. There were flies everywhere. After the bodies were removed we withdrew from the city.

I wish they would have let us finish the battle the first time because I think we could have taken the whole city without any losses. We lost some good men. We lost a good friend of mine that I had gone all the way through the marines with. Watching Greg get killed by the train station really pissed me off because he was in this tower the lieutenant had put him in with no cover. He was from Illinois and was only 19 years old. We lost him on April 11. We lost another great guy who went in first while checking a building out. From what I heard from his buddies, right when he turned in to the building he said "Oh shit" and then took a whole machine gun blast.

We withdrew and did a couple more missions with the Navy SEALs. We just supported them [with] firepower. After that, that ended my second tour.

After we returned to the States for a while we got word that we were going to deploy again. We were leaving early because they were having their first elections in Iraq and they thought it was going to be terrible, a lot of trouble and fighting. The third time is pushing your luck. There were a lot of guys in the unit that were going for the second time too. I started going nuts, tearing everything up in the barracks, so I went to talk to the chaplain. The chaplain told me that because I and some other guys were so pissed off, the company commander was granting all of us 10 days leave. We got 10 days leave instead of the normal 25 days leave, but I got to see my family again before I left. When they took me to the airport, I started crying and I told my little sister that I didn't think I was going to make it back this time. She started crying and told me I would make it, I had made it this far.

A battery used by insurgents to help set off IEDs discovered by Cpl. Brown in Fallujah, Iraq, in 2003 (Neal Brown).

We did a week's training and then we went over and straight into Fallujah again. It was like a ghost town. Our job was to let people back into the town and keep security on the city. I think our town was the only one that didn't receive any fire or trouble during the elections. We had a very successful election for the people. There were a couple of fights, but that was all.

Then towards the end of our tour things started really stepping up. The insurgents got word that there was a big general coming through town and they hit the convoy. When it was over they found out there was no general. The insurgents received about forty casualties.

Then they started hitting us with mortars. One day they hit my truck and my buddy's life was saved because a piece of shrapnel went through the driver's side of the truck and hit a metal plate in the truck. If it hadn't been for that he would have gotten hit in the chest. Right after that I took over as a Mark 19 gunner. We worked along a road that we called Iron Road because from one city to the next it was nothing but IEDs.

About two months before the tour was over I got hit by an IED driving into Fallujah. We turned a corner and a IED went off. I don't remember getting hit. The only thing I can remember is some of my buddies getting my vest off to make sure I didn't have any wounds on the inside of the vest.

Bombs and wiring to rig an IED discovered by Cpl. Brown in Baghdad, Iraq, in 2003 (Neal Brown).

I got shrapnel inside my elbow and hearing loss from it. They say it wasn't that big of an IED.... Never did receive my Purple Heart. That tour three of us got wounded. They gave us a day or two of light duty and then sent us back. That's why we made fun of the army sometimes because if they got hit the least little bit they got sent to Germany. We got a couple of days off and then back on patrol.

I joined the Army Reserve and I could be looking at a fourth tour in Iraq. The Guard is working on my Purple Hearts because the colonel saw my medical papers and he said, "You were wounded twice." I was wounded the first tour but it wasn't bad. It has taken a long time because there is a lot of paperwork. That's why I don't know if I want to fight [to get] the Medal of Valor because I have that piece of paper from all my buddies as witnesses. My staff sergeant took the credit. The funny thing about it is that I confronted my staff sergeant about it. He said, "It's not your medal, I told you to get that truck." I said, "It doesn't matter if you told me to go get it. It's like telling a corpsman to go get a wounded marine. You told me to go and I ran under fire to go get it."

On December 24, 2003, before we went for our third tour Staff Sergeant Lark got the Medal of Valor. The citation said that he ran to get the

Ace bulldozer under fire to knock down the wall inside the palm grove. His actions were above and beyond the call of duty. In the formation you could hear all the men saying this is bullshit that medal belongs to Brown and Drake.

My second tour I put my buddy Nickels in for a medal because he saved my life. We had these two teenage boys that had a kid's wagon and they had an antiaircraft gun on it. I raised to fire at them and my gun jammed. I yelled at Nickels and said kill them and he saw what was going on. He starts running toward me and the kids are loading the gun. I froze and thought I heard him say get down, but I'm not sure. He started firing and took them out. He saved my life and I tried to put him in for a medal. I liked Captain Dillback, he brought us back home twice. He knew how to kill the enemy. When the rules came down restricting our firing on the enemy, he always found a way for us to shoot back, but he was still shady. He would not give out medals to those who deserved them. He stayed on a gun more than anyone else when we were in the city and he knocked out a lot of insurgents. But all the ass kissers got medals. Anybody who was a corporal on down could not get a medal for valor. A gunny wrote himself up for a Bronze Star and got it. One of my buddies was in mortars and had to put out stakes for the mortarman. He went out under fire and placed the stakes. The last stake was where some concrete was at, so he laid there under fire for about nine hours, not being able to shoot back, and held the stakes in place. He didn't get a medal.

I joined because of September 11. I just wanted to get back at those people who did that to our country. Right after Christmas break my buddy Junior came up to me with tears in his eyes and said, "We are going to war." I said, "What?" and he said, "We are going to war." I started crying because it actually hit me that this was the real deal. Then when I finally got over there I wondered if I would be able to do what I was trained for, but when that first round zipped by my head it was just a natural instinct. Hearing men scream when they are wounded or seeing a dead American gets to you. Then when you take that first life, you're saying to yourself, I got that son-of-a-bitch then when you're alone at night you begin wondering if you killed someone's father or brother and it starts getting to you. Then you wonder, when you encounter the next enemy, are you going to hesitate. I didn't the next time, but it is weird, sometimes you see the faces of the people you shot so you see the effect. Then when you see people blown up and there are no body parts it is different. It is all difficult to deal with.

CHAPTER 4

Staff Sergeant Stacey Miesaloski

U.S. Air Force:
506 Expeditionary Squadron

IRAQ • OCTOBER 2003–MARCH 2004

We arrived on October 3, 2003. When we first got there we were asked to turn over our weapons we brought with us because the army was in control of the post and was doing the fighting. We did and then we were assigned tents. Within three hours we were mortared and we couldn't do anything because our weapons had been taken away from us by the army. All we could do was hit the ground and crawl to the nearest bunker for cover. The army guys was laughing at us because they were used to the mortar attacks and they were up just walking around laughing. The second or third day we got assigned our jobs. I was assigned to the recreation tent.

The first day on the job they came by to find out who may have mortuary experience. They found out I went to school for it so they chose me. I was assigned to the lieutenant and he and I along with two first sergeants set up a mortuary tent. When we went out to pick up a KIA we didn't have to identify them. The medic would do all of that and I only had to bring the bodies back.

A couple of days went by and we got a call on a wounded soldier. The lieutenant, first sergeant and I went out to bring the soldier back. They wouldn't let me do anything but just stand there and it really upset me because I want to know what I was doing there if they weren't going to let me do anything, especially since I had the most experience.

That was the only person we had for a couple of weeks. During that

25

A white Christmas in 2004, Kirkuk Air Base, NE Iraq (Stacey Miesaloski).

time I had made friends with a number of the locals who would come in and work on our base. Some of them had been in Saddam's army, but as time went on they began to be replaced by new locals. The new locals were mapping out our base. We didn't know at the time they were marking off strategic locations within the base where we had weapons, headquarters, and other areas of importance. They were mapping out the area and taking it back to their local units to be able to mortar our base. They were able to find out some of our routing areas for supplies coming in.

We had a supply truck that was due to come in and was a couple of days late. It was assumed by the commanding officer that the truck had been hit by the enemy, so we were sent out to find the truck. The commanding officer said that I couldn't go because I was a single parent. I went anyway.

The lieutenant, first sergeant, and I went out and found the truck. It was still running and the refrigeration was still running in the truck in the back. It hadn't been there for [long], because some of the items were no longer any good, but the ice cream that was in the truck was still frozen. We found the driver in the front seat of the vehicle. The insurgents had cut his head off and set his head in the front seat. The driver was a local and we brought the body and head back and had some locals from town come and get the body.

I got in trouble for going. I lost one rank and they threatened to send me back to the States. They didn't send me back to the States, though, and I was able to continue with the mortuary unit.

As time went on I began to prove myself to them because I had had more experience than they realized. They found that I was not freaking out and was able to handle the situations better than most of the other soldiers, so they began to allow me to do more and more on the missions. Some of the people and my unit began to dislike me because I was being able to do and asked to do many things that they could not do. They thought I was being privileged — like going out and picking dead bodies up is a privilege.

Most of the troops that were killed were on convoys. They were going in and out, day and night, for a variety of missions but mainly looking for Saddam. They would get hit by IEDs and then we would be called out. Many times the IDCs were set off by a cell phone. When we were called out, most of the time the vehicle would just be in pieces. Many times we would find just body parts. We would pick up an arm or other parts and bring them back to the base. You then take the body parts, clean them up, and place them in a black body bag. We then placed the bag in a box and it would be shipped out. We never identified anyone with just body parts. We would only indicate who we believed it to be because of the possibility that at the last minute people could've switched off on a mission. We didn't want to send incorrect information home to families.

We began to have more and more funerals as activity picked up. Then we began to have the missing funerals. I had never seen a missing person's funerals before. They would have their boots, their weapon, their dog tags, and helmet. These funerals were held for people where there were just pieces of a body left and the remains had already been transferred back to the States. They would have roll call and when they came to that person's name they would call his name three or four times. They would have people who knew the individual to stand up and have something to say about the individual, then they would have roll call, the twenty-one-gun salute, and play the taps.

As time went on I became numb. Nothing bothered me. When we were being shot at we didn't pay any attention to it, but that was probably because they were such poor shots. For example, they used to have these donkeys pulling a wagon and they would have a mortar on the back of it. They would be going along and then stop and shoot the mortar hoping the round would end up hitting on the base. Very seldom did the mortars hit anything. It may hit outside a base near the maze or it may hit the base, but seldom did they hit anything.

We started doing searches on homes. We would go out in the trucks and stay in the trucks until they called us with someone who had been wounded or killed. It was getting close to Christmas and through the holidays everything

Landscape outside the Kirkuk Air Base, NE Iraq, in 2004 (Stacey Miesaloski).

was fairly slow. I was trying to make a call home, as I remember it, and then all of a sudden it was like we were having bullets rained on us. They were coming from everywhere. We all took off and headed for the bunkers. When it finally ended we found out that Saddam had been caught and that was the reason the rounds were going off. All the locals were shooting in the air in celebration and of course what goes up comes down. We ended up with a couple of people wounded but nothing serious.

Around Christmastime it snowed. I would've never thought it would do that in Iraq but it did. The weather went from one extreme to the other — it was hot much of the time and there wasn't much humidity, but it would get cold. It would get down to, say, forty or fifty degrees, but it was a bitter cold. They also had a rainy season and I can remember it rained for a day or two straight, just hard rain. We had a truck that got stuck and actually turned over on its side because of mud and rain.

My daughter Gracie was only two years old when I went over. My family took care of her while I was gone. I am a single parent. I missed her terribly and worried if she was okay while I was there. I worried I may never see her again. I was grateful I made it back and that we are home.

CHAPTER 5

Lance Corporal
Dustin Whitehead

U.S. Marine Corps:
2nd Battalion, 8th Marines

IRAQ • MARCH 2003–MAY 2003

I was a senior in high school and around March or April 2000, I decided I was going into the Marine Corps. I went and talked to the recruiter and signed up. I went to San Diego in July of 2000 for boot camp. After boot camp my first duty station was Camp Lejeune. I was attached to Headquarters Battalion Truck Company. I was a truck driver and drove trucks for the infantry and supply. We did a lot of training while I was there.

Everything began to happen on September 11. We were put on alert and knew we were going to deploy. The anticipation and emotions ran high among the troops. We didn't know when we were going to leave, so we watched TV to see what President Bush was saying and what he was going to do. Finally in February of '03 we were attached to 2nd Battalion, 8th Marines. They were short on truck drivers. Then we were informed that we were going to deploy. We didn't have time to do anything but make phone calls to our families.

We flew into Cherry Point, North Carolina. From there we flew into Kuwait. Kuwait was considered a hot zone. We never knew what to expect. We found our trucks and joined the other units in the middle of the desert. We had some large tents and set up camp. President Bush declared war and the very next day we were in Iraq. We didn't take any roads. We were in the

Turned-over truck of L/Cpl. Whitehead's unit after attack near Fallujah, Iraq, in 2003 (Dustin Whitehead).

middle of the sand. It was follow the leader. I was driving a truck for Gulf Company. I couldn't even see the truck in front of me because of the sand dust. The ride was hard on the 20 troops in the back with all the sand dust. My ride was much better because I could roll the window up as I drove. We got into Iraq a day and a half later in a southern city called Nasiriyah.

We were going to take control of the city and the bridges that crossed the Euphrates River.

We could see the city as we approached it and everyone's adrenaline was really going. You could see the helicopters flying in and bombing the city. Smoke was going everywhere.

The companies started splitting up and as we came up on Nasiriyah we saw trucks on fire so we knew that something bad had already taken place. We were coming up on the bridges and we started taking fire. We stopped because we didn't know where it was coming from at first. Then we spotted a bunch of Iraqis in some ditches firing at us. The troops dismounted the trucks and started returning fire. In a short time we had control of the situation with most of the Iraq soldiers dead. We set up a perimeter after that and set up for the night.

It was about three weeks into the war. Me and a couple of other trucks

Burning truck of L/Cpl Whitehead's unit after the attack near Fallujah, Iraq, in 2003 (Dustin Whitehead).

were sent back to the main company. We were getting supplies for the troops. We got everything loaded up and by then it was dark. The first sergeant told us we would just stay the night with the main company and take the supplies back to the troops the next morning. I met up with some of my buddies and set up for the night. I took my boots off and my helmet and laid back on my sleeping bag. Then suddenly we started hearing rounds being fired. I had been there for three weeks and had gotten used to rounds being fired so didn't think much of it. Then the firing increased. I decided to get up and dressed and suddenly we were getting mortared all over the place. I moved for cover. The mortars increased and we were taking more incoming rounds than we ever had since we had been there. We were really surprised and thought we were in trouble. RPGs [rocket propelled grenades] were hitting our trucks and in no time four or five of our trucks were just destroyed. The firing lasted for a good thirty minutes. Then everything settled down. We didn't have any KIAs but we had a lot of wounded marines. We started treating them and getting them evacuated. The firepower we faced that night was unbelievable. We just didn't think the Iraqis had that kind of firepower.

We were up all night. The next morning when everything cleared we started cleaning up. We had a lot of damage. If there was anything in the trucks it was toasted. My truck survived the attack. The only thing that happened to mine was I had a 30-millimeter hole in the trailer. A number of

Rocket damage to L/Cpl. Whitehead's truck after attack near Fallujah, Iraq, in 2003 (Dustin Whitehead).

marines had kept their backpacks in the trucks and lost all their personal items.

Come to find out a small group of Iraq soldiers came between my unit and a small Light Armored Recon unit. They started firing on the armored unit. Unfortunately when the unit started firing back on the Iraq soldiers their rounds were coming right at us. It ended up that friendly fire on my unit was the worst thing that happened to us while I was over there.

We took some mechanics with us and went to a group of army trucks that had been hit when we first went into Basra. They were on the side of the road, and the mechanics took parts from them and in a couple of cases got the army trucks themselves running. We used them to get what equipment and supplies we had back to the troops.

We were always on the alert. We had fifty percent watch all the time. We had two men to a foxhole and one marine would stay on watch while the other slept. You didn't want to get caught sleeping on watch or you would get a rifle butt in the back of the head by the first sergeant, besides considering the safety of the other marines.

When we got [to Nasiriyah] it was like a ghost town. The Iraqi people got the word that we were coming and many left the city. The ones that stayed

Suspected insurgents captured by L/Cpl. Whitehead's unit in Fallujah, Iraq, in 2003 (Dustin Whitehead).

caught the wrath of our unit. We went on a lot of patrols and the Iraqis had the advantage because they knew where they were going in the city, but our orders were that if we saw an adult male and he looked suspicious we were to take him out.

We would be on patrol and all at once you would see an AK-47 come out of a window of a building. We would take cover and just blow the building to pieces. We would call the helicopters to come in. Normally they came in two at a time. They would circle the building a couple of times and then all at once stop in midair and the missiles would go flying.

The radio operators would call back to the artillery units and call in exactly where they needed their rounds. It was obvious that the Iraq soldiers didn't have much training. They couldn't hit sand falling off a camel. A few times we would walk into buildings and we would find Iraq snipers sleeping. We would take them in as POWs. We would put a sand bag over their head and zip ties on their hands and then have to stand guard over them. We would have them for hours on end like that and you would almost feel sorry for them, but if we hadn't they would have been trying to kill us.

After we had been in Nasiriyah for a few weeks we had pretty much cleared the town. They decided that we were going to go into the city and pick up dead Iraq soldiers. It was a terrible smell. We would try to pick them up and their legs would fall off in your hand. We had dozers come in and we would have to bury them.

We were in Nasiriyah for several months. We anticipated moving on to the next city but never knew which city or when we would move out. We were tired most of the time because of the lack of sleep and sleeping in fox-holes. We all missed a good meal and we all missed our families. The only thing we did when we had down time, which was very often, was play cards.

We were guarding a bridge. One day I went up to take some supplies. We had snipers on the bridge. Their orders were to kill any adult male within certain areas they were assigned. There were a few Iraqis that came in the areas that they weren't supposed to be and it would be lights out for them. We got to be familiar with a few Iraqis that lived on the outskirts of the city. They begged for food. You would see little kids that were starving. We would throw them the things that we didn't want out of our MREs.

It was extremely hot. Many evenings we would have sandstorms. It was one of the most dangerous times. The Iraq soldiers were used to them and we would take a lot of fire from them when the sandstorms hit. They knew how to adapt to the storms, and we had goggles and used a shirtsleeve to keep the sand out of our faces. You couldn't see two feet in front of you, but you could sure hear the rounds coming at you.

The next city we went to was Al Kuk. There were a lot of riots going on. We were supposed to take control of the city and sort out the good from the bad. We didn't take much fire in that city. You could tell that our presence wasn't appreciated by the Iraq people. Many protested and threw rocks at us.

The city was actually an Iraq base. We stayed in their barrack and we could see an area for training with obstacle courses. Nothing had been used for a while. There were no beds or anything like that in the barracks just concrete floors and a bunch of empty rooms. It stunk pretty bad and lots of flies and mosquitoes were terrible over there. I believe I counted about 70 days without a shower. We had baby wipes to clean ourselves up with but thank God for toothbrushes and toothpaste. We didn't have any American cigarettes so you would have to buy them from Iraqis. They tasted like dirt but it was better than nothing. It was three months before we started receiving packages from our families.

The men that we were over there with grew a bond that no other friendship could compare to. The support that we had for each other is what kept us going. It is something that you would never want to take back in your life. A good friend of mine that I went to high school with was in my unit. I didn't know it and saw him four or five months after we were there. It really felt good to see him and have someone from home over there with me.

The morning that we were supposed to head back we had the trucks lined up. I was in a tent sleeping and I wasn't where I was supposed to be sleeping. I was in a tent a few hundred yards away from the truck. I missed the wake-up call. I heard the trucks firing up and all at once my tent flat opened and someone yelled, "Whitehead, let's go!" The whole battalion was waiting on me. I left the tent and all. I got an ass chewing and the supply sergeant was pissed because I left my tent. We headed back to Kuwait and took the highway back this time.

We got back to Kuwait. They had trailers set up. They were shower trailers. It was 114 degrees in Kuwait and we had two companies of marines trying to crowd into two shower trailers for showers. We were there for a few weeks. We slept on open mattresses that were there. I don't know where they came from.

After a short period of time there we packed up and came home. It was a wonderful feeling to be back in the U.S.

CHAPTER 6

Specialist Daniel E. Baker

Police Mentor Team,
Iron Horse Infantry 11B

HELMAND PROVINCE, AFGHANISTAN •
DECEMBER 2008–SEPTEMBER 2009

When we got in country we weren't sure who we were going to be with or what our mission was going to be. We were told that we were going to be busted up and sent to different teams. When we got to Kandahar I was put on a team of twelve men…. They needed a driver and I got the job. We went outside the gate and it was the first time I was out and was scared to death because I didn't know what to expect. Our radio would click and every time it did I would expect something to blow up. It was nerve-racking. As I look at it now it was okay. I drove into the main city of Kandahar. We met the police force we were going to be working with, and then drove back into Camp Bastion.

I learned my mission was going to be to work with Afghanistan National Civil Order Police. We called them ANCOP for short. The other team packed up and went home and in the first week we went to Helmand Province for our first mission. We shared an area with the British. We had an American spot called Camp Diamond. We went to Nad Ali. We sent the national police out to be trained and we were to bring civil order to the town. We would get control, bring civil order, then bring in the national police and turn it over to them and we would leave.

The first night we went down it was dark by the time we got there. We didn't know where we were going to stay and the British let us stay at one of

36

Afghan National Civil Order Police making arrest in Helmand Province, Afghanistan, in 2009 (Daniel Baker).

their areas the first night. It wasn't really a base, it was just a bunch of compounds that they had built and put fences around and claimed as their own. We really didn't know what was going on the first night and we just slept out around the trucks that night.

The next day we found that they were building a police station. They had the concrete walls up and we decided to move in there. For about the first three weeks we just circled our trucks there and slept around the fire pit.

And we ran our missions out of there. It wasn't very far into it when we had our first firefight. We were driving around and setting up precincts. We would take so many police officers and place them in the different precincts. We went to one precinct and were dropping off some of the officers at this old schoolhouse. The ANCO were terrified. They didn't want to leave their area. They had trip flares set up around their area. Then we found out that every time we left the compound we would start hearing gunfire go off. They were getting hit hard. The area where they were had open walls and they had no protection. They had four ranger trucks. No armor, no protect, so we spent several days trying to build up that area. And that's the area we did most of our fighting in.

We spent four days there. We got hit real bad. It happened Christmas night. We repelled the attack and started back to our compound. Our commanding officer contacted us and told us to go back. We spent four days there. They had to fly food supplies and ammo in to us. After that we would go out on missions for two or three weeks at a time. We went without showers the entire time we were out. The only time we would be able to go back to the compound would be when we ran real low on ammo and fuel and no one could run it out to us. Then we would have to go back to our compound to resupply. We could get showers in at that time. After a month or so activity started slowing down. We were able to go out for about three or four days at a time and then come back into the compound to resupply and take showers.

The very first trip we made to Lashkan Gah it had rained and we weren't sure if we were going to be able to make our route. It was through the desert, through low spots, and the roads were bad. With the weight of the trucks we thought we were going to be stuck constantly. We were looking for the route and we were in the desert. There were no roads so we were just trying to pick a line and stay on it. The route ran right through Marja. We wanted to avoid Marja. It was the last Taliban stronghold so we wanted to stay out of there. We were going along and realized we hadn't gone far enough out to miss it and were going to drive through the edge of the area. We stopped the trucks and we could see Marja but we were way out from it. One of the trucks was about to lose his load. I was sitting on top of this hill and I could see this driver get out of his truck to shift his load. It is hot and I am out on top of my gun turret eating my MRE. All of a sudden a gunshot rings out. With the first shot one of our Afghan police officers just falls. The first shot was right in his neck. There goes my MRE. My helmet is on and I start the truck down the hill. A mortar round lands about fifteen meters from me. I'm thinking, "These guys are dialed in, this is not good." Rounds were flying everywhere. I get teamed up with my other truck, and as soon as I do another

Christmas in Helmand Province, Afghanistan, in 2009 (Daniel Baker).

mortar hits about 10 meters from the truck. I knew then what it felt like to be in an ambush. We were caught in a crossfire. Five minutes ago I was eating my MRE and now we are in a crossfire in the middle of nowhere. It's the worst feeling in the world. Having no control, not running a mission being vulnerable. We finally got turned around and out of the area. I had a bad headache and the medic said I had a concussion from the explosions.

The first couple of months we were real excited but after that we begin to get used to the environment and activity around. About February everything begin to develop into a natural pattern. We would spend about four days out and then come in for a couple of days of rest and resupplies. That's when we started having clearly defined missions.

On February 4, we received information that there was a guy that was a mechanic building IEDs just north of the checkpoint at Argyle. We had a plan for a mission to take some of the police with us and get this individual. They had shipped us down tents that we had set up. We didn't have power so we set up generators and wired them up. It was about an hour before we were going to go on the mission, and here comes my dad. He is with a lieutenant and another team of police — they are going to wire these generators

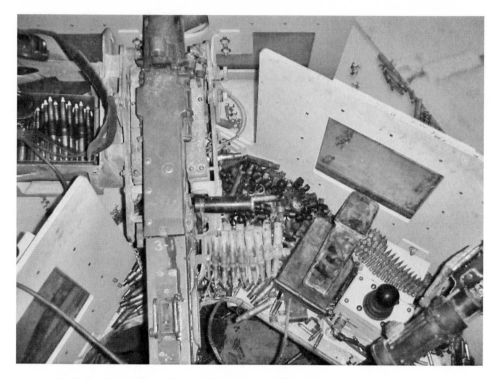

Firefight aftermath in Helmand Province, Afghanistan, in 2009 (Daniel Baker).

so we could have some power. We had all these extra people so we decided we would all go in a massive force to complete the mission.

We headed out on this mission. We expected to receive a little enemy resistance. The plan was, when we left the checkpoint and hit the center section, truck one was going to go straight, truck two to the right, truck three to the left and truck four set in the middle. All others stayed behind. I remember before truck one was in park, the first shot rang out. We got our truck parked and we immediately started getting fire from the enemy. We were firing back for about ten minutes before we realized we were going to have to do the entire mission like this. We had all taken cover and were trying to figure out which compound this guy was in so we could arrest him. It didn't even dawn on me that Dad is sitting back there a few trucks away and he isn't even seeing anything. About an hour into the fight, truck one was low on ammo. We were starting to run low too. A team had gone in and made the arrest. They had more info and the information had been right. He was making bombs. We stuck him in a truck and were going to go back. About that time the team in the rear calls in and they are taking fire. We were trying to get turned around and we figured out that they had massed on us for about two klicks back [a klick is equivalent to one kilometer]. We were so busy looking to the front where we were taking fire that we didn't realize they had been moving down the sides. It took us about thirty minutes to get the trucks turned around and fight our way out of the area. On the way back we had a guy have a RPG fly right by his head, it bounced and hit another guy. We had to evacuate two men because of head concussions. That was all that was hurt on the mission and we felt we were fortunate with that after we had had so much contact with the enemy.

We left him in custody with local police. Then we redistributed ammo to all the trucks so we were prepared for more contact and another mission the next day. We were laying there that night in the compound. Shots started coming from everywhere at the checkpoint north of us. We had to go out and repel the attack.

Then two or three days later we started and resumed our regular missions. We were still pumped up from the fight a couple days back. We got word that they had made an IED and left it buried in the road. We went to check it out. We had stopped our trucks in the middle of this bridge. A team went to check it out. Pretty soon the commander came back to me and said, "It is buried in the road, but it is okay." He said he had already disabled it and handed me the battery out of it. This commander was a real expert on IEDs. He had disabled a lot of them and wasn't afraid of them at all. We decided to let the local police handle it.

This one didn't work out that way. It was booby-trapped. They were taking it out of the hole and it exploded. Our guys that were watching them take it out of the ground were killed. We lost four guys that day. We all felt, when we had been in the firefight a few days earlier and we only had two men with concussions, we thought we were invincible. That day we lost our invincibility.

We went out to pick up the pieces and get as much of our friends back to the United States as we could. We drove back with the body bags and went to the British base. We called in a bird. The bird flew in and we put a tag on their body bags and they were flown home. We got two days off to go to Kandahar for that. It put the war in perspective at that point. When you really see what it is you're doing it begins to make sense.

From that point we tried to continue to make missions. We had to let them know that they wouldn't win so we kept taking the fight to the enemy. We went to new areas we hadn't been in and we would set a point and push further and further in the different precincts with our patrols. We were there for about another month and a half till about the end of March and then the national police came back and it was time for us to move to another area.

Nad Ali was the area while we were there that we saw the most action and as a result it was the area we thought we had done the most good.

They sent us down south to Marja after that. Contact was minimal. The British had been there for a long time. They had run missions out of there for a very long time and there just didn't seem like there was very much for us to do. We watched a lot of movies while we were there. We did do a few missions where we were sent in by helicopter and cleared villages with no incidents. We would get information they were making bombs. We would go into the villages, line up and check all huts. Most information was bad, we found very little when we went in and caught the guy that planted the bomb. Don't know if [it was] our intelligence or theirs, but we found him and arrested him. The problem was that there is a lot of corruption in the country. The police were offered a bribe and he was let go. I don't know if we were making progress or not but we were sure trying.

When we were finished at Marja we were supposed to be done. We were supposed to pack up and get ready to leave. And we had got a new command and he had heard how well we had done at Nad Ali and so he wanted to get the press involved. He got some reporters from *Rolling Stone* and he says we are going to Nawa before we are done here. At that time it was the second known worst area in the province. He told the press that he had hand-selected the team. I don't know if it ever got printed because we tried to let the press know it wasn't correct info. He had come in six months after we had been there to relieve someone else. That's the only reason we went to Nawa, so he could put names and faces on *Rolling Stone* magazine. We were with the Second Marine Division. We had no business there and the marines didn't want us there. They wanted our police officers but they didn't want us there.

After a while we went to Camp Phoenix and in a couple of months returned home. It was good to be back in the U.S.

CHAPTER 7

Sergeant Joseph Napiorkowski

33rd Brigade Combat Team, Illinois, 11B Infantry

EAST CENTRAL AFGHANISTAN •
OCTOBER 2008–SEPTEMBER 2009

I was in the Guard in Afghanistan, a sergeant. I arrived in December 2008 and assigned to a FOB [forward operation base] in Salerno. I was on a twelve-man PMT [police mentor team]. Then about six months after I was there I transferred to an EET [Embedded Training Team]. The EET team mission was to train the Afghanistan army.

We were doing missions with the Afghan police—patrols looking for IEDs. We had this same route that we took every day. There was a bridge we had to cross to go into the local village. When we would get to the bridge we would always check it and under the bridge also. Then we had a spot that we would stop and take a break. The locals were nice to us most of the time, but they were always watching us. One day we got to the bridge and started checking underneath like always. When we were done the lieutenant said we were going to take a break. Just as we stopped an IED blew up. It was in the exact location where we normally had stopped for a break. We just happened to be about seventy-five yards from it when it blew, because we didn't stop in the usual spot. That was when reality set in for me that this was the real thing.

We moved on into the village a little while later. Usually we had no problem with the villagers, but on this day they were rioting. We weren't prepared for that and dealt with it the best we could, trying to break up the rioting and maintain order. When we got back to the base we tried to find

43

out what was going on that caused all the upheaval. Come to find out some Rangers had been in the village looking for insurgents. They had shot into a compound and accidentally hit a woman holding her baby. The woman was killed. It took us two weeks to get order in the village after that.

What we did most of the time was to go into the villages and try to meet and greet people. We wanted to win their hearts and minds over to our side rather than to the Taliban. It was difficult to do because when we weren't there the Taliban soldiers would threaten them with torture and death if they didn't support them. Then when you have an incident like with the accidental shooting it makes it real difficult.

We were in the village one day doing what we called meet-and-greet missions. As we moved through the village we spotted a truck parked in behind some buildings. We went to check it out and found the truck full of HME [homemade explosives]. It ended up having six thousand pounds of explosives in it. At the time I think it was the record for the most explosives found at one time. There were AT-4s, the insurgents' version of rockets, a couple of AK-47s, and all the explosives. We took it all back to our base and we blew up three hundred pounds of explosives at a time to get rid of it. It took us two days to dispose of it all.

I had a mission that I had to do by myself. I had to take seventy ANP [Afghanistan national police] up north to this base for training. I was in the back of the plane with my interpreter and 70 of these police. You really don't know who's legit, who's not. They act like they are your best friend and when your back is turned some would stab you in the back. When we get there I am outside the wire, trying to get seventy of these guys into the base. There was about four or five American troops there, a couple of air force, maybe two or three army and one marine. The base was real small.

We got all of them inside the base and the other troops and I were sitting and talking. All at once we started hearing *kadunk, kadunk, kadunk*. We had a German base that was about two hundred yards from ours and they just started getting hit with mortars. They were closing in the gap and the mortars were getting closer and closer to us. There were some contractors on the base and they were yelling for all the military people to get to the front of the base because the insurgents were going to try and storm the gate. Then we started getting hit with rockets. I grabbed my gear and ran to the front along with the rest of the troops — all five of us. We heard some yelling outside the gate and were preparing to fire when we heard some engines firing up. We looked over and the Germans were sending tanks out. They started firing and the whole fight ended just about as quick as it started. It was a real scare with no more of us than we had to fight back. We finally settled down for the night, only to wake up the next morning to another rocket attack. No one was hurt though. I was there for about three more days and we had no more attacks. I helped train the police for that time. Then one day I got a call that I was going back to my base. I was put on a plane and flew back the next day

When I got back I was put on an EET team. We were working with the Green Berets and the Afghanistan National Army. We were to train them on how to find the IEDs. The U.S. had hundreds and hundreds of brand new Ford Rangers they had sent over for the Afghan army. They were stick shift and still had the plastic on the seats. The Green Berets said when we went outside the wire to just grab one and that was how we were going to do our missions.

The lieutenant came to me one day and said that we were going out the next day and look for IEDs. It was going to be a sergeant with three or four Afghan troops with each team. There were going to be three teams including mine. The problem was that the other two sergeants had no training at all for tracking IEDs. They had spent their whole time on FOB [forward operations base] security and had never left the base. I was the only one with any experience. I had been on about a hundred and thirty missions. I told the lieutenant that I didn't think it was a good idea because of their lack of experience. I told him that I have seen what IEDs do to armored Humvees with the troops in back and we have Ford Rangers and two teams with no experience. The lieutenant said the colonel wants the mission to go tomorrow. It's going to go.

The next morning we started out. Each truck had about five Afghan troops in the back. We were making our sweep and we were about to go over this hill. All of a sudden *boom*—one of the trucks in front of us got hit by an IED. There were some casualties. The truck behind the one that got hit had the lieutenant in it. All of his Afghan troops bailed out of the truck and started running. He jumped out and started yelling at them to come back. They just kept running. None of my team was injured. But that's the way it was. There was a lot of bad decisions made by the chain of command that got people killed. We lost a lieutenant, a couple of squad leaders and I had a good friend of mine killed because of bad decisions by the chain of command. It was my biggest pet peeve, the chain of command's bad decisions.

One of the biggest questions that I and other troops had was what are we doing there. I don't mean what are we doing in Afghanistan, but what are we doing that is making any difference. We are doing all these missions with these Afghan troops and they are just asking for more and more from us. They want weapons, ammo, armor, trucks and anything else they can get from us. We found caches of weapons that was sent over by us, and the weapons were being used against us. If they want a building built we built it. Whatever they wanted we would provide. And in the end we were just getting our troops killed by the same people we were providing and trying to help. When it is all over we won't have changed a thing.

CHAPTER 8

Warrant Officer Tim Baker

33rd Brigade Combat Team, Illinois, 11B Infantry

HELMAND PROVINCE, AFGHANISTAN •
DECEMBER 2008–SEPTEMBER 2009

I deployed with the 33rd BCT as a warrant officer, and originally I was there in signal. I was to go to Camp Phoenix to work with the J-6 shop. I was to be their representative to the J-3 planning section. When I got there I got introduced to everybody in Kabul in Camp Phoenix. I was supposed to work with an air force lieutenant. The first three days I was there I would go to the lieutenant and ask, "What have we got going?" He would tell me, "I don't have anything for you." After three days I couldn't stand it anymore. I have a real extensive background in wiring. I heard they needed electricians, so I went over to the engineer shop and I met the colonel there and told him what I could do. That day they had come down with a mission in Afghanistan called "Task Force Power." What had happened because of faulty electrical systems in Iraq, eighteen people were killed. Some got electrocuted in showers. Some got electrocuted because of other faulty systems also. We had to solve the problem in the Afghanistan Theater. Myself, Major Jeff Gilly, Lieutenant Mark DeThorne, who was an engineer, and Sergeant First Class Jeff Chapman became the electrical shop team. We wrote the SOP [standard operating procedure] for electrical work in Afghanistan. It was adopted in the entire nation by all the military. Once we completed the SOP we were assigned to go around to all the areas. There was one north, south, east, and west. These are commands. There was one in Kabul. We were to brief all the commanders. Train

Father Tim Baker and son Daniel Baker before they left the U.S. at Fort Bragg, North Carolina, in 2008 (Tim Baker).

them on how to do proper grounding. Then we were to go into all the camps and do inspections to ensure electrical systems were set up properly and to help with repairs. It took us from January when we left to go to Kabul and then up to Karr Air field. We needed to go north but couldn't move that direction at the time so we headed south and ended up in Kandahar around the first week in February.

Then they sent myself and Mark DeThorne down to Helmand Province. We started at Lashkar Gah. On February the 4th we got sent down to Nad Ali. That's where my son Dan was stationed. There was just a small team there. When we went out to these small camps when we weren't doing electrical work we would help the teams run missions. Everybody was short-handed. We hadn't been there three hours and we went out on a mission. We were sent to apprehend a high-value target. We went into a town called Marja. We dispersed north of the town. We dispersed four vehicles. Two vehicles were sent to get the high-value target while the other two vehicles stayed about two klicks back from the target. The two vehicles approached the target and we started taking small arms fire and rockets. This high-intensity exchange went on for an hour. We took out the target and were returning to base. We continued to receive fire all the way back to the base, and just as we were approaching the base a loud sound like frying bacon went over our heads and a rocket landed right in front of our vehicle. It was our lucky moment. It bounced off the ground, hit the gunner in front of us in the head and knocked

A mission south of Bagrham Air Base in Helmand Province, Afghanistan, in 2009 (Tim Baker).

him out but the rocket didn't explode. We had two men evacuated out when the mission was over.

We went back to Nad Ali and about four hours later when it got dark they hit the base from three sides. We had to go back in. The lieutenant and myself were the only ones without night vision. We were at firing points and all we had to shoot at was muzzle flashes. After an hour or so the shooting stopped.

The next morning we had to go to Kandahar because we had to retool, clean weapons and get resupplied with ammo. We went back to Nad Ali. On February 8, 2009, First Lieutenant Mark DeThorne and myself were with Team Iron Horse at Nad Ali in Helmand Province. The U.S. camp was on the outside of Camp Argyle. First Lieutenant DeThorne and I were working on their generators and power distribution to their tents. At approximately 0900 we were informed an IED had been located approximately 400 meters from the camp. It was decided First Lieutenant DeThorne and I would remain at the camp while Team Iron Horse, which included my son, Specialist Dan Baker, went to investigate the IED. Approximately 20 minutes later I heard two explosions approximately one second apart. I looked in the direction of the explosions and saw a vertical column of debris resulting from the explo-

Helicopter ride to Bala Marghab, Afghanistan, in 2009 (Tim Baker).

sions. At that moment I thought my son had been killed and almost vomited. I had no choice but to continue with my task. The entire time I was sick to my stomach trying to figure out what I was going to do, what I was going to tell his mother, my wife.

Approximately 15 minutes later an interpreter returned to camp covered in blood. He said everyone was looking for First Lieutenant Jared Southworth and Staff Sergeant Jason Burkholder. My first question was, "How is Dan?" The interpreter indicated he was all right. At that moment my thought was that I was glad it was someone else. When the team returned to the camp the bodies of First Lieutenant Southworth and Staff Sergeant Burkholder were in bags along with their equipment. Some of their remains were splattered on the front of the vehicles. My son, several other members of the team and I went into the tent where we cried about our losses. I tried to provide as much comfort as a father can provide. Their remains were then hosed off of the vehicles into the ditch.

We were just sick. We had lost the lieutenant, the sergeant, and an interpreter. We wanted to go down and help them, but we didn't have any way to get down there and we were told to just sit tight, they were bringing everyone

Over watch with Italians at Bala, Afghanistan, in 2009 (Tim Baker).

back. When they came back, they pulled their vehicles in. We were all beside ourselves. We all went into the tent and busted out crying. There were no John Wayne speeches, no music to play. Everyone was just sick to their stomachs and crying their eyes out. The sergeant hadn't been married a year and I felt like his wife had been cheated. The lieutenant had four kids.

Shortly after that they moved us out of the Helmand Province. When we went down the road there were several trees close to where the IED had exploded. There were still some body parts in the trees. We had some missions in the south and east. They made us turn in our weapons two weeks before we left, and I'll be damned if we didn't get hit two or three times before we left. We had a vehicle IED that went off and killed a couple of Americans and several civilians. And on my birthday we got hit by about twenty insurgents. They killed two of them and then they ran. To show you what was going on, a number of officers were actually running to the gate where the action was to try to get their Combat Infantry badge. They didn't care about the fight, they just wanted those badges. They couldn't keep us there long enough. We were there two months after our replacements came in because some of the officers wanted to get time for some medal or badge.

CHAPTER 9

Major Greg Settle

Headquarters and Headquarters Company, 2-130 Infantry

BAGHDAD, BABYLON, IRAQ • 2004 AND 2006

HELMAND PROVINCE, AFGHANISTAN • 2009

War is a complicated endeavor. As an individual a human being will experience every emotion in the human spectrum during a war. You are happy, you are sad, you are excited, and you are scared. You experience all of them. It's only the war itself that really gives you that spectrum of feelings and emotions. I spent two years of my life in Iraq right after the surge, the initial invasion. Then I came home for six months to almost a year and then went back again. The environment always changes but the war itself doesn't as far as the emotions that you feel. You make bonds with the men you serve with that are just lifetime bonds that you can't get anywhere else other than in war. Sergeant Strong was my gunner during our last deployment in Afghanistan and he saved my life numerous times, and that experience we had I can't share with anybody else. There is a bond between you and your children, but it is nothing like the experience of bonding in war.

I have a very strong wife. She is very understanding, but then again I feel for the families because their significant other, their husband in my case, is gone. She still has a family to run and still has a house to take care of and there's always that uncertainty that she has. I mean I would go weeks at a time not being able to contact her. She doesn't know if I'm safe or if I'm not. The mental strain is difficult. Then we come home and you see a lot of soldiers

Captain Settle, Kabul Range, Kabul, Afghanistan, in 2009 (Greg Settle).

having issues with their families. Things have changed over the year or eighteen months they have been gone. It is different and hard for the soldiers to adjust. With my wife it is better than average. We have our differences, but she is a strong woman and she always supports me and I don't think I could have come home and adjusted being back in the States as well as I did if it wasn't for her and her strength and her willingness to help me with that.

Operation Iraqi Freedom/Operation Enduring Freedom time frame and what we experienced when we came home was a lot different than those from the Vietnam era. I feel so, I don't know if I want to say sorry, but hurt by how the men coming home from that war were treated. The general public was atrocious. It was disrespectful. I'm very fortunate and every man and woman that has deployed during this war is very fortunate that we have received the support from the public that we have. They help us. They are behind us and it is good to come home and you are proud to wear the uniform. Everywhere you go people thank you and you want to tell people don't thank me anymore, I did what I was asked to do. I did my job, and that's what you will get from almost every soldier.

I think back over the sixteen years I have been in the military and realize

I have done a lot of things. I joined when I was seventeen years old as an enlisted man. It was in the mid–90s and you never thought about being deployed. You just went one weekend a month and you drank beer with your buddies and it was like being in a club. That all changed after 9-11. It all became real. The possibility of deployment was greater and we were like, "Wow, we might get to do what we signed up to do." I had been promoted to second lieutenant and I was always proud and believed in honor, duty, and country and I lived it.

I got picked up to do the home security mission, basically guarding some air bases in Illinois. I was stationed in Springfield in the G3 training office. I was young and didn't know anything and working with some really high-ranking officers. Then there was some other lower-ranking officers in offices next to mine and they heckled me every morning. They were always giving me a hard time. Then one day one of them stuck their head out of the office and said, "Any you clowns want to go to Iraq?" He was the mobilization officer for the state of Illinois. I said, "I do." The army had just got into Baghdad so it was right after the initial invasion.

They put together a team of us to go. I was the lowest-ranking officer and we had several majors, a couple of captains and one enlisted man. We deployed to Babylon a Hillah Babylon area and worked on the division staff. I did aviation requests for people and it was an eye-opening experience to learn when you're twenty-three years old what goes into making the army work. It was the massive amounts of things that happen day to day. It wasn't a hard mission and I was gone a year of my life, but I learned a lot. I learned that all this stuff that goes on in the movies that you watch, the blow-'em up, kill-'em-Rambo-commando type stuff isn't really what goes on. The fighting aspect of it really is done by a very few.

After a year in Iraq I came home and went back to the company I was in only to find out that they were going to deploy to Iraq in four months. I'm a lieutenant and my men are preparing to go to Iraq. I didn't feel as their platoon commander I could say, "Sorry guys, I'm not going," so four months later we strapped on and went back across the pond. This time we were in Baghdad. I was a platoon leader for a force protection company and our mission was to provide security for the vice president of Iraq. Anywhere the vice president moved we provided security. We did that for a year.

It was a big difference working on a staff and then having to juggle forty-two men with different personalities, ideas, and expectations. I am twenty-four years old managing all of this firepower and twelve million dollars' worth of equipment and that is a lot of responsibility. We were on the ground and working every day, but you just grow and you learn a lot as you grow and I think it just makes you a better leader.

I screwed some things up. We were providing our security at a compound for the vice president and one of my guys, I don't know if he dropped his weapon, we will never know the full story, but he dropped his weapon and somehow it went off and the bullet ricocheted off the ground and hit an Iraqi security guard in the ankle. It didn't kill him and wasn't a malicious act. I wasn't on that mission that day, I had to go do an investigation on something so I wasn't anywhere around. We had six investigations on the incident. It is like you're guilty until proven innocent in every situation in the military. I was scared, I mean I thought my career was over. I finally got a letter of concern in the end.

Iraq was a unique place. The people there are the infrastructure and a lot better than Afghanistan. We would be moving the vice president from point to point and Baghdad was like driving downtown Chicago. It's a nightmare and then our rules of engagement were, "You will not stop this convoy." We welded our bumpers on the trucks with two-inch pipe and we didn't stop. We were like a demolition derby, but that was our job. I don't know if it was right or wrong, but I feel bad for some of the civilians that were just trying to get to work and provide for their families and we are running into their cars and tearing up their one crappy car.

You learn a lot. With each rank you get a little bit higher. I am now a major. Your priorities change. As an enlisted man you care about what big Sarge tells you. Then you become a lieutenant and you have a handful of sergeants you have to manage. Then you're captain and now you have a bunch of lieutenants to manage and now major. It's like a learning process and you grow with it.

My last deployment to Afghanistan was a difficult one. We had a very challenging mission. Our mission was to eradicate poppy and to provide security and mentor the Afghanistan National Army (ANA). It was a hostile environment. There was a lot of combat and a lot of days you really didn't know if you were going to make it. For me it was all about trying to make sure the men around me were safe and doing everything you can to take care of them. Fear is a powerful tool. It makes you do a lot of things that you didn't think you could do. It makes you go a little bit longer and a little bit faster.

We had been in Helmand Province about a week and we set up a screen line just outside of a stronghold of the Taliban. I was outside of my vehicle working with ANA counterparts trying to establish the screen line. I remember a couple of mortars came in but they really weren't right on top of us. We knew it wasn't going to take long for them to figure out exactly where we were at. At that point an enemy AGS 17 (automatic grenade launcher) begin walking in on our position. It hit the front of my truck as I was coming back to the truck. It was just a big cloud of smoke and blew both tires on the front of the vehicle. I was being chased by a machine gun at the same time and it is like everything is in slow motion. I could watch the bullets coming up the ground at me like in slow motion. They went right between my legs. It all happened within a matter of a few seconds, but it seemed like a lifetime. I got on the radio and started yelling to Sergeant Greg Strong to just start shooting them. It's experiences like that, that you never forget.

We had a couple of ANA counterparts wounded in action and tried to advance on an enemy position to pull them out. We were pinned down pretty good. We had our own Mark 19's and mortars firing and we finally got into the compound but was pinned down again. We lost a couple of ANA that day. It was a long day and one you will never forget. It makes a man out of you real quick.

I wouldn't trade any of it for anything in the world. The people I have met in Afghanistan, the people themselves, most of them are warriors. You have to respect that whether they are fighting for what they want or to put food on the table, it doesn't matter. They did what they had to do.

Hopefully you can take the kind of experiences that you have learned and as you get older and hopefully a little bit wiser you can pass the experience on to the younger generation and make it a little bit better, because we made a lot of mistakes, no doubt about it, but hopefully we can give that information over to the younger generation of soldiers that are going to fight and maybe they won't make some of the mistakes that we made.

CHAPTER 10

Sergeant First Class
Gregory L. Strong

*Headquarters and Headquarters
Company, 2-130 Infantry*

KABUL, AFGHANISTAN •
AUGUST 2008–SEPTEMBER 2009

I arrived in Afghanistan in August 2008. We started out in cheesecloth tents. It was horrible. We were told to make the best of them so we did the best we could with what we had. They were not waterproof and we were there during the rainy season. They would stretch out and we would have to use two by four's or tent poles to hold the roof up. We would have to make tarps to put over the top to get the rain to run off. Then we got Alaskan tents and they were nice. They were fifty by forty tents and we actually had electricity in them because we had generators and were able to have heat also. Something we had little of with the cheese tents. It was funny, after we got the Alaskan tents one day we came back off of a mission and our tent had blown away. There all of our stuff was, laying there in the open.

Living conditions were rough. We didn't have any American support on the food, it was all an Afghan national vendor so we got a lot of curry with the bone still in, chicken curry with the bone, and rice. We were ecstatic if we got Tater Tots or French fries. The lamb smelled delicious but it's tough as shoe leather and you get one bite per lamb chop. I lost close to fifty pounds and other guys lost a lot too because the food was atrocious.

Our mission In Afghanistan was unique. We had a special mission to work with the Afghanistan National Army (ANA), Counter Narcotics Infantry Kandak, Afghanistan National Police's Poppy Eradication Force and DynCorp International's Poppy Eradication Force to eradicate poppy and support the national goals on reducing illicit crop production. We worked in Helmand Province. We went to Camp Dubs, which is across town from Kabul. Camp Phoenix was just across town from Kabul so we were just across from the main headquarters.

Our job was to set up security. The way it worked was we would put one of our trucks with each Afghan company so that made four Americans with each company. Then we would set up security lines in a rectangle two klicks by two klicks. We and the Afghan army had three sides and DynCorp had the other. Once we had the security lines set up, then DynCorp would go inside and eradicate the poppy. We were very lucky in one aspect because we didn't lose any American lives nor did we have any American casualties and that is a big feat because we had daily fighting. We did lose Afghan National Army lives and Afghan National Police, but none from DynCorp.

It isn't the farmers who want to grow the poppy. They are forced to by the Taliban. We are up against the same problem that the Russians were. They went in and wanted the farmers to grow wheat. The farmers take the wheat and then the Taliban comes in and takes it away from them and makes them grow poppy. Our problem is that we are going in and doing eradication and the Taliban is using the wheat and fertilizer to make bombs to use against us. We did the same thing, now we are getting blown up with our own fertilizer. The farmers of course would do what the Taliban told them because they would threaten to kill the farmers' families if they didn't grow the poppy. When we were engaged with the enemy a lot of times the Taliban would go into farmers' houses and kill then and then the tabloids would come out [saying] that we were killing innocent farmers or their families.

The problem we incurred was that the Afghan National Army soldiers are not very good shots at all. Part of the problem is that the AK-47's they had have fold-out stocks instead of wooden stocks on their rifles. It makes it difficult to be a good shot. The ANA listen well, but the problem there is eighty percent are illiterate. On the other hand, they can read you in five minutes whether your BS'ing them or whether you're talking the truth. But there were other problems as well. They aren't very clean people, although they do wash their feet before they pray. Their weapons were often dirty and jammed. They had to load their own machine gun belts which were an enduring problem. Another problem was they had no organizational skills. We are very organized and they don't understand it. When we would get into a firefight we couldn't advance. It's hard to tell them when you're in a firefight

SFC Strong receiving Combat Infantryman Badge and Bronze Star in Kabul, Afghanistan, in 2009 (Greg Strong).

and we just had to try to stand and hold the line. They wanted to execute all the time so it was hard for us to keep them in check. Where the respect came in was, we would go out and make contact. Then the next day do the same. The ANA saw we were sticking with them and we gained more and more respect from them. It got to the point they would fight beside you and then by the end they were really laying it down for us. They even got to the point of trying to protect us.

Our forces were very far apart from each other. You're talking two klicks apart and one Cougar armed with fifty-cals and Mark 19's as well as saws for backup weapons and our M-16's, but the eradicating went very well. On top of our Cougars we had six helicopters above us at all times. We also had a Predator above us that helped us with communications and [to] stay in touch with everyone.

We did not have night vision and the wind storms didn't help any. But the Afghans' instincts were amazing. For instance, we would be on line and looking around, and no one is doing nothing, and you do a line check once some are sleeping, and you do another line check and still nothing, and all at once the ANA would posture up. And they were ready to fight. You knew it was coming. We would be in a firefight in minutes.

Truck on watch next to poppy field near Kabul, Afghanistan, in 2009 (Greg Strong).

All our trucks had a name and ours was War Pig because it got hit the most. We had this terp [interpreter] and he always went out with us. We called him Big Paws because he was big for an Afghan. When we would go out he would look around like a dog sniffing the wind, then he would say, "They will attack from here." He was right every time. One day Major Settle asked him how he knew they would attack from a certain way. He said because he was a military man. He had fought in the south and he knew their tactics. He could even give you the time and we were never surprised once.

The Afghan National Army has a real trust factor. Half of them are Taliban so you don't know who you can trust and who you can't. One time we were at a site and a fellow soldier of mine told me that his interpreter saved his life one time. He told the soldier he couldn't go out because his brother was a Taliban and they were going to fire on the guys when they went out. If the terp doesn't go out, then he doesn't get killed, and neither does the soldier.

Our terp one time got out of the truck when we were out and he had a ANA scanner so we could understand their language and try to interpret from that. The terp tells me that he had been Taliban at one time. I think he still

Typical campsite in Kabul, Afghanistan, in 2009 (Greg Strong).

was. He had been a sergeant major in the ANA army. He says to us, "If they see me you will be fine." On another day we were out and knew where the enemy was located and we were holding up. We were next to a person's house that was an upper Taliban. He was on vacation and they wanted to fire a 107 rocket at us but they wouldn't because if they missed and hit this guy's house it would really make him mad. Major Settle, knowing this, ordered the terp to get in the truck. The terp said, "No, we are safe right here." There is an expression the Afghans always get that tells you when you're in trouble. They get wide-eyed and he was wide-eyed. The major told him to get in the truck or he was going to shoot him himself. He got in the truck. We drew the fire from the enemy and engaged in a firefight. The terp was in the back of the truck scared to death the whole time.

I was in the turret of a Cougar during a firefight once and we were drawing fire. I was looking in my binoculars to locate where the fire was coming from. I had just put my binoculars down and was looking over the turret. This breeze went by my face and I thought what the — — —, but nothing came out of my mouth. I heard an explosion behind me and that of course

Original tents when we got to the Helmand Province in Afghanistan in 2009 (Greg Strong).

started the engagement. It had hit a tree behind my position and fragmented. It was a 107 rocket that missed my head by about six inches. It had been ground-fired from about 300 meters away. I brought back a piece of the rocket and have it in my office.

When I came to the unit I was the oldest man on the team. My nickname was Big Papa. I worked for Major Settle and you couldn't have asked for a better officer. His record speaks for itself. He has three Bronze Stars for valor. For his age he's heads and shoulders above me on wisdom. We used all nine lives, every prayer from back home, every rabbit's foot, and every ounce of luck we had. It all worked out to our favor because the good Lord was watching over us. While there, there were so many near misses and near catastrophes and close calls, but the good Lord and our leadership saw us through it all.

CHAPTER 11

Sergeant Chase Salmela

Headquarters and Headquarters Company, 33rd Brigade Combat Team

KABUL, AFGHANISTAN •
DECEMBER 2008–SEPTEMBER 2009

I enlisted in the military in 2005 and went to basic training at Fort Leonard Wood in the spring of 2006. My first drill was with the Brigade Headquarters in October 2006. Shortly after that we got rumors of deployment. Then I got orders to help the unit out with the mobilization process and was on orders for a year until we finally deployed in 2008. I was at the brigade level and worked with a lot of top brass there and it was a pretty interesting experience.

I am an intelligence analyst which is 35 Fox MOS. Although I have that job I worked in the S-3 training section before deployment. Being an intelligence analyst is challenging. There's only so much you can do with the IPB intelligence preparation of the battlefield and do field manuals, but with the technology today and it changes every day and is real challenging because you don't get the real feel for it, and on drill weekends it's more concentrating on getting company stuff done so there wasn't a lot of platoon section time and we had to go through all the checklist and briefings for deployment. As an individual I put all I could into it to do the best job I could.

The first week of October 2008 we moved out. We were in Urbana, Illinois, and they had a ceremony at the assembly hall at the University of Illinois. The center stage was all lit up and we marched out and the commander went through with all the family members and they got to see a company formation and a drill ceremony. Deployment is emotional. The families know you are in the military and you have a job to do and the ceremony kinda gives some closure to the situation. It is emotional for all of us. At the time I was engaged to my high school sweetheart of eight years and it was stressful on our relationship. I don't know how to explain it, it was like there was tension in the air.

It was difficult on my parents also, back when I joined at 20 years old. We are originally from Illinois but my family moved to Colorado in 2005 and I stayed in Illinois. They made the trip to Urbana for the deployment ceremony and they understood why I was in the military, but also misunderstood it and it was a constant give and take as far as talking about it. When I initially told them I was joining the military, they didn't want me to do it because it was too dangerous. I was independent and joined anyway. My mother had the hardest time with it. My father was in the marines in Vietnam so I don't know if it was a generation thing or what, but things were different back then and obviously Vietnam was different than Afghanistan and Iraq. I have to calm [my mother] down every time I go out there to Colorado to visit them. They always asked about what is new and is there news on deployments. My mom thinks I have a computer chip in my arm and am a major spy. I have to constantly reiterate that she is stretching things, so in October of 2008 it was a emotional and stressful time for them.

We left the armory with police escort all the way to the airport and then flew directly to Fort Bragg, and that's where we did our pre-mobilization site training. We were there for about two months and that's where we really started getting into sectional and MOS training. We started picking up computers and really working into the training.

I had accumulated some leave and I had about three or four days coming right before Thanksgiving. It wasn't enough to come home so I had my girlfriend to fly to Fayetteville, North Carolina, and I got a hotel and we stayed there for a couple of days. We went to Myrtle Beach for a day and visited a few other places. It wasn't as hard to say goodbye this time as it had been when we left the armory in Urbana. I don't know if it was the whole initial process leaving home and all, but it just wasn't as hard.

We left Fort Bragg on December 1 and it took us a couple of days to get in country, and we went to Camp Phoenix and we were relieving the 27th Brigade out of Georgia. We met a number of the guys from the 48th and spent some time getting to know the layout of the camp. It was an interesting and new experience. All of the 33rd wasn't there yet and we spent time going around finding out the locations of the towers, helicopter landing pad, the LZ, and the rest of the layout of the camp so we could get some sort of routine in order to expedite the transition of the guys coming in, and shortly after there was actual change-over between units.

My responsibilities were the ARSIC Central Intelligence analyst. We were primarily a training unit to train the Afghan forces and because of that we didn't have a lot of responsibilities, land holding, mission oriented or actually conducting missions. They obviously wanted to know what was going on with the enemy, but it was more like relaying the information to headquarters than going out in the cities and different provinces and doing raw intelligence collection. It was computer based and we in my ARSIC shared information on what was going on in different provinces and what trends we saw in that kind of information and I did that for six months.

We had ample ways of being in contact back home. We were able to use the Internet in our own individual rooms and we also had a center where there was Internet and we could get on civilian e-mails and had access to Facebook. I didn't use Facebook but did use the e-mails and we could get phone cards at the PX to call home. I called my girlfriend about once a week and my family too, but not as much. It was kinda tricky calling because there is a thirteen-hour difference between Afghanistan and the States so I had to be careful when I called. As for mail, it took about a week and a half to receive mail. I got a lot of goodies in the mail from time to time.

We really didn't see a whole lot of activity where I was at. We woke up of a morning and worked out, showered, shaved, grabbed some breakfast and then to work for twelve hours and then your shift was done. I would clock out, go back and maybe watch a movie, and go to sleep and then do it again. There wasn't a whole lot going on so it was hard to find things to do with your time — write e-mails, watch a movie, hang out with your friends, play cards, and I did that for six months.

In April 2009 I went home on leave. Going on leave is an adventure in itself. If I had it to do again, I probably wouldn't do it because it is hectic. It is nice to go home and see your family, but the aspect of catching helicopter rides from point A to point B and then to point C and D and then fill out paperwork to get to point E and ten more paperwork to get to point G is a real hassle. Then I went home for two weeks' leave and back to Afghanistan. Going back I would wait for as much as three or four days to get a helicopter ride from one point to another. My leave was two weeks and I was actually gone for about three and a half to four weeks trying to get there and back. When I returned I picked up where I left off.

In June our company had to start an Embedded Training team to train the Afghan National Army. A friend of mine said they were looking to grab some extra guys for the team. I was halfway through with the tour and my reaction was to jump on it and have a chance to get a different experience than just sitting at a desk and I wanted to go out so I jumped on the opportunity. I told my platoon sergeant and he checked into it and I was on it in a couple of days. It was definitely a last-minute deal.

In the two days I had to [change from] a noncombatant to a combatant status. I went to supply four or five times to get supplies I needed over the two-day time, and at the same time checked in gear I had that I no longer needed. I also contacted my girlfriend and told her that I was moving from a desk job to a new assignment. I told her I would get in touch with her as much as I could. Then two days later I reported to the team.

When I got to the team they were doing an ammo check and inventory. They were pulling out fifty-cals, Mark 19's, AT4's, grenades, I mean just pallets of stuff and my first thought was, "What did I get myself into?" I get out of the Humvee and this guy says, "Put these four boxes of fifty-cal ammo in the truck." I am loading up the truck and trying to see what's going on and was trying to learn who everybody was and there were four or five guys from my company that I knew. There were two guys from the Arizona and Indiana National Guard as well as our guys. We had the trucks loaded and the convoy set up and I realized I hadn't been given an assignment yet and I didn't know where I was sitting in what truck, so I found the captain and asked what my assignment was and where I was sitting. He told me I was driving the lead truck in the convoy. I was shocked. I had driven a regular Humvee, but this was an armored Humvee and I had never driven one before and I was supposed to be the lead vehicle for a three-vehicle convoy.

Well, we left at about midnight and I was driving the lead vehicle. Here I had come from intelligence and now three days later I am driving the lead Humvee. We drove for about eight hours and I was alert the whole time because I had heard all these stories about IEDs. I was really nervous and watching the road and both hands on the wheel. There was an IED that went off about one hundred meters ahead of my truck. What they had done was put the IED in a culvert underneath the road, and instead of it exploding upwards it exploded out the culvert so I don't know what kind of damage it would have done. Mentally, emotionally and physically it didn't bother me, it was just more of, "It happened, now just drive on." And I did and we drove for about eighteen hours and we stopped at an American base, I don't even know where it was, and grabbed about eight hour's sleep, refueled and got back on the road.

It really amazed me how many IED holes there were in the road. How fresh they were, it was like driving through a parking lot full of cones. It was turn left to swerve one then right.

We finally got to Kandahar and were there for about a week just resupplying and getting some rest. When we left we had to go through the city and some of the 33rd was going to give us an escort. There were three or four of their vehicles and a couple of ANA vehicles in front and then my vehicle and the rest were behind me. We had been driving for about fifteen minutes and an IED went off. We called back and informed the rest of the convoy. The IED hit a Humvee and hit on the front wheel of the passenger side of the vehicle. When we come in on it the vehicle was on its roof, wheels in the air, and the doors were open. The guys were still trapped inside. The guy manning the gun had been thrown from the vehicle and was laying in the road in front of the vehicle. I wanted to go help, do what I could, but we were in the middle of Kandahar city and we had been told about these complex attacks, so I called back to my team leader and stayed in the truck. We called for a medic.

The lieutenant said, "Let's pull security," and told me to pull up and block the road in front of the Humvee, which I did. Because we might take fire I had to stay in the vehicle so I could maneuver it, and the lieutenant got out with the medic to assess the situation at the explosion site. I was about a hundred meters from the vehicle and I was on the radio keeping the team leader informed about what was going on. It was difficult because the one guy was on the ground in front of the vehicle, but there were two in the vehicle that I could see, but I didn't know if there were any more in the Humvee.

After about ten minutes of going back and forth I got out of the vehicle and told the gunner he was the radio and I was going up there and see what I could do. There were three people in the vehicle. The same concept as we had in our vehicle, the vehicle driver, TC, and the gunner. The gunner had been thrown out, as I said, and the other two still had seat belts on, trapped upside down. They had actually got the driver out and he was conscious, but the other two weren't and we didn't know what kind of condition they were in. Me and another guy concentrated on getting the other guy out of the vehicle. It was difficult trying to pull a two-hundred-pound guy out of a vehicle when he was upside down in this small opening in the Humvee vehicle. We were huddling and trying to get a hold of him and the door was partially off and it fell on me and cut my upper arm. It is an armored door so it weighs about three hundred pounds. The cut wasn't that bad, but we finally got the guy out of the vehicle. We had a couple more medics by then and we checked the unconscious guy for vital signs. He had no pulse but there was no external damage as far as blood or anything broken so we were kind of baffled. The medic wanted to do a tracheotomy so I held his head between my legs while the medic performed the tracheotomy. It took him a while to do it and then we got our stretcher out and put him on it and put a neck brace on him.

I think what happened was that when you're in the Humvee and you have all your gear on and the helmet and all, your head is only about an inch from the roof. The Humvee went into the air and landed on its roof, I think that it crushed his head down into his neck. I think that is what it was, some kind of neck injury, but about that time the medevac was coming in and they wanted us to pull security for the incoming helicopter, so I ran back to the truck and pulled off ninety degrees. We were supposed to mark the site with either purple or yellow smoke. We had some Canadian soldiers with us and one of them threw out smoke and it was the wrong color. The helicopter came in and saw the wrong color and peeled off. We had to make contact with them and it was about ten or fifteen minutes before the helicopter came back. After the guys were taken out by the helicopter we were there for about another hour just trying to clean the area up.

I had blood all over my pants and I still have them today. I remember when we got back in the vehicle the lieutenant was asking me if I was all right. He knew I wasn't an experienced combat soldier and he knew it was pretty bad. I told him I was all right. I knew that I was fine. You have the initial reaction because of the sudden surprise, but I was calm when I got back in the truck.

I found out that all the guys in the Humvee were from this unit. The guy that did the tracheotomy was from this unit. The guy that had the tracheotomy was from this unit also and he died that day. The gunner died also, but the driver made it. He had a broken leg and foot and a couple of discs in his back. I actually met him a couple of months ago here at the armory. We got to talk and I had a chance to ask him what he remembered. He has been in therapy for ten months after the incident, but he is walking, he is alive and one of the other guys on that team in the escort is in this unit. We were talking one day and realized that we were both in the same convoy in trucks next to each other.

After we left the IED site we went to Helmand and we were there for about four months. We worked with the British and Danish and did missions with them. About a week after we got there, one of the Afghan soldiers that we were responsible for got killed because they were driving reckless in their vehicle. They would flip and roll them because they were like Ford Rangers, just little trucks, but they would have like four or five people in the bed of the truck just sitting around as they were going fifty miles an hour down the highway and hit a pothole or swerved a little bit and those guys would fall out of the back. It was literally once a week one of them would get killed falling out of a truck.

I don't know if it was the U.S. presence or because we were trying to help them out, but they just expected us to hand them over a new one. It was like holding out their hands and waiting for a new set of keys. We told them they couldn't keep doing this, we weren't going to give them new trucks over and over. They just didn't understand why we wouldn't.

One night we were assisting the ANA doing a night patrol. We had sat upon these berms, like strategically overlooking this bridge. There were like two or three ANA vehicles to our one. There was a helicopter team and it was going to be in the area for a couple of nights to assist us. We were stretched out maybe a hundred kilometers, like one vehicle every twenty kilometers. We get this radio traffic from the anti–IED helicopter and they reported that they had come up on an IED emplacement team putting an IED in the road. They had killed some of them but they wanted us to assist and go to the site. About half an hour later we were at the site. We finally found it and there was one enemy dead about ten meters from the road. There he was with pick-axe, a bag of explosives, and a shovel beside him where he was about to place an IED.

The helicopter informed us that there were two others and one had run to this house. We went to the compound and there was an enemy machine gun in position at the corner of this garden in front of the house. There was a blood trail so we followed it and went to the house. We told the ANA that they had to go in and clear the house. They had the hardest time understanding why they had to do it instead of us. I don't know if they were just scared or these were friends of theirs because you couldn't trust all the ANA. The house had a wall around it with the house in the center. One Afghan guy goes over the wall, doesn't see anything and comes and opens this gate so we could all get in. We started through the house clearing one room at a time. We got to the last one and it was scary because it was like underground. It was like twenty steps down in the ground and there were a lot of booby traps around. It was at night when we were there so it was hard to see. We were there for about eight hours and it was morning before we left, but we didn't find anyone else.

The next morning I did the biometrics analysis on the dead enemy soldier. I did his iris scan and fingerprints and all of that and he wasn't in the system. He had been laying there for a while and rigor mortis sets in pretty quick so trying to get fingerprints was difficult. Then we had to wait for the Brits to get there because there were quite a bit of explosives there and they were responsible for destroying them. After that we returned back to the base.

They had the election in 2009 and we were told we could not be near the election sites. We took positions on the berms or hills and provided some security while the elections were going on. A couple of days later we were literally packing up to go home. We were replaced by the marines and the process took about two weeks. Then on September 11, 2009, we landed at Fort McCoy, Wisconsin. We got a police escort from there back to Urbana,

Illinois, and it took about four or five hours. We drove to the assembly hall for the welcome home. We had people putting up signs on overpasses saying welcome home. When we got in formation our commander told us he was going to say give our thanks for the support, a prayer, and was going to release us. We weren't in formation but about five minutes and we were released to our families. It was a happy time for those of us who made it back.

CHAPTER 12

Staff Sergeant Scott Edwards

C Company, 2-130 Infantry

BAGHDAD, IRAQ • 2006

HERAT, AFGHANISTAN •
DECEMBER 2008–SEPTEMBER 2009

The 123 Field Artillery out of Galesburg, Illinois, was put on alert and then called up to go to Iraq. They filled their Alpha Bravo companies, but didn't have enough to fill Charlie Company so they tasked our unit to fill Charlie. I didn't have to go but decided I wanted to because I've been on active duty before and I thought, I support the guys here so I'm going to support them over there. We went to Fort Dix, New Jersey, for our training in January. We trained for about 90 days. It was great to go train for Iraq in a foot of snow. That's the army, who knows what they do or why they do it. We went straight to Kuwait from Fort Dix for two weeks of acclimation and then into Baghdad. I was stationed in Baghdad, Iraq, in 2006.

When we arrived in Baghdad we assumed the mission of security detail for the president and staff of the Iraq president. Because I was the administrative guy I wasn't too much hands-on at first. Our line platoons were broken down into details so that we had one platoon would provide security for the president, another for his secretary of defense. We just did security for them in Baghdad.

When they went out of Baghdad they would fly on a chopper, but in Baghdad they took vehicles. The Navy SEALs were actually in the vehicles with the dignitaries and we would form details and be the outer security. The

SEALs were a good bunch of guys. I basically stayed in the office and did admin stuff at first. Then guys started taking leave and I pretty much had to fill their spots. I did everything. I drove the vehicles and sometimes was on the gun.

We really didn't get to work with the Iraq army much, but we did work with them some. Their soldiers really don't want to do the job — they wanted us to do the job. When we wouldn't and demanded they do the missions, they would get mad and say we weren't trying to help them.

We didn't have a lot of attempts on the dignitaries. During the first elections we were really worried about possible attacks. But it went okay. During the time I was there we had mortars come in on us and we had VBIEDS (vehicle borne improvised explosive devices) at the checkpoints, but they were not really close to us, and we had no direct threats. When we first got there we got RPGs (rocket propelled grenades). After a while they realized we were a hard target and they couldn't do much to our vehicles so they started targeting the Iraq army trucks because they were soft-skinned Ranger trucks. Our mission was successful. We never lost a dignitary.

I went to Afghanistan in December 2008. When we first arrived I was basically on a security detail for a FOB (forward operations base). I was the sergeant of the guard. If there was activity going on in front of the perimeter I would have to check it out. Most of the time it was nothing. We were actually inside a ANA [Afghanistan National Army] base. The Afghan soldiers were just being ignorant, out wandering around doing whatever they do. The FOB wasn't too bad. We were on the east side of Afghanistan and there wasn't much activity. It was pretty relaxed. We had some enemy mortars come in a few times but that was about it.

After about four months into the tour we were reassigned. Me and nine other guys were pieced out to an ETT [embedded training team]. We went to Kabul and me and two other guys were assigned to UH, 3–6 Special Forces team. We took on a brand new Afghan battalion to train. The Special Forces were in charge of their infantry training and me and my team were in charge of logistics and mentoring. One of my guys, a 13 Fox 4 observer, and the other guy were put in jobs that they had no idea what they were doing. Because I had been on active duty before, I knew the army and knew the system so I was able to get the job done and help the other guys in the team do the same.

The Special Forces were less than cooperative with the Afghans because the Afghans' training was substandard. They didn't know what they were doing and the Special Forces had all this high-class training. It was like trying to teach a bunch of second graders how to do something. A lot of times the Special Forces would get frustrated and just say, "We are done," and leave. Then the Afghans would come to us and say, "We need to do this training."

Afghanistan National Army soldier posing for photograph in Herat, Afghanistan, in 2009 (Scott Edwards).

The Afghan soldiers were like the Iraqi soldiers. They want us to come there and train them, but when they were done they were done. Like it might come one o'clock and they would say, "We are done," and we would say, "No, we have all day training," and they would say, "No, we are done," and leave. They just had a different mindset than we did. They wanted us to do the job also. They didn't want to do anything.

One big difference with the Iraqi soldiers and the Afghan soldiers was that the Afghan soldiers would fight. If we got into a firefight they would stay and fight really hard, but Iraqi soldiers, they would run and hide. They wouldn't fight at all.

We finally took the battalion from Kabul and took them to the west side of Afghanistan. It was a three-day convoy. That was to be their area of concentration. While we were in the west they had an election. It was their first ever. Basically they just did security missions and nothing big happened. It was pretty calm in that area the whole time we were there. Most of the conflict was in the south. They were also trying to get more troops in the north area and began to get more resistance because that was the Taliban area. Most of

SSgt Scott Edwards and Afghanistan National Army sergeant major in Herat, Afghanistan, in 2009 (Scott Edwards).

the problems was with IEDs placed in the road blowing trucks up. We were there for about two months and then our tour was over and we turned it over to the 82nd Airborne.

The training of the Afghanistan soldiers was definitely a challenge. They wanted us to do everything. Winter would come and we would ask them if they ordered firewood. They would say, "No, you do that." We would say, "No, that's your job." Unfortunately we would be talking to the officer that was supposed to order the firewood. He wouldn't order it. He didn't care. He was in an office where it was warm so he didn't care, but his troops out on post had no firewood. They have poor mentality and I don't think it will ever change. They don't do good planning. Iraq was the same way. They had poor planning. Once we are gone and time for them to take over all the operations by themselves, I think they will just go back the same way the countries were when we came.

CHAPTER 13

Sergeant Michael S. Mormino

Headquarters and Headquarters Company, 2-130 Infantry

KHOST, AFGHANISTAN •
DECEMBER 2008–SEPTEMBER 2009

I started the deployment process before the rest of my unit because I was being sent to Raven school. I did two weeks of Raven certification at Fort Bragg. Raven is a small unmanned surveillance airplane and they taught us how to use it. Then we went to Afghanistan in December 2008. We were at Camp Phoenix for a couple of days and then shipped out to our FOB at Camp Clark, which was out east in Afghanistan.

I did gate guard for the most part and had the day shift so I didn't see very much action. We got hit pretty good at night though. It wasn't as bad as I thought it would be, but bad enough. In the morning I would get up and make sure the rest of my team was up and running. I had one in the tower and one patting down locals as they came in to the base to go to work, and then whenever they got done they would get patted down again and sent to their home. Camp Clark was a FOB inside a larger Afghan FOB. It is just a little chunk of land. We had two gates, the main gate and then we manned an Afghan gate. We worked with the Afghans trying to search the trucks coming in. They had these things jerry-rigged. It just surprised me. The batteries were sitting in the cab of the truck running the stinking radios and stuff like that. We were always looking for bombs and it kept you on your toes and you didn't want to get complacent, but the whole truck would look like a bomb the way the wires stuck out all over the place, but that is just how they were. We went with the Afghans to search because you couldn't trust them. We had navy personnel, air force personnel, and a larger army unit there besides us as well. Everything that happened, happened at night. We got mortared about seventeen times while I was there. It all happened between 2200 hours and 0300 in the morning.

I got to fly my Raven over an enemy foot patrol that we had come into contact with and I lost the Raven because I rammed it into a mountain. We had to take a foot patrol out to get it and climb the mountain. We took a platoon of locals with us and they made fun of me all the way there and back because I got winded climbing up the mountain. We retrieved the plane and came back.

The second time I lost the plane was with a fly-over of a suspected mortar site. It hit some rough wind and it downed the plane. The next day they sent out the 101st Airborne on a patrol, but they couldn't find the plane. Then the next day I went out with a squad of National Guard soldiers and we found my bird and brought it back.

They did a move in the middle of our deployment and Georgia came in and swapped us out. We did our right seat training with them and then went back to Camp Phoenix for a couple of weeks, then we were sent to Camp Stone which was in the west. I was administration, putting packs together for awards and guys going home. We were there during the election and we got thumped pretty hard there as well.

The camp hadn't been hit for three or four years and we got hit one night with about sixteen mortars and four or five rocket-propelled grenades. There were no casualties on our side. It lasted all night. We had just got there that day and I was working the night shift because the regular army was working in the offices during the day. They said that around 1800 we could come in and start doing our work. Me and one other guy were in there plugging away, doing our admin work. The alarm went off. We heard the first mortar hit and so we ran to our bunker. While we were running for the bunker another round came in and hit, but they were hitting outside of the wire. No one was really scared because since we had been in country we had been mortared so many times that it became a normal thing for us. We got in the bunker and was thinking, "When are we going to be able to go back in and get our work done?" They took a roll call and me and some of the other guys sat there and told jokes until we heard the all clear and we could go back to work. About the time we were out of the bunkers [came] another volley of mortars and rockets with it this time. We were in the bunkers for a long time.

It was a culture shock when I first got there. We thought we were going to be in the mountains all day fighting in the shit. It was hard seeing grown men walking around holding hands and kissing on each other, but the locals were friendly to us and seemed to like us and wanted our help, but after time we could tell that when they shook our hands they were just trying to see how much money they could get from us dumb Americans.

I did a lot of soul searching over there trying to figure out what we're fighting for and figure out what these locals were after. We had this interpreter, his name was Sunny. He was a pharmacist, but made more money being an interpreter than he would as a pharmacist or doctor. He could speak excellent English and he came in one day and said, "Sergeant Mormino, I want you guys to just drop nukes all over this place and level it and then we will come back in and rebuild it later." A lot of the locals believed that way, but at the same time most of them wanted us to do everything for them. They didn't want to do it for themselves.

Our main mission was to train the Afghan National Army. I thought this was a good idea because we were saying, "We are going to come in and fight for you, but we are going to train you and you can fight for your country yourselves. You're going to fight the good fight." Problem was one in ten wanted to fight the good fight and the rest wanted something given to them.

We did some humanitarian type things while we were there. We would set up a clinic and all our medics would come in and let the kids and older people come and get checkups. We gave out shoes and clothes and soccer balls and other stuff. It was mainly for the kids, and I was just there handing out shoes and stuff and it gave me a warm and fuzzy feeling inside because I was doing a good job and doing the right thing. I had finished one day and I saw an ANA soldier smacking the shit out of this little kid, I mean just beating him, and me and my buddy went over and told him to knock it off, you don't hit kids like that. Then we took the kid and made sure he was all right and the little bastard stole my pen out of my coat. Over there they see kindness as weakness.

My experience wasn't near as bad as some of the other guys. It was like a vacation for a little bit, other than getting mortared. I had a gun and got to go out on log runs and I flew ... missions, but one night I was on duty and Dog Company out of the 101st Airborne was out. I was near the radio and they engaged in a firefight. It wasn't bad, but here I was back on base just listening to them get shot up. Then we went out where they were the next morning and it was the first enemy combatant that I had seen. They drug him up by my truck and left him there. We ended up being there for about eight hours, but it was rough on me. I didn't kill him, but I can still see his face.

The first time we got rocketed I was playing cards with my lieutenant and a guy named Mike Wallace and Mike Zine. Mike Wallace was a specialist on my team and Mike Zine was a civilian contractor. We were sitting and

Sgt. Michael Mormino and his Raven at Fort Bragg, North Carolina, during training in 2007 (Michael Mormino).

playing spades and I was beating my lieutenant's ass and the rocket came in and hit. I didn't know what it was, it just whistled and then exploded about fifty meters from where we were at. Everyone froze, just froze and looked at each other. The lieutenant made the first move and he got up quick and his chair fell back and everybody just scrambled out the door. It was chaos outside, everyone was running. I looked back to see if the lieutenant and the other guys were behind me. Mike Wallace is a big guy. I don't mean tall and strong, I mean big and fat and I never saw him move so fast. We went into the bunker and after a while they sounded the all clear. It was only one rocket that came in so was nothing crazy.

I was told to go to the tower for watch. I went and scanned my sectors and just waited and waited and waited. Nothing happened and finally they called a second all clear. I went back and gathered up my cards and went to sit down, and my lieutenant came in and said I needed to go and guard a hole in the wall where the rocket had come through. I got to see the damage from the rocket. The bastards had hit our refrigerator, there was ice cream, pudding, and Otis Spunkmeyer cookies everywhere. I guarded the area all night. While I was there I realized for the first time that I could have died seeing how close the hole was to where we were sitting and playing cards. It was just nuts. There was a civilian contractor that lived in a utility shed that was about four or five feet from where he was at and he needed to take a piss and left the shed. About a minute later the rocket hit right where he had been sitting at the computer and just peppered the walls with shrapnel. He would have been dead. It just made you realize how easy it could happen. It was the first time a rocket hit inside the wire.

As time went on we would hear the mortar tubes go off and they were just throwing mortars. They didn't care where they hit, they just wanted to mess with us and keep us up all night. We got to where, when we got hit we would just pick up our cards and go to the bunker and finish our card game with our headlights on and our body armor on. It almost became routine.

We got hit once during the day and that really scared a lot of people. What happened was, we had a company go outside the wire and go to the range to get some trigger time in. Whenever we went out there the locals would come up and pick up the brass because they could go sell it, and there was a kid that had wandered out to get some and they didn't see the kid and a ricochet round hit him and killed him. The local village near our base was Taliban friendly and didn't like us anyway and we were getting hit by them instead of the Taliban for retribution for the kid. They had tried to save him, but by the time they got to him it was too late.

They put us on high alert that night but nothing happened. We thought, "Well, maybe we got by with this one," but the next night we got hit pretty hard. I saw rockets coming in, mortars and one of the rockets that hit was an old Chinese Willy Peter rocket and it hit a Hesko barrier, which is a wire cage with gravel put in it, and I saw the rocket. My buddy was outside calling in incoming and he didn't have any armor on and he said, "Hey, Sarge, come here and look at all this shit coming in." There were tracer rounds and all kinds of stuff coming in and it looked like it was coming right at us. I pulled the guy in and said, "Get in here, you dumbass," and as I'm sticking my head out to pull him in I watched the rocket hit the Hesko and this liquid fire just rolls over the top of it. It was the most beautiful thing I had ever saw in my life. When I came to reality I was like, "Holy shit, I better get in because they are really getting close to us," and that was just nuts for me to have done. They left us alone after a while and the next day we were all rattled because of the attack and knowing we had killed the kid. It was an accident, but it still was a terrible feeling.

A few days later we lost a kid from Dog Company while they were on patrol. They hit an IED. He was just nineteen years old and they did a memorial for him. It was the first time I ever saw a battlefield cross with the rifle

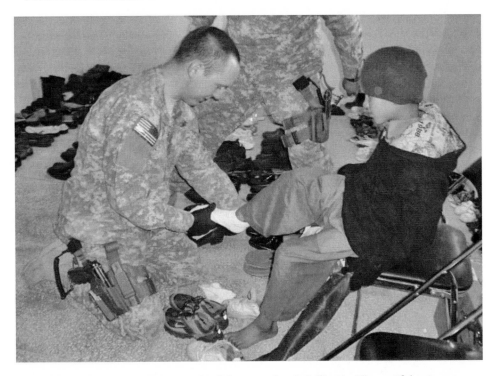

Sgt. Michael Mormino giving a pair of shoes to a local civilian in Khost, Afghanistan, in 2009 (Michael Mormino).

and the boots and the helmet and the dog tags. Nobody said a word for him. None of his fellow soldiers stepped up and said anything and it was a shame. We're all brothers and nobody knew this kid well enough to say something for him. Maybe nothing needed to be said, but I would hope if that happened to me one day someone would say something for me.

Then during the summer Georgia came in and relieved us again. We were sent back to Camp Phoenix. We were the 33rd without a mission. Rumors started floating around that they weren't going to send us home because the one-star general wanted to get another star for being there for a year, but nobody knew. There were all kinds of rumors floating around above my pay grade. I was supposed to do what I was told and that's what I did.

Camp Phoenix was a different world, soldiers singing and dancing around, a freaking Dairy Queen in the middle of the desert. Well, it wasn't the desert in Afghanistan but people were walking around all day long, nobody had anything to do, fifteen thousand soldiers sitting there twiddling their thumbs. The only guys working were the ones guarding the gate. Thank God they were working.

A couple weeks later we went to Camp Stone and it was quiet for a long time. In country and drinking is a big no-no. Guys were bragging about how long it had been since they had been hit. It was the night before the election and somebody got some kind of fifth of rum and just tore it up. Since it had been so long that they had drank they were really smashed. The person was pretty high-ranking. I went out of the bunker and this guy is walking around. I asked him what he was dong and he said that he was looking for his truck so he could get his gear and go to the bunker. About that time rockets started coming in and I got him to the bunker. Then while we were in the bunker he and several others needed to get air because they were getting sick. We told them to calm down and stay put. The rockets stop and they go outside and start puking. Then the rockets started again and this one guy is trying to take charge but he is too drunk. We got back in the bunker and he lit a cigarette and started puking. He said it was from the cigarette, but we all knew better because he reeked from booze. Little did he know the commanding officer was in the bunker. The next day four of them got in trouble and were shipped out by the commanding officer.

We lost a kid named Talbert and we lost another kid named Garrett Smith during that time. They were involved in a IED attack. I knew him and he was a medic and had been part of my platoon back at Fort Bragg, but because he was a medic he got pulled and went elsewhere. He was a good kid and had a girlfriend at home. I wouldn't let anybody say anything about him or his memorial service. It was the rollover that got him and Garrett Smith got it by friendly fire. I don't know what happened exactly, but he lived long enough to make it to the helicopter and then he died. A lot of people say if we would have just came home we wouldn't have lost him, and other people say it wouldn't have mattered if we came home because when your time is up it is up.

We finally came home and arrived in Wisconsin and it was glorious to get back onto American soil. We were just sitting there breathing it. When you go to other countries some of them have a funk to them and Afghanistan has a terrible funk and you breathe it and then you come home and it smells good. We were there two or three days and then they bused us back home. It was the longest ride I ever took. They trucked us to the Marion Pavilion and we were released to our families. There were so many people blubbering and crying all over the place. Parents hugging anyone they could get their arms around not even their own kids. There were signs all over the place and it was a life changing experience.

War is a scary thing and it would be hard to lose any of my men, but I didn't. We all made it home safely and I thank God for that.

CHAPTER 14

Staff Sergeant Christopher Niemeyer

Headquarters and Headquarters Company, 2-130 Infantry

NAWBAHAR DISTRICT, AFGHANISTAN •
DECEMBER 2008–SEPTEMBER 2009

I was in Afghanistan from mid–December 2008 through September 2009. I spent my first three weeks on a police mentor team. We checked their records to make sure they were in line with the training regulations, had the police personnel at each police station that was required, and measured their levels of training. That was short-lived and after three weeks my duties changed.

I was sent down to Zabul Province in Nawbahar and joined a six-man embedded training team. Our job was to train the Afghanistan soldiers to get them proficient and to make them battle ready. The guys on my team were basically a bunch of good guys. Three or four guys on the team had been there for several months. Me and one other guy were brand new.

It was harsh landscape, hard ground, very mountainous, very difficult to move around in. We traveled in Humvees and as matter of fact the first month we couldn't move anywhere because we had snow on the ground and just couldn't move. We finally started doing missions about a month after I got there. We got a reality check about mid–March when we were going on a mission just outside our sector. We had about six miles on this mission to a village. On the way we hit an IED. It was an Afghanistan army truck that was hit instead of one of ours. We lost four Afghan soldiers and several severely wounded. We got all of them medevacked and continued on our mission. It wasn't even two hours later after our mission was complete and we hit another one on the way back to base. This time we lost two Afghan police officers and four others were wounded. It was an eye-opening experience that I will never forget. That's when my deployment started in my eyes because before that it was kind of smooth sailing and then you get a reality check and you realize this is the real thing.

We were at a small FOB [forward observation base] and we only had six guys on our team. It was very primitive living. We literally lived inside mud walls that served as a barrier for the FOB and we had a twelve-foot-wide living space. We felt very protected because the walls were about eighteen inches thick, but on the other hand we had no security, we had no land support for about four hours from us, and air support was scarce. If we got hit it would take about 45 minutes to get any air support.

Our first firefight was on April 29. It was at a nearby village and it was very chaotic. We started getting RPG rounds and small arms fire. I got my first confirmed kill that day. It was a camel. It was very hard to see the enemy and a very long distance firefight, but again another reality check. When you got bullets literally hitting all around you, you realize how real it is and how quick you can get killed.

It just got worse. Our FOB got hit many times by mortars and rocket attacks. Our job was to train the Afghan police and Afghan Army and we did our job, but every time we went outside the wire we were a target. We just hoped the enemy would fire at us so we could make contact and eliminate them.

We went to the villages and we tried to win the hearts and minds of the people in the villages, but the harsh reality is that the economic situation in this very rural area has no financial structure and the people have to do what is best for them at that moment, so if they have to follow the Taliban in order for their families to survive that day and tell us what we want to hear the next they will, to help their families survive.

We understood their situation. We were limited with only six of us and visited about twenty villages on a regular basis. We met with all the people and usually a big group of men or elders that listened to our story and the Afghanistan commander's story. We promised humanitarian aid. One of the problems with the humanitarian aid was we did get lots of school supplies, shoes, and clothing, but one large supply was flour. I found that kind of interesting because we wanted to eliminate poppy seeds and replace it with grain to give them some kind of other economic structure, but yet we were giving them tons and tons of flour which eliminated the need to grow grain. I found it kind of comical.

Toward the end of our deployment we had elections on August 20, the first democratic election in the country. We expected trouble and went out on patrol that morning at 0500. The people of the villages told us they needed us to come to their village and tell them to go vote so that they could tell the Taliban that we forced them to do it. The Taliban had threatened the villagers with death of their families and torture in some cases. We had an issue with the election before it started because the Taliban had taken most of the villagers' ID's for voting so they could not vote. We dealt with it and let them vote anyway.

When the polls opened we had Afghanistan National Army at the high ground to keep an eye out for us. We had all three of our trucks down at the election site. We got word from one of the Afghan army troops that they had found an IED at the top of the hill. While there they were drinking their chai tea and one of the troops kind of swept his leg when he was sitting on the ground and found a pressure plate. We take two trucks and start for the top of the hill to defuse the IED. About fifty or one hundred meters from the IED site we were just hailed with mortars, rockets, and small arms fire. I'm talking about hundreds of rockets and mortars. It was just crazy, like something out of a movie. Every time I saw a mortar or rocket hit on the election site it looked like a good hit, and when one would hit near the people the same thing. I was on high ground and my view was perfect. I thought at that very moment we had lost hundreds of people at the election site. We got on the radio and called the commander, who was down on the ground at the election site. It seemed like twenty minutes that we tried to get a hold of him and there was nothing. Then suddenly he was on the radio yelling. He was in a chaotic situation and trying to check on the people. It seemed like every time he moved in the vehicle to go check on the people a rocket or mortar would hit right there. It was by the grace of God they didn't get hurt or killed.

When the smoke cleared we tried to figure out where the enemy was located. We begin to fire in all locations that we thought the enemy was in to try to draw fire, but after the initial attack they did not respond. When the smoke cleared, about an hour later, we threw C4 on the IED and blew it. It was the biggest IED that I ever saw. It left a four-foot hole in the ground.

We went down to the election site and not one person had a scratch on them. I can't explain it. It was just by the act of God. I was supposed to have come home on August 14 and here it was August 20 and one of the most scary days that I had spent in Afghanistan. We had had numerous attacks on the FOB, but nothing like the one on election day.

The experience in Afghanistan was fantastic. I learned a lot about myself.

I learned a lot about the culture of Afghanistan and I learned a lot about mentoring and being a leader. It was just a humbling experience because you just don't realize what you have until you see what other people don't have. The Afghanistan people where I was had absolutely nothing, and the funny thing is they are good people. They were the most generous people and would literally give you the shirt off their backs. I call it my year-long camping trip and that is kind of what it was, but I don't look forward to going back and I hope and pray I won't have to go back, but I wouldn't trade the experience for anything in the world.

CHAPTER 15

Sergeant First Class
Heath Clark

*Headquarters and Headquarters
Company, 2-123 Infantry*

HELMAND PROVINCE, AFGHANISTAN •
DECEMBER 2008–SEPTEMBER 2009

We arrived on December 1, 2008, in Afghanistan. It was me and Lieutenant Southworth that took over the Scout Platoon section at Helmand Province. We did a five-day process and then headed out from Kandahar City. We headed down Highway 1 to Highway 601. It took us eighteen hours to get what would have taken a normal individual about two and a half hours to drive. The roads were all bombed out. When I say out I'm talking about twenty, thirty-foot-wide craters, cars on fire, trucks on fire, split in half, bridges were down to one lane. These bridges weren't bridges like you what you'd see going over the Mississippi. They were like twenty or thirty feet wide. It was something like out of a movie. As we were driving along we were getting shot at. We could hear the AK rounds and the RPGs coming at you and that's when we knew it was real.

We got to Laskar Gah and started to get settled in. It was Christmas when we first started our engagements with the enemy. We had three teams. I had Dagger, then there was Easy Rider and Iron Horse. It was around a seventeen- or eighteen-man configuration with four trucks each team. We were embedded with ANCOP (Afghan National Civil Order Police) police and Easy Rider was embedded with the border patrol down in southern Helmand

85

so we didn't see them much. It was our mission to go out and take out the police in each district a little at a time and send them to training. There was just so much corruption and the ANCOPs were an elite police force. The regular police force knew the right things to do. Traditionally they do the right thing but when you're not with them they kinda revert back to their own ways of life, which is corruption. And when they don't get paid they have to deal with that in getting what they want to survive. The retraining was supposed to change that for the regular police force. We trusted the ANCOP group completely, but not the regular police. Considering their issues we were in fear of getting shot by them. Even though it was a possibility, our main focus was on the Taliban when we went on daily patrols.

When we arrived there about ten or twelve businesses were open. When we left there about one hundred and thirty businesses were open so our mission was a success, but not without human cost. In February we had the governor of Helmand Province coming to visit the PEF [poppy eradication force]. We heard there was an IED in the road and we were going to confirm that there actually was one in the road. Team Iron Horse, which included Lieutenant Southworth, Staff Sergeant Burkholder who were running the team, and a new captain that had just joined the team a couple of weeks before, were at an abandoned checkpoint that the Americans and Brits had built. They went out to check it out and it exploded. It killed Lieutenant Southworth, Staff Sergeant Burkholder, our interpreter and one ANCOP. A major with the ANCOP was injured, but was released from the hospital a week later.

It changed the attitude of all the men on all teams after that because it was our first personal loss. Me and Southworth had taken the team over and at Fort Bragg we told them that we were going to go to bad places and we are going to do things that you have problems with later on in your life but we will do our best to bring you home alive and probably everyone won't come back alive. We knew we had talked about it. We sat the younger kids down before we left and told them probably ten times and the last time you could see in their faces they were somewhat scared. I had bounced around from team to team and had filled in when guys went on leave but I wasn't there when it happened. It was probably best that I wasn't because the lieutenant and I had a great relationship and we were great friends. We had a different relationship than most lieutenants and platoon sergeants because on active duty you come and go, but in the National Guard we spend so much more time together. It was tough on me but unfortunately in the military you don't have time to sit there and get drunk or whatever. You have to deal with your emotions by yourself in your personal bed and you just have to keep going. We got to go to the memorial service and then we came back, regrouped, and hit it again.

When I say hit it again I mean we tried to provide stability and find the bad guys and make the bad guys go away. There were areas where we would go and we were shot at every day. We just knew it was going to happen and then there were areas we would go and damn near have a picnic and there was no issue at all. I think a lot of people are confused about the Taliban. Where I was at, a lot of people were picking up arms against us because we were with the police and they had been beaten by the police, or they had been stopped at a checkpoint and robbed, or their crops taken, and they are aggravated due to the corruption within the police themselves, and now we are bolstering the police, so that was what we were facing. We could be driving down the road and when the women and children started walking out in the fields we knew that within minutes we were going to be engaged.

We didn't have high-value targets we were engaged in regular patrols. There were days we would sit on a checkpoint and talk to people and get their point of view of things. Some of them could speak English and they would tell us they had been beaten up by the cops. They would tell us they didn't want us to ever leave, they liked us. After a while the engagements slowed down because they begin to realize we were there to help them, not take from them. We were there for three months and then the police came back from training and took over and we would move to another place.

We were the only American team in southern Helmand Province. We were embedded with all Brits so if we needed air support we had to coordinate it with the Brits. It was British airspace. We had no communications between our radios and theirs. We had blue force trackers and they had them at our headquarters so they knew where we were all the time, but the Brits didn't know where we were because they didn't have the same equipment. We just weren't using the same equipment or radios so it was complicated.

If we found IED's or caches it would take hours and hours before we could get the Brits in. They would come in and destroy them and we would have to wait for them to get it all done and then for them to get extracted because we didn't have the capability to take them out of there. The Brits did their mission and we did our mission. It wasn't that we worked for the Brits but we worked closely with them.

On a daily basis our missions would change. We were there with the provincial reserve team Prowler. Prowler basically took all the new recruits, about a hundred and eighty of them. We got them to school and left two American personnel with them through the training and then they brought them back. We would then take them out and try to teach them the right thing to do. The problem is you're dealing with illiterates and we would do drug tests and about twenty or thirty percent of them would drug test. About sixty percent would test positive for drugs.

They had an Afghan lieutenant in charge of them and we told them not to go out without us. We told them to come get us and we would go out with them. They went out one night and didn't come to get us. The lieutenant went out one night about two or three in the morning and his truck hit an IED. It blew him up and the truck and ended up killing about four or five of them. We had been trying to get them trained to be a quick reactionary force and the first week the lieutenant gets killed after just finishing training. We were back to square one.

It was difficult because they wouldn't listen to us, and we kept telling them to let us go out with them so we could keep teaching and training them. They had gotten a lot of confidence during the training and they would do what they wanted and it would prove to be disastrous and fatal. We were down to about eighty of them between them being killed, quitting, or secretly being pulled by the police to put them somewhere else.

We were pushing our ideas on them, and the way we thought they were supposed to do it and the way they were supposed to do it just wasn't the same. One of their older leaders felt he was just as wise or wiser because he was used to that type of warfare, and we would recommend what we thought they should do and they did it the way they wanted. It was very frustrating because we knew it wasn't going to pan out for them and there were a lot of losses because of it.

In September we were pulled back to headquarters. We had been having trouble getting supplies like the big FOBs [had] and we were running out of water and our uniforms were ripped, so we got pulled in to resupply and for a briefing. It was frustrating because we saw people in the big FOBs with all this new equipment and all that we couldn't get and could have used when we were out on patrol. There was a big displacement on the way that the equipment distributed. We took all these sniper rifles over and other gear and we just didn't get the luxuries the big FOBs were getting, and they never left the bases. We kept requesting this equipment we couldn't get. We got trucks, we got crew served weapons, we got bullets, and we got MRE's and water. We never got hamburgers or hot dogs that we requested, they would just send us perishables because we had reefers. We would get thirty thousand styrofoam cups and plates but nothing to put in them. We got a mechanic to come and look at our equipment finally, but it took forever. We were just jacks of all trades. If you can't get it you just make it. It got ridiculous in the end.

We as a group just pulled together and were tight after Lieutenant Southworth was killed. We had a few other casualties. A second roommate of mine got shot by an AK-47 in a little town up north on Highway 601. It was about sixteen to eighteen kilometers from the dry junction. We went there on a joint mission with the Brits and the intelligence said there would be little resistance.

Of course, that's just the opposite of what happened. It was on July 4. I was in [Camp] Bastion at the time the engagement was going on and it took me four days to get back. I ended up jumping on a little attack helicopter and flew to a place where I could catch a flight. There is no accountability over there. If the chopper had went down it would have taken them months to figure out where I was located because there is no manifest. The only one that knew was us and we knew what we had to do to get back to the fight and that's what we did. [My roommate] was okay. A bullet had gone all the way through him and went underneath his body armor on one side of his love handle and came out the other. It missed all his vitals and he recovered.

I went on leave with Josh Melton. He was another squad leader of mine out of Kandahar. During the time we got stuck in Kuwait for five days and I got to hang out with him. After we got back about two or three weeks he was killed. He was another team leader of ours that got pulled for security detail. That was in June and the guys took that one real hard.

We also had a driver that hit an IED and was injured. He was cousins with Melton and he had some vertebras broken in his neck. That was our three casualties that we had in our platoon, but it brought us together. Some of the guys had some issues and it bothered them and we have worked on that since we have been home.

A lot of people have asked me what good we did. We did our job and it's not for me to sit and go through how successful it was. If you look at the news you might think that since we left, things had gone the opposite direction. We got called up and we did our job well and we gave it our all. We stuck it out. Things got messed up some. We were the first ones in and we were the last out. There was no relief situation. You had a lot of areas where guys saw no combat, but you had areas where guys saw combat weekly. I'm not going to say daily but weekly and monthly, but if you wanted to see it daily you could. There was so much down there you just couldn't do it all. The Marine Corps came in and we gave them some advice and started taking over and they actually took half of Helmand as we were pulling out. I didn't get to see the success or any of the issues that they had to deal with.

We pretty much stayed out of Marja when we were there. The town was around eighty thousand and we couldn't get close to it. They had some surface to surface air missiles that I know 7th Group and 5th Group took out, but there was still another one there they were looking for and hadn't found. We couldn't get close to the town. It was a Taliban stronghold. I mean we had four trucks and eighteen guys and we would sit there and throw as much at them as we could, but we were too small a unit to assault them. We just stood and fought as long as we could fight and tried to push through.

We were successful in January. We captured three guys we had been looking for and we actually had two teams with eight trucks at the time. It was Team Prowler and Team Iron Horse. We engaged for about two and one half hours, roughly around ten thousand rounds of ammunition. I had to medevac two soldiers because of an RPG hit. It would literally knock a person out from the concussion. Once we got hit we got down and we had no ammo. You have two Mark 19s and two fifty-calibers and you have 240s as secondary, and when you start running low it's a bad feeling because that's your firepower. It was hard to get air cover unless it was predetermined that we could get it, but sometimes the Apaches would go in on raids with us and escort us places. They would fly right above your truck and all around because Highway 1 and Highway 601 was so dangerous. We had occasions we had to get escorts going and coming on missions just because it was so dangerous.

The Brits were in charge of Highway 601, which went to a dry junction, which met with Highway 1. It is called a ring road and during July and August it got so bad that they couldn't get supplies through. The Brits were running out of supplies and we took patrols and went out daily and nightly. There were engagements and there were IEDs blown up and there were enemy casualties, but we had no one hurt. We got the supply route opened back up.

We had a hundred other missions that came down the pike and we were shifting and adjusting. We dealt with the equipment that we had and made it work. We tried to mentor the police as best we could but we couldn't be with them twenty-four hours a day and there was a lot of damage control that we would have to do when we came back in to resupply ourselves with fuel, food, and water.

Once we were on Highway 601 and a truck driver pulled up. He had a truck load of watermelons and he was bleeding, had blood all over his face. We asked him what was going on. He said at the police checkpoint the police had beat him up and took a bunch of his watermelons. It's like everything you had tried to do for the past six months was just destroyed. We bought some watermelons from him and paid him and that's what we had for lunch that day. He had good fruit.... We went down after that and tried to talk to the police and of course no one knew what we were talking about. It was like that everywhere.

I sat in nightly with the Brit general and there were a lot of reports of corruption. It was hard to accept that the police were stopping people at checkpoints and beating them up, taking their cell phones, money, and food, but they were doing it. It was frustrating and infuriated me. We tried to teach them the best that we could, but they were raised in a country that was corrupt. In many ways it is what they are taught.

I can't look back and say we could have done it differently. We went toe to toe with the enemy and we had no one killed. It was all with IEDs, bombs in the ground, improvised explosive devices that you don't see, you don't know they are there, and if you do know they are there you still have to confirm it. When they go off it is just one of those things. It happens so I don't sit at night thinking we could have done something different.

The leaders were the only ones that got killed in our platoon. They were the ones that led out front and tried to keep the younger guys out of harm's way. They got killed doing their job, not doing something stupid. I look back at it and say what did we do was, we were successful for the amount of time that we spent over there. We had our ups and downs but we felt that we had done the best that we could. The marines came in there with ten thousand marines and replaced three eighteen-man teams. I think they have and are doing good things over there and they will till they leave.

When I think of it we had an Afghan general that was blowing up the Russians in the 1970s and we were calling him a terrorist and now he was leading me. It was difficult trying to figure out who the enemy was among the police that we were mentoring. We would try to give humanitarian aid to the same people that would pick up arms and shoot at you.

There is a wheat seed program over there that the U.S. government funds. They have wheat, cotton and corn. I sat in on all the cultural classes. They taught us all about the culture for the northern part of Afghanistan and had classes in the language. When they sent me to southern Afghanistan the language was just the opposite. Some of the cultural differences were wrong. I was thinking they couldn't get me in the right classes so it almost felt like you were set up for failure before you started.

We lived with [Afghans] and when we were embedded with them we were from two different worlds. We left the politics out of it and that's why they didn't have a problem with us wanting to kill them and them wanting to kill us. When they worked with us they were top-notch, but I just don't know how they were when we weren't [there]. We hear of the beating and robbery, but most people don't want to hear about that. If you have someone that is sixteen years old shooting at you and you have to pull the trigger to go home that day then you do it. If you're getting shot at from a house from every window and you have to drop a five hundred pound bomb on it and make the whole house go away and you don't know who else is in it, we don't like it, but it happens. It is war.

I don't regret anything that we did. I don't regret anything that we didn't do. Yeah, looking back we could have done more, but looking back at anything in life we could have done more or something different. I can honestly say we gave it our best and tried to accomplish as much as we could in the amount of time that we were there.

CHAPTER 16

Staff Sergeant Jason Thompson

Headquarters and Headquarters Company, 2-130 Infantry Scouts

IRAQ • 2005–2006
WARDAK PROVINCE, AFGHANISTAN •
OCTOBER 2008–JULY 2008

In January of 2005 we mobilized out of Fort Stewart, Georgia. We trained there until about mid–April of 2005 and then we deployed to Kuwait. We did about two or three weeks of training there and then we found out we would be leading a convoy up to Baghdad. I was a team leader, assistant squad leader, and our job was to provide security for the battalion's convoy. We did that from northern Kuwait all the way to Baghdad. The convoy was pretty uneventful.

We got to Baghdad about three in the morning and unpacked our gear. We had been there for about three or four hours and some of the guys went to the PX to pick up some supplies. We got hit by a rocket attack and four guys got wounded. One was sent back to the States right away and the others got purple hearts out of it. It pretty much told us what our deployment was gonna be like.

We were basically just responsible for combat patrols in the Abu Ghraib City district of Baghdad. It was on the northwest side of Baghdad. We would load up all four patrol vehicles for the patrols. We always had two patrols out at any time in a sector so we had mutual support if we needed it. It was an area about five or six miles wide and another three or four miles deep. We patrolled the entire area.

We were the first unit to come through with new uniforms and a bunch of the guys in the unit we relieved had spread the rumor with the locals that we were Special Forces, so the first month or so we didn't make much contact. Then when the insurgents figured out that we were not Special Forces, we were just regular soldiers with new uniforms, we started taking some IED's and other contact.

The area where we were at had a pretty bad reputation. There had been a lot of guys wounded and some killed in the area before we got there. We fought with local insurgents, but had some foreign fighters as well. We could always tell when we were getting hit by the foreign fighters because they would drive a lot of times on the canals that were there and they had no problem with blowing the roads up and blowing the canals up and cutting off water. The locals wouldn't blow up their own water supply so we knew we were getting hit by foreigners.

We didn't take any major casualties in Abu Ghraib district, we had some small scratches from IED shrapnel, but no major gunshot wounds. Engagements as far as direct fire was pretty much few and far between. In the urban environment they didn't have any good escape route. They would take pot shots at us, but it was quick and then they would leave.

The IED's started getting pretty bad about two months into it and after three months we actually changed areas and went out to a farm area to the west of Baghdad International Airport. Our mission was to stop the indirect fire from coming in on the Baghdad International Airport complex. When we got there it had been patrolled for about six months to a year. The unit before us wasn't a big enough unit to cover the area properly. The area was probably fifteen miles wide and seven or eight miles deep so it was at least twice as big as before. We knew since the other unit wasn't big enough to cover it that the insurgents were pretty well in place and had time to place the roads with IED's.

It proved to be right. On my first patrol out we got hit with a triple stack 155, a hundred-and-fifty-five-millimeter artillery and it also had a hundred-and-twenty-millimeter mortar round. I got lucky because I had some electronic countermeasures in my truck so it kept it from going off directly under me. It went off about ten meters behind me. That was a wake-up call from that point on.

The first month that we were in that area we got hit by 46 IED's and then after that it just leveled off. It was in the thirties and well over a hundred IED's for the battalion in the three months that we were there. That's when we took our first major casualty. We had a group of scouts doing a route clearance and they were checking alternate routes and they rolled over a pressure plate mine. It destroyed their Humvee and it peeled the driver's arm from the wrist up to his elbow. He ended up losing his arm. We had other guys that got knocked silly every day from the IEDs and one guy that got a big hunk taken out his leg from one, but he didn't lose his leg. A piece of vehicle went through it. That was the worst injuries and no fatalities.

In this area they would also try to get us into complex ambushes. Charlie Company was in our sector just south of us and we saw a motion cloud rising up about five miles away. I mean it was a huge explosion and we heard it. We started rolling down towards it and by the time we got to there we could hear them over the radio that they were engaged. They had set in an operation post on the road and had several IEDs placed on the road. They were going to try and take out the IED team. Apparently they knew the IED team was there and they rolled a vehicle-borne IED in on them, and luckily a gunner on one of the vehicles that was picking up the OP saw the vehicle coming, and when it refused to stop he engaged the vehicle and it blew up about a hundred meters from the IED team's position. It was ineffective, but right after that they opened up with light machine guns and RPGs and we had two guys hit on that one. One of the guys was ours, he got hit in the leg by shrapnel from the RPG and lost some use in his leg, but was okay. The other was an interpreter and he was knocked out from the explosion. There were three insurgents killed in that firefight.

Another time we were out on foot patrol and I saw something weird on the ground. I just moved it with my toe and it moved some. We kept moving more and found a huge cache with a bunch of mortar rounds and gas masks and mortar tubes, RPG rounds, RPG tubes, and TNT. That's when we learned they were burying their caches. They were using the berms along the canals and they would just bury it into the side of the berm. We ended up finding tons and tons of munitions that way. That turned out to be good because once we started finding the caches the indirect fire pretty much came to a stop, which let us sleep easier at night.

After about two months out in the western farm area we had the roads pretty much secure. Our job then became going out looking for caches. We were real effective at doing that and found a lot of them. Then in November of 2005 we were moving out to Anbar Province and when we got there it was pretty much the wild wild west. Fallujah had been invaded in 2004 and when they did I don't know if it was a displacement from the invasion, but most of the insurgency went to Ramadi and we went to a little place between Fallujah and Ramadi called Alpha Quantum Air Base. It was about twelve miles from Ramadi on the west and another seven miles to Fallujah. The IEDs were really bad there, but once again we didn't have many people hurt. They hadn't really gotten into using what they called the EFP's. It was like explosively formed projectiles so we never really dealt with them and we weren't as limited to roads out there either. We could drive off road a lot so it kinda minimized their use of the IEDs. We did take a couple of direct hits. One of our gunners got really lucky cause it blew basically his whole truck apart and knocked him out, but he never received any physical wounds. We left that area in April and came back home. By the time we went back to Kuwait and all, it was June by the time we were back in the States.

When we found out we were going to be deployed to Afghanistan we didn't know until about three months before we went what we were going to be doing. They told us that we would be staying together as a unit, but come to find out later they pulled people from everywhere. They were trying to spread out skill sets and get guys that were good in all kinds of areas. We also had high-level officers in the teams. My team leader was a major. We were going to be mentoring teams. We also had a security force connected to us that was usually about eighteen to twenty guys on top of our eight- to ten-man mentoring teams. We went to Fort Riley, Kansas. We were there for about two and a half months. We went through all the training, all the schools, and then once again flew out to Kuwait. From Kuwait we flew to Kabul International Airport.

The thing about Kabul is that it is about sixty-three hundred feet above sea level. I mean you're higher than Denver and it was not good because I was in real good shape and I could barely carry my rucksack to the end of the ramp. I thought, "Oh, man, I am in a different world," and couldn't breathe. It took a good two or three weeks just to get acclimated to the air. The air quality was just horrible. In Kabul it was like breathing pure feces.

We trained there for about ten days and then they shipped us to Camp Dubs. It's a little camp on the southwest side of Kabul. We were there for about another ten days and then we found out we were going to Wardak Province. The province was one province away from the one we were at, southwest from Kabul. We were at an airborne base camp FOB. It sat seventy-three hundred feet above sea level. We were even higher than at Kabul.

During the wintertime it's pretty slow because the fighters can't sustain themselves as well as in the mountains so we had about two months of rockets two or three times a week. They would shoot three or four rounds and they were always really ineffective. We never took any casualties from the rockets.

We were assigned to mentor the police. As a police mentoring team we were assigned to the entire Wardak Province. I don't know how many districts there were but we worked in the Jalrez District, the Maiden Shar District which is where the province police headquarters was located, as well as the Nirkh District. The police chief of Nirkh was dirty. He was a known Taliban supporter and he made no bones about it. He really didn't even try to hide it. We would go out and count his weapons and he was always short ten or fifteen pistols. He had sold them to the Taliban and everyone told us he was selling them to the Taliban. There was several times we tried to get him relieved and in order to get him relieved we had to go to the Provincial Headquarters. The police chief in my team was a general in the police force and before he was a general in the police force he was a commander against the Soviets. We knew he was bad also and he had deep ties with the Taliban. We had to go to the Ministry of the Interior and of course everybody knew the guy and would say, "Oh, he's my buddy," and would do nothing about relieving him.

The thing I noticed about mentoring the police was that there was about twenty percent that were there because they believed in their country and wanted it to be better. Then there was about another twenty percent that were on the farther end of the spectrum that knew once they got the badge they would be able to extort money from people, and then you had about sixty percent that were in the middle. They were there because they needed a job to raise their families. The ones in the middle and the ones that liked their country, you could work with them. You could actually trust them for the most part, but the twenty percent on the far end of the spectrum that were just there to extort people and were trying to get into our heads to see what we were doing to fight the Taliban were the scum of the earth. They kept themselves in a pretty low profile because they didn't want to be detected and we didn't always know exactly who they were.

The problem we had working with the police is we could never tell them ahead of time what we were going to do. Normally, we like to have a prepared force going into an operation so they could bring the right equipment, so they can rehearse, so they know what they are dealing with, but if you told them anything the people would know instantly about it and it would always be a dry run.

Most of the police we had were willing to train and they were pretty willing to work so we basically made raid teams out of them. According to the Afghanistan constitution, anytime there was an American that went into an Afghan house you had to have a Afghan police officer with you, so we focused on raid parties and we got them pretty proficient. We took them out and cross-trained them with Special Forces groups so that they could go on raids with them also. We didn't focus on training like regular police training in maintaining evidence and that sort of thing, we just trained them in how to survive. Things like when you take direct fire instead of running at the direct fire to engage it, which they did, we told them to take cover. We started teaching them American tactics and how to set up bases of fire because if they fought their way they just got annihilated. It took them a long time to figure out that you can't run into the gunfire, but after a while they started to get it.

Once they were trained pretty good we started doing humanitarian aid missions. We would go to a local village, the police would secure the area and we would supply the police and the Afghan army with rice, cooking oil, blankets, heaters, little coal-burning stoves, and the police would get the village elders and try to win the people's loyalty. It didn't work, but there was a lot of poverty over there and we got a lot of families through the winter. We did that until March of 2009 and then they moved my police mentor team back to Kabul.

At Camp Dubs we started mentoring what was called ANCOP [Afghan National Civil Order Police]. It was basically their national SWAT team and we had a brigade of them. It was nice working with them because they had to be able to read and write and be a sergeant or above and have a fairly financial stable situation. We were trying to cut out some of the corruption and these guys were not corrupt because they cared about their country and wanted to make it a better place. It made working with those guys a lot easier. They were easy to train, they shot well, they moved well, they communicated well, and you could tell they were professional about it.

When the police force was originally formed they just took whoever came, gave them a badge and a gun and they were an Afghan police officer. The ANCOPs would go into the districts where the regular police were and take over the district. The untrained police officers were sent to the National Police Academy. The entire district would go. To show you the difference between the ANCOPs and regular police, when the ANCOPs were done with the mission and the regular police were returning, the people would tell them that they couldn't leave. The people would say, "You don't rob us or threaten us, you're actually trying to help us." Of course, we never stayed. Hopefully, when the regular police got back they had been trained at the academy and knew the difference between right and wrong, but it didn't seem to work when they returned.

The corruption was everywhere. Corruption is expected out of the leadership. Our leadership in America is different. Leaders take care of the people below them and help them out. They are completely opposite in Afghanistan. The leaders at the top expect the people to be giving them gifts and giving them money and do them favors. The average salary is about one hundred and fifty dollars a month and the leaders expect twenty of that to go to them and they would actually take it right out of their paychecks. It was infuriating and there was nothing we could do. We sent reports in about all of it and there just wasn't anything done about it.

I was pretty lucky over there. I never got a scratch on any of the missions. I had a couple of zingers but never really thought, "Oh, shit, this is it." I had a couple of places where I was like in a really bad situation but never thought

I was going to die right now. I did lose four friends there and my platoon leader and a fellow squad leader were both killed. It was a pretty bad situation. It was our last month there and the Taliban wanted to take out one of our Cougars and there weren't any Cougars on the road that day so they took out his Humvee. It killed them both.

The scout platoon took a pretty big toll over there. They had three guys killed, one sent back to the States from wounds, and a bunch of guys came back just messed up psychologically from all the stuff that happened to them. One of my best friends was a sniper squad leader in Helmand Province and it was like the wild west there. Every time they went out they were in a firefight and some of them would last three or four hours depending on how fast [someone] was able to get there to help them out. About the only thing that would get the insurgents out of Helmand was our air support because they knew if the A-10s or Apaches got there they were going to die.

I learned a lot from my experience there, the complexities of war. There was one time we had an observation on a bunch of insurgents that included at least one key leader. He had a couple of secondary leaders with him along with about fifteen bodyguards. It would have been easy to just drop a Hellfire missile on him, but the Afghan commander wouldn't make the call. The American commander couldn't make the call, so it went all the way to the Pentagon trying to get permission to take these guys out. The lawyers at the Pentagon said that we couldn't do it without permission from the Afghan leader because it would cause too much collateral damage politically. They never got a scratch and it would have basically ended the war effort in our province. It was pretty disheartening. We dealt with a lot of that.

We had the bad guys in our ranks and we knew who they were and we couldn't do anything about it. They would smile at you and offer you tea and there was nothing you could do. It was just like when we were going to go on a humanitarian mission. The Afghan general would call and say he wasn't feeling well today so he wasn't going. We knew as soon as he said that we were going to get hit because he didn't want to be there when it happened. And every time we would get hit. The leadership is just corrupt.

July was the end of our tour and we deployed home. It was good to be back in the United States and I hope we never have to go back over there.

CHAPTER 17

Specialist Mark Ferrell

Headquarters and Headquarters Company, 2-130 Infantry

KHOST, AFGHANISTAN • SEPTEMBER 2008–AUGUST 2009

I joined the army when I was eighteen years old. I graduated from the infantry school and came back to my unit. The first month I was back I found out that we were going to Afghanistan in about six months. It was a shock to me. We started getting our equipment together and we started training. We trained real hard for those six months.

The roster came out with names of the soldiers that were going to go over. I wasn't on the roster and we were trying to figure out why I wasn't on it. Then I found out that I was pulled by another unit and was going to go over about a month before I thought I was. I had about two days to get ready so I packed all my stuff and it wasn't long before we were in North Carolina. We did mobilization training there.

We shipped out to Kuwait and then from there went to a FOB [forward observation base], a small outpost called Chapman on the eastern border of Afghanistan. We were the only army unit there. All others had since been removed. It was a nice place to be. We spent the whole year there on the eastern border. It was known as the coast bowl, surrounded by mountains, but we were in the lower area so it wasn't the safest environment.

I was nineteen in combat and we did see suicide bombers and car bombers but there wasn't a whole lot of people shooting at us. We were close to the Pakistan border and there was a supply chain coming through that area for the enemy.

We had a good group of people at the base, about twenty-five army guys and about the same amount of navy guys. We were on a combined team, the Provincial Reconstruction Team. We would take out engineers two or three missions a day. We would go to far out sites to visit village elders. We determined the needs they had for each village we went to. We built schools and orphanages.

We did three-week rotations. Two weeks we went on missions to the villages and one week we would do security for the post. We had two towers and a couple different gates we had to guard. We got hit with rockets several times and one gate got hit with a suicide car bomb. That was the biggest danger we had at the post.

The Afghanistan culture was different, to see how the people lived, and we went to some of the villages that were far out in the mountain regions. We got to places really far out where there hadn't been any people for a long long time. It looked like in three or four hundred years. It was neat to experience the culture of the people. The ones that worked on the base could speak pretty good English and were nice to be around. They were always trying to bring us food and get us to drink their chai, the tea they drank there. It wasn't my favorite, but the bread was pretty good. The people were good overall.

The mission was a success in my opinion. We built two different orphanages for the kids. Providing security is one thing, but to know our guys was making stuff happen for the kids... It doesn't matter what kind of war it is, it isn't the kids' fault. They don't choose where they get born and they don't choose where they are going to end up so it's not their fault. To open an orphanage for them and to see twenty or thirty at a time just smiling, playing with soccer balls, it just felt good doing that. The war is a whole different aspect. You know any second you could be in a fight but you are in a different country and you did get to help someone, so that was my favorite part of the whole experience.

I was there for twelve months and it takes about the first two months to come to your fullest development. I had a birthday in Kuwait. I turned twenty there. The most tragic thing that happened to me was when I came home on leave. I was very close to my platoon leader and the day I got home on leave I found out he had been killed. It was very tough for me and I wear his bracelet everyday as a remembrance. He was like a father to me in the army. I was eighteen when I went in and he knew I needed guidance. I was scared when I knew we were going to war and he took me under his wing and taught me the right way to do things. He really was the last guy you would think would get hurt. He was a hard charger and a good guy that knew his stuff. His death definitely changed the course of my life. It made me really think about where to set my priorities in life. He had four small children. He was a police officer back home and the scariest part was I knew that he was probably the most well-trained guy I knew. If he could get killed I knew it would be much easier for me to get killed and that really scared me.

I had only been about fifty yards from the car bombing that had hit our gate. Just to be that close to the blast and get a little shrapnel was all I got. I was lucky I had my vest on because it caught the shrapnel and I didn't get injured at all. There were two Afghanistan security guards with me but no one else was around. There was a kid on a bicycle, but he just got blown over, but wasn't hurt. It was supposed to be a multiple attack. The car bomb was supposed to hit the gate and take out the security and then there was a dump truck that followed that supposed to drive into the base and pretty much destroy the whole base, but that fell through. The car was over-packed with explosives and left a crater, and the dump truck got stuck in the crater and didn't detonate. It was loaded with over a thousand pounds of nitrate, a few mortar rounds in it. If it had I wouldn't be talking to you right now.

The first month of deployment you think this is absolutely craziness, this is not normal life. The middle part you just go with the flow, it's your job for the day, you get it done. The last month is scary because you made it this long and now you are getting ready to see your family and see your friends and everything is good, but you got to make it through that last month. It gets in your head. You don't want to get hurt and it is creepy.

After I got home I was sitting in a college classroom in two weeks. I had all these other kids around me and it was totally different. I have definitely got a different outlook on life than the other kids that were in my class. I finished college and graduated with honors. I am real proud of that.

CHAPTER 18

Sergeant Alicia Edwards

Detachment 1, 1344th Technical Command

KABUL, AFGHANISTAN •
NOVEMBER 2008–AUGUST 2009

I had just finished boot camp, school for my MOS, and returned home on August 1 of 2008. Approximately five days later I found out I was going to be deployed. I was really surprised because I wasn't expecting it. I was really nervous and had a lot of fear of the unknown. I only had about two weeks to prepare before we deployed and I just didn't know what to expect at all. I went with Echo Company 634th. They were a support battalion and so we prepared and left for Fort Bragg on August 25 for training. We finished our training at the end of October and prepared to leave for Afghanistan. Then we found out what we were going to do when we got over there. We were going to provide security for an FOB [forward operation base].

We had a lot of fear. Fear of the unknown and not knowing what to expect. Then once we got there and started our daily routine it wasn't too bad. It was kind of neat. I enjoyed all of my experiences, like when we first got there we went through training. They call it right seat, left seat, and what I did was work at an entry control point. I was at Camp Edgars at this time and working at the entry control point. What we did was basically check the local nationals that would come in to the base. We would check their ID's and make sure they didn't have cell phones on them and we would search them to make sure they didn't have any weapons or bombs on them.

Sergeant Alicia Edwards in Kabul, Afghanistan, with Afghan children in 2008 (Alicia Edwards).

A couple of days after we were there we had kind of a funny story. We had a guy come in and he had an ID that didn't look just right. We checked it with some of the other ID's we had and it wasn't correct. It was actually a Turkish ID. It had Turkish writing on it. We searched him and he had weapons on him and I got really scared. I had only been there for about four days and I thought, "Oh, my God, this is what my whole deployment is going to be like." He was detained and interrogated, but come to find out he was just lost. He was supposed to be at a different base. After that he was released and sent to the area where he was supposed to go. I think we overreacted when he first came in, but we were really scared.

When we got there it was pretty warm. A hundred and twenty to one hundred and thirty degrees and that was in November. My living conditions were pretty good. We lived in two-story Conexs. I had a roommate and it was pretty good daily life. We just got up, would eat, get ready for work, and go do our job. I lived at Camp Eggers and it was a very nice FOB. We had a lot of officers and generals so the conditions were very nice. We had a PX and Green Bean coffee shop, so if you have one of those you are definitely doing well. We worked twelve-hour shifts. While I worked at the entry point I learned a lot of the biometrics, the stones, the eye scans, and the iris. Although we did our jobs we also had a lot of training like riot control, how to detain.

The holidays were sad, but the command really tried to make the holidays special for us. There were lots of gift bags and special dinners. They always seemed to bring in camels at holidays and I always found that interesting. It was still sad though because we all missed our families.

I bonded with my roommate. We became really good friends and we had a lot of fun together. We really got to know each other very well and understand each other and if we were having a bad day or missing home we supported each other. I struggled in the beginning a lot because my daughter was two years old and she didn't understand why I was gone and that was really hard for me. The time on the phone was hard too. There was a ten-second delay when we talked and she was just two and didn't understand that and we really didn't get to talk that much. It was the hardest part of the deployment for me, not being able to see her and communicate with her.

They did everything they could though to make sure we had Internet and phones and to try to set up free phone calls. They made sure we got plenty of time on the computers so we could go to the Internet and do e-mails. I usually worked the day shift, but someone went on leave so I switched to the midnight shift and I liked that because when I was off in the morning it was evening at home so when I was finished with my shift I could talk to my family.

On January 17 I got off work and I went and took a shower. I was in my Conex and I decided to talk to my sister for a while. After that I watched a movie and then stayed up a little longer than I normally would and went to bed around 10 P.M. I'm not sure exactly what time I went to sleep, but shortly after I did I heard and felt this sound. I don't know how to explain it but I'll never forget how it sounded. It shook the whole Conex and the windows were rattling. In seconds I was up and was thinking, "What was that?" and then the sirens came on. I did think about what I was going to do, I just got up and started putting my gear on. I put my boots on without socks and finished dressing really quick. I ran out the door and I thought people would be running everywhere and I didn't see anyone. I panicked because I didn't know what to do. Then I saw my squad leader running toward me and he started shouting, "Come on, come on," and we ran for the bunker. After we were in the bunker we were just waiting to find out what our position was going to be. Finally I got out of the bunker and was just standing in the road to be told where to go and what to do. Then the squad leader came running up and said he needed five people. And so me and four others just started running with him. We didn't know what was going on. We saw medics running and we finally got up to street where the gate was located. There was this huge hole in the road. There was a fuel truck and it just had fuel running out everywhere. I saw the hole and I saw the fuel truck, but I still at that point wasn't putting everything together as to what happened. It was kind of like a blur and then things slowed down for a few minutes and then the squad leader came up and gave us directions in what we were going to do. We were to set up a perimeter and ID people who were trying to come through the gate. There were reporters already there and Afghan police were there also trying to come in to the base. We were checking them because we had incidents of people in uniform not really Afghan police trying to get into the base that hadn't been police at all. We were just trying to make sure that the right people were at the scene.

I felt like everything was moving really fast, but actually time was going really slow. I heard them talking and heard several names. They weren't sure of the casualties at that time, but there was a female that was in my unit and she was running security on the fuel truck. They were putting fuel in the truck when the V-Bid [bomb] came up and went off. It was her name and one other that I heard. Both their names were Robinson, but there was no relationship. I hadn't heard anything about her yet, but I kept hearing these screams and yelling and I was so concentrated on what I was doing I hadn't really looked around very much. One of the guys I was working with said, "Oh, my God, look at that." I looked up and all around the gate. We had concertina wire and huge barriers with concrete and sand in them to help absorb blast. The barriers were really tall on and top of them concertina wire. There was a soldier that was wrapped inside of the concertina wire. They got him out and was airlifting him to BAF, which is an air force base that was a couple hours away. He ended up dying before they arrived at the air force base. Later that night I heard that the female had survived and that they had shipped her to Germany. They had to amputate one of her legs. She had a daughter my daughter's age and I really felt for her and her daughter. It was just a really long day for all of us emotionally, physically, mentally, I mean you are just drained. We also had two people in the platoon that had brain injuries, and they were sent to Germany also and then home later. They had memory loss and had to have rehab because the injuries were so serious. We were out all day looking for secondaries, but we didn't find anything. It is funny how after something like that happens you hurt, you are sad, and you are angry, but still nothing changes. Life is still the same. I was out there all day and then came back in enough time to take a shower and go to work.

You have to do your job and nothing changes. You would just think that there would be enough time to take a moment to gather your thoughts and your feelings, but you don't. You just carry on and do your job like nothing has happened.

A few days after that we found out that my platoon was going to be moving to a new FOB that was about ten minutes away from Camp Eggers. The FOB was still being built and nobody lived there and we were going to go and be the security force at the FOB. Myself and a lot of the other people in the platoon were really nervous about leaving Camp Eggers after the bomb went off because we knew we were going to be the only platoon there and the new FOB was in a bad location. It was located right under a mountain and you could see right down into it. We had a lot of bad feelings about it. Then after the V-BID bomb hit us we figured we wouldn't be going, then a few days later we found out that we were going. The morale was really low in the platoon after the bombing and the loss and injuries we had had. We had been there for three months before the bomb went off. Unfortunately, we get complacent because everything is just a daily routine and you begin to think nothing will happen. Then it does happen and we were really shook up and on high alert.

We moved to the new FOB and it was really nice. Everything was brand new and we moved into apartments and they had brick buildings and all. They had bigger rooms and it made us feel safer. We had been there for a couple of months and nothing happened and we begin to get complacent again. We had a blast. We did everything as a platoon. We played volleyball and all of us got really close. They brought the food to us from Camp Eggers and it was never very good. We had no Green Bean and that was most people's biggest complaint.

People started moving in slowly and we started getting officers and we had a lot of air force and navy people moving in too. We just did our jobs and it seemed like our morale was slowly getting better. We had some issues in the platoon with some of the people and the leadership, but that was getting changed out and everybody was doing a little better. We did have several hand grenades that went off, but none inside the wire. We were surprised that we never received any mortar fire. I worked a vehicle scanner which I loved. It hooked up to a computer and when the local nationals would come in it would scan the vehicle and X-ray the inside and we could see the entire inside of the vehicle. There were a few times when we saw something that we needed to hand check and searching the vehicles was a scary moment and nerve-racking. We never found any bombs and the rest of my tour went really smooth.

My husband was deployed at the same time I was, but was in a different location. I got home a month before he did and that was difficult. I came home from taking care of myself to being a mom again and although I loved it, it was scary. I was very short-tempered, I had lots of anger, and I didn't know why. It made me feel bad that I felt that way. I felt guilty that I felt that way and I thought, "Well, Scott is going be home soon and everything will go back to normal." I thought that was why I was having the problem. He got home and it wasn't as wonderful as I thought it would be. We were just getting used to each other again and living together. Deployment is so much different than living at home. You can eat when you want and everything is just different.

I was suffering from post–traumatic stress disorder and did not realize it. Maybe I realized it. Maybe I just didn't want to admit it. My husband and I both had a lot of bad dreams. I would beat him up in his sleep, which he wasn't a big fan of at all. One of the biggest problems was I could hear the screams in my sleep of Sergeant Robinson from the blast and could see him wrapped in the wire. I could hear him all the time. I would wake up really scared and it was just a very tough time. I had a lot of depression. My husband was very supportive, I just refused the help. Finally one night my daughter heard some of my dreams and was crying. I thought oh my God I need help because it was bad on my husband and her and we weren't connecting or talking. I was very distant from everyone and I didn't enjoy life. It was like every day that went by I got worse. We started marriage counseling and that's when I guess some of the things I had been saying and been dreaming came out in the counseling. The counselor told me that I had PTSD. She was a counselor and she couldn't prescribe medication and she wanted me to go to my doctor. I had a really bad experience with that because I didn't want my doctor to know so I wanted to go to someone else's doctor. My mom told me about the doctor that was in her church and I went to him and told him what my counselor told me to tell him which was that I needed something to help me sleep and that I needed an antidepressant. The doctor got up in the middle of me talking and asked me what I was experiencing. I started telling him and about the dreams and what I was hearing and as I was it got really intense. I was in different places and I could smell burnt flesh and I kept talking and the doctor got up and walked out of the room and wouldn't come back in the room. I thought "Oh, my God, I shouldn't have told him, I was too open, I just shouldn't have said that." Then I thought the negative, that he was being rude and that he was probably against the war. He wrote me a prescription and he gave it to the nurse. My mom was really upset about it and she went to find out why he did that. Come to find out he had been in Vietnam and when I started telling him what I was experiencing it brought up his own experiences and he just couldn't take it. I never saw him again but it was a strange experience for me.

My goal wasn't to stay on the medication, but to take it for a while to get through it. I don't know what I would have done without the support of my husband. I mean now, three years later, if I hadn't got some help. I went about three or four months without any help and now I just think that's three or four months that I lost of being healthy and happy. I do great now. I still get sad for the loss. The female that was injured in the blast passed away six weeks after they amputated her leg. They thought she was really coming through it but she just had too many internal injuries from the blast so we ended up losing her. It was a sadder day when we found out that she passed away than it was the night of the blast because we all hung in there and we thought she was going to pull through. I knew her, we weren't really like super good friends but I saw her, and we talked, and we shared our stories about our daughters here and there, but I just felt sad for her, but I really felt sad for her daughter, that her daughter would never grow up really knowing who she was or what her mother did or the sacrifices that she made.

The biggest thing for me is that I don't think people understand what we do. Like where I work, I work with a lot of veterans and they say, "Well, you're just National Guard, you're almost army." I hear it all the time and I don't think they get what we do. I just don't think they understand. I might do flood duty or ice storm duty, but I deployed. I have done some really awesome things and experienced a lot of sadness but have had a really great camaraderie that you don't get anywhere else. You can have that in the service, but I don't think you can really get it until you deploy with someone and you have the situation that you have their back and they got yours. I don't think people really understand camaraderie until you experience it to that level. That is the only thing that I take offense to is that I am just National Guard. I feel I am doing something. I love it. I was supposed to deploy again in April and it got cancelled and was really sad because I love deployment. I don't like leaving my family, but I love the feeling that I am doing something when I am deployed. I'm accomplishing something every day. It feels good to lay your head down at night and know you are accomplishing something. I feel like I'm showing my daughter or leading by example. I'm not just telling her about loyalty and honor and integrity, I feel like I'm showing her by my actions and that's really important to me. That is huge in our house and she is a little older so she doesn't say it anymore, but it used to give me this awesome feeling when we would go by and see an American flag. She would always say, "That's my mom's flag."

CHAPTER 19

Corporal Levi Wampler

Charlie Company, 133 Signal Battalion

BALAD AND ABU GHRAIB, IRAQ •
JUNE 2003–MAY 2004

One of the first things my recruiter told me was, "The only way to tell if a recruiter is lying is if he is moving his lips." He was right because one of the things he told me was our National Guard unit was so low on the priority list we would never go to war, and I spent one year in Iraq from 2003 to 2004. That was just his opinion and that is the way everybody pretty much felt. What we didn't know was that once we are federalized we can be attached randomly to any army unit. Our actual battalion we went over with was from Iowa. However, for them to have a full contingent they had to pull from Michigan, Wisconsin, and two companies from our unit out of Illinois. It was just a hodgepodge group shoved together to make the unit and that is why we went through so much training. I am doing a 9 to 5 job but am home at night, and then all at once we are shipped to Kansas for three months of training, then to Kuwait, and finally into Iraq.

There isn't much in Kansas but when we got there they didn't have a place for us to stay. There were about a hundred of us stuck in a training barracks that was suitable for about eighty people. They were just shoving National Guard units anywhere they could and we were like living in huts and barracks that weren't big enough for everybody. We lived there for a while in the middle of nowhere, nothing to do but train all day. We would train all day into the evening, go back to the barrack, sleep and get up and train all day again. It was like a small basic training, but very well run.

Then we went to Kuwait and that was supposed to be our acclimatization. To get us used to the weather, to get us used to what is going on over here, and to bring us up to speed on what's happening in country. The best explanation that I can give you as to what it was like is to say if someone could put you in an oven and then get a fan and blow sand in your face. It was hot all the time, from a hundred twenty degrees to a hundred fifty degrees. There were times during the day that we couldn't do anything because of the heat. We would just go sit and try to get used to it. We had got over there early and there was no AC yet, so the one good thing about that was they couldn't work us as much because we just physically couldn't do it because of all the heat, so we did a lot of sitting and waiting for orders to come down on where we were going.

While we were waiting it was like a part of the theme of Kansas. We weren't really sure if they had a spot for us or not. The orders would change from day to day on where we were going next. Then we were going to be attached this unit and then the next day a different unit. They never really seemed to know what was happening with us. We did a lot of training, sat in the carpool area a lot and went over our vehicles and made sure everything was right with them.

Then we finally got orders to Baghdad, Iraq. That was where we were going to go to initially. The convoy from where we were at in Kuwait to Baghdad was two hundred miles. At that time they didn't have the sophisticated IEDs that they eventually had after bringing people into Iraq and training them, but they did have IEDs. Early on the best things they could muster up was pipe bombs. They would throw pipe bombs off the bridges or would go medieval and just throw rocks and bricks off the edges.

The Humvees we had were not armored. We didn't even have time to paint them and they were green. They were the old canvas tops and it was kind of funny, while we were in Kuwait they had us cutting pieces of plywood and trying to affix them to the canvas of the Humvees, as if that would help us in case of an explosion. We had to put sandbags under our feet and stupid stuff like that. The plywood, if anything, would have added the shrapnel of an explosion.

The drive across Kuwait was no big deal, but when we crossed into Iraq there was a big sign, "You're Now Entering a Red Zone. Welcome to Iraq, Helmets and Flak Vest Are Required." When we crossed it wasn't bad on the convoy because it is pretty desolate on that part of the border and there are no towns. As a matter of fact there was nothing but sand. As we went along we would pass people and they would give us the thumbs up. The problem was that in the middle eastern culture thumbs up is the same as the middle finger, so we never knew if they were, "Thumbs up, we are happy you are here" or if they were flipping us off so we just gave thumbs up back. We had to make several stops, but I can't remember how many. They were smaller camps and we kind of camped out there as we stopped. Then we got to Baghdad. We didn't know exactly where everybody was going. It was very early on and we were still moving into parts of Iraq. We got there the day in June that President Bush said the war was over.

We camped on top of the Humvees because there was a little bit of a breeze so we would throw our cots on the hoods of the vehicles and sleep there. We had done that in Kuwait and the first night in Baghdad. Everyone was still living in ripped-out palaces. You could see the bullet holes and the blasts on some of them. All weren't damaged, but they were gutted out because right after the fighting stopped the civilians went in and took anything of value. We lived in them when we first got there. There were no doors, no windows, mosquitoes everywhere. We had to have our mosquito nets out to sleep at night. We were lucky they had outhouses set up by the time we got there. Most of them were wooden structures. They got the plastic ones later.

We stayed there for about two weeks and then my team got shipped to Anaconda, which is near Balot, Iraq. On our convoy to Balot we got stopped in the middle of Baghdad. We weren't supposed to let the Iraqis get close to us in a convoy because we didn't know who was who early on. It wasn't really bad, the bombing and all. The insurgents weren't organized as of yet and a random convoy was hard to hit, but there is a crime of opportunity thing where someone might try to pull something off. These kids came running up to our convoy and at first we were trying to keep them a few feet back and were trying to talk to them. We had been taught a small amount of [...] the Arabic language. It was a few words they taught us like "stop," "put your weapon down," "surrender," and words like that. What was so ridiculous about it was it was strict Arabic and the guy teaching us [said] that it was like strict English. There is American English, British English, and Australian English. There is inner-city slang and things like that, only it was at a higher level of Arabic language and most didn't speak it so we didn't try it very much. We were trying to keep them back and one kid came up and gave me a big thing of pita bread. I accepted it without thinking and then some MPs came and said we needed to keep them way back. The kids stayed back, but were giving us a kind of disappointed, upset look because they thought we were a new toy in their neighborhood. The kids were like five, eight, ten years old, not teenagers. We had to make the kids go away and they were angry at us. I felt kind of bad for them, but at the same time we were trying to learn what life was like in a war zone.

It was the first time we had encounters with civilians. When we had been in Kuwait and up to this time we only dealt with and communicated with other military personnel. We had one other encounter with a civilian on the convoy. This guy was in traditional garb of the robe and the red checkered headdress like you see in the movies. He was like the traditional stereotypical Arab-type person. We were stopped and he came up and he wanted photos with us. He wanted to post photos with us for us, like it was our cameras. I have a photo with this guy and it is a funny photo too because my flak vest is open and I felt like I was in Kansas. We still hadn't got into the mindset of being in a war zone yet. We felt like we were in Kansas, but it was just a lot hotter and nothing but sand everywhere.

We got to Anaconda and it was nice because it was being set up as an R & R facility so they could send people for weekends to relax. I have talked to guys since I came back and they said they finally built an Olympic swimming pool there. There is a giant gym and a Burger King. Those were being built while I was there.

I was in a team of six people and my job was a switching phone operator. We would pull into an area and we would have two shelters. One shelter sets up an antenna called a cell phone antenna and the other operates the switchboard. We would pull in, set the cable antenna, then run phone lines basically and give people their phones and teach them how to use them. A lot of people didn't know the army had phones so we kind of offered an infrastructure. A lot of my experience was sitting in a shelter. We had air conditioning, thankfully, which was for the equipment, not us in the shelter. The shelter is just this big steel box on a Humvee. It isn't bulletproof, it is just insulated for the air conditioning and the heat. We did have some relief from the heat because we could go hide in our shelter when it was our shift.

The facilities at Anaconda were better than some of the guys had in Baghdad. My team was on Route Red Fox which was on the natural preserve right outside of Baghdad. It was Saddam's personal nature preserve. People had come through and tore off the gate and there were animals out running around like hyenas and such that hadn't been caught yet. There were some bombings, but most of those were at the airport. The camp was like five to ten miles across and the bombings took place on the airport side, but we still had to react.

We had concertina wire around our compound and we would go out and sit at the edge of the wire and see people walking in the dark, and we couldn't tell if it was our people or somebody else's people. We had a few times where people tried to break through the wire and try to do some random destruction, which was all they had left to do, little random acts at the time. At first we would run out to the wire and then someone realized that it was kind of silly because none of these people were actually combat trained and here we were military trained with all the weapons, so they decided we should just go to the bunkers for safety when incidents happened.

In military life people make decisions at a level that are smart, but by the time it gets to the bottom it was dumb. They wanted us to be in the best shelters possible so when a bombing occurred we would be in a shelter, but we had to leave that shelter during the bombing and go to another shelter so we were in the safest one.

Another thing is that we had to be in uniform when we went to the bunkers. One time I woke up in the middle of the night and I had on my physical fitness gear and the bombs go off. I threw on my boots, threw on my flak vest and Kevlar and go running for the bunker before the next round of explosions. They made me go back because I wasn't in the proper uniform. Well, I didn't go back into the building I just stayed in the bunker because I wasn't going to risk going outside with bombs coming in.

It was really boring there because my job was technical and I never left the base. I just had to sit there. I wasn't an MP or infantry or anything like that. I never saw any enemy face to face. I never shot my rifle. The enemy just tried to bomb the shit out of me. As long as our phones were working we didn't have anything to do. We watched movies. We all brought laptops while we were over there. Most of us had our families ship them to us. We played video games and worked out a lot. Then we would get bombed.

We were moved to Abu Ghraib, which is the famous prison over there and we were just supporting the MPs with phones. We were kind of like a MASH unit because we had just six guys living in a tent together and since we were attached, I was in Charlie Company and we were attached to Bravo Company to be attached to the 22nd Signal Battalion out of Iowa, and then when we got there we were separated from the 22nd Signal and attached to whoever needed phones, so we didn't know anyone except our six guys. I heard there were thousands of people at Anaconda and am not sure of that but it was a big base, but we didn't know anyone else so we just hung out together the whole time we were in Iraq. We just hung out together and got to know each other really well by the end of our deployment. We pulled pranks on each other and were always doing silly things to break the tension.

In Abu Ghraib it was really crappy. It wasn't set up like at the other place it was like a true base. We were living inside what looked like a garage. It was just a big open bay, but we could walk around and we could see what the prison life was like because everybody was living in the prison. The MPs actually lived in the prison itself. They lived in the cells. They had the doors tied open so they wouldn't accidentally close and lock them in. The area we lived in, I never figured out what it had been used for. It was just this big open area and had a big door that had been ripped off. It had been replaced with a giant piece of plywood with those giant sandbags that were four by four and ten feet high. They had to bring in earth movers to do that and they were good barriers. We pulled our Humvees inside the building and made sandbag walls on each side of them and it was really safe.

We started putting out phones and we were pretty popular because we had a home to home phone because we had an outside line. It was just sitting right there and a lot of people came through to use it to call home. We didn't have much conversation with them, we were just there for the phone. It was nice, though, because when no one else was using it we could call home. It was difficult because there is a ten- to twelve-hour time difference and so you had to call at the right time when everyone was off work. The line had a lot of static and you couldn't always get an outside line. It was like a crapshoot. You would spend half an hour just dialing to be able to talk to someone for two minutes and it would just drop the call. The thing of it, though, is that it was better than what a lot of people had because at least we could call out. We also had Internet so we could send chat messages and e-mails. That was the benefit of being in communications.

We did twenty-four-hour shifts there. One person would be in the shelter and if anything went wrong that they couldn't fix they would wake all of us up and we all went out to work on it. Then when your twenty-four-hour shift was up we had seventy-two hours off. We erected a tent inside the garage so we would have some kind of privacy because people were coming to the shelters to get information and to use the phones to call home. We had pretty comfortable living conditions because we had a lot of spare time and we did a lot of reappropriating, which is really stealing, but it was what we had to do there. We didn't steal personal possessions, it was just equipment. We had a general that had moved in down the road from us, and the only time we used our night vision goggles is when we drove down there and stole lockers and cots. We were attached to so many units when we were over there, we didn't get the equipment that everyone else did. Everyone else was getting footlockers, cots and even air conditioners, but the people we were attached to put us at very low priority because the attached unit was supposed to supply us, but it wasn't happening. We took what we needed.

We had to go on convoys down IED Alley from where we were to Baghdad. It was about a fifteen-mile stretch and we made the convoy about twice a week to get our MREs and other supplies. They had a PX in Baghdad and we would stop there too. We didn't have a lot of attacks on those convoys but several times the MPs would just suddenly [swerve] off the road and go different random dirt roads, or sometimes just stop everything and did what they called herring boning, which is everybody turns toward a 45 degree angle, stops the vehicles and everybody gets out and in between the vehicles for protection. We would be there for twenty or thirty minutes till they would figure out what was wrong or defuse a bomb that would be in front of us. They never told us what it was. We just stood guard. It began to work on me a lot. I wanted to kill something. I was just afraid. The namelessness, the facelessness of it kind of bothered me. It was IEDs, we had mortar attacks and rocket attacks and we had to just sit there helpless. I would sit there in the bunker and clean my rifle, then reload it and then clean it again. All I could do was try to count the bombs. One time we got so many we made the news. We got bombed like eighty times in one night by rockets and mortars and again all we could do was sit in the bunker helpless and count the bombs. The worst bombing was while I was actually on leave. It was lucky but unlucky. I was lucky because I was home on leave running around drinking and having a good time with my friends, but it was unfortunate because I didn't want my team to get hurt. The bottom line, though, is that we never saw the enemy. We couldn't fight back.

My drill instructor in basic training said that if you told a war story you had to say, "No shit." There I was in Abu Ghraib and at this point I was desensitized to the bombing and explosions. My cot started to sag too much and it started hurting my back so I was outside with plywood which we had liberated from somebody else and I was trying to fit a piece for my cot. All of a sudden bombs started landing and I just ignored it. You know. No big deal, it happens all the time. My sergeant came out and made me come back inside and put my flak vest on. I put it on and when he wasn't looking I went back outside and started sawing on the plywood again with the bombs going off. He had to come out and make me go back inside again. Once I got yelled at by an officer because we were in a mortar attack and I went outside with a camera to take photos. At that point I just felt like nothing could really happen. I hadn't even been hurt and I felt if I did it really didn't matter. I am out taking photos of the explosions on the other parts of the base and he came out and made me go inside. Once I cussed out a sergeant major because he made me leave the gym during a mortar attack. He was new, like he had just got there. We were in concrete buildings where it was safe and they always wanted you to leave and go outside where it wasn't safe. I tried yelling at him that it wasn't safe outside, it is safe where I am at. I got in trouble for that but I didn't care.

I was put on what's called advance party for the convoy back to Kuwait. They wanted so many of us to know the route back in case the convoy got separated so the week before we were to leave I went to Baghdad. I began to believe during the bombings that they were after me. I was the target and when I got to Baghdad for the advance party we started getting bombed. It just reaffirmed in my head that they were out to get me because the area in

Baghdad had not been getting bombed and as soon as I got there they started bombing. They were trying to catch us when we were getting out of lunch so about 1 or 2 P.M. there would always be a missile attack. Then we had to start eating lunch early and then go hide in a shelter.

Everyone had diarrhea the whole time we were there. The diarrhea was caused by the food that they fed us, and if they didn't get the right amount of bleach in the water it caused it, plus the constant stress. I really had to go and so I am out there in 130- to 140-degree weather. It was just freaking hot. I took my flak vest off and I was done caring at that point and I sit it down next to me and I started using the bathroom, and all of a sudden a rocket hits about forty or fifty feet down on the other side of the road, so it's like one of those raised or elevated roads and the Porta-Potties were down on the side and so the rocket hit on the far side of the embankment, but it was close enough that the pressure changed in the Porta-Potty and I watched the walls like enclose and then flop back out from the pressure of the explosion. I had the choice of grabbing my gear and pulling my pants up and running for the bunker or I could stay and finish. I just stayed there and finished what I was doing, I didn't care.

That same week we were all hanging out right outside of one of the barracks and there was a sandbag wall two or three feet in front of us. We were hanging out between the door to the barrack and the wall, smoking. It had been about an hour since the last rocket attack. The airport was across from us. A plane takes off. This sergeant was with us. I am five foot five and he is about six foot three inches tall and a firm-built boy. He thinks it is another rocket attack. He shoves me, but out of the way, and runs in the building. I never stopped giving him crap for that.

A buddy of mine was out at the Porta-Potties, which were sandbagged. He goes in to use the bathroom. The biggest explosion I ever heard went off and we couldn't go out of the building. All we could do is peek out to see if the Porta-Potties were still standing. They were still standing up, and here he came running and his face looked like just a white sheet of paper. He was shaking and freaking out. Come to find out Explosive Ordinance Detection had set off a bunch of weapons cache that they had found right outside of the camp. They didn't tell anybody, they just set them off. Everybody was freaking out. Every phone on the base was lit up and people were calling all over the base to see what had happened. Some people got an ass-chewing for not letting anyone know they were going to be setting the explosives off.

We talked about our feelings and emotions among ourselves about what was going on around us. There were a lot of feelings of helplessness and the lack of control, just no control over your life. There was the idea of being bombed all the time and not being able to do anything about it. The faceless attackers, and I'm not saying that's worse than seeing your attacker, but I didn't like it because I couldn't do anything back. All I could do is sit there and wait for it to stop and hope I didn't get hurt. My inability led to hopelessness which led to just giving up. I didn't care anymore.

Coming back home we did the normal stuff. We did the convoy and we went to Kansas but only for a couple of weeks this time. They let us drink when we got back and I drank so much my kidneys hurt. I just drank to try to drown it all out. Then we came home and did all the nice things and said hi to everyone and then me and my girlfriend at the time stayed drunk the entire summer. I'm married to her now and we still have trouble figuring out what happened. It was just like a haze for like three or four months and all I was trying to do was drown it all out. She didn't know that. She just found that out recently. She just thought we were having a good time. To go along with the lack of fear of death I bought a motorcycle in the first three days I was home and that was a bad idea. I bought a two-hundred-dollar pair of sunglasses because I had a cheap pair over there and I still have problems in bright light. I didn't have any kind of training for the motorcycle and no one showed me how to use it. I was pretty sure I wasn't going to die because if God or the universe wanted me to die I would have done it in Iraq. It just wasn't going to happen. I was on a back road and just trying to figure it out. I tried to force it into a 90 degree turn and almost hit a truck. Finally I had some lessons and that made it worse because I could do more dumb things. I started to pass a car one time and another car was coming and I just stayed on the yellow line between the two cars as they passed each other. It was a stupid thing to do, but I really didn't think I could die.

I started school and had a job in camp, but I begin to have problems. I would be going to class or work and would wake up in different parts of the campus and didn't have a clue why I was there or how I got there. It was intrusive thoughts. I did the same thing with driving. I would take off and end up in different parts of town and didn't know how I got there. I had to go to a doctor at the VA and I found out I had PTSD. The worst part was the night terror. I would wake up hearing mortars coming in and I couldn't sleep, that is why I drank so I could sleep. Explaining it to people is hard. If they have been in similar situations you could talk to them, but you have people ask you about it that haven't been there and it is hard to explain. They don't understand it so I would tell the ha ha funny stories and leave the rest out.

We went to a movie one time after I got home and it was a Michael Moore movie, something about 9-11. It started out with a bunch of guys in uniform in Humvees in Iraq and they all get blown up. I was up and out of there. My girlfriend needed to understand, like, "What is it you're afraid of?"

I didn't know how to explain it to her, that I didn't die, if that's what she meant, but getting bombed happened on a daily basis and I didn't know how to answer her so I just gave her a dumbfounded look. I just couldn't talk about the hard stuff.

I had put in for a job at a university that had a little bit more money and responsibility. I had a co-worker I almost slapped. I got a number three on the test and you get five points for being a veteran and I told him I took the test and I was number three on the list. He said, "Yeah, you veterans always get those five points." I did all of what I did and you get five fucking points and this guy is going to complain. I wanted to choke him. I think that a lot of people think that way. You join the military and you really don't do anything and you get all those benefits. All I can say is that I did my duty and I am damn proud of it. I love my country and I don't regret a minute of the service I gave.

CHAPTER 20

Staff Sergeant Patrick Tullis

Headquarters and Headquarters Company, 2-130 Infantry

BAGHDAD, IRAQ • JANUARY 2005–JANUARY 2006

KABUL, AFGHANISTAN •
DECEMBER 2008–SEPTEMBER 2009

I joined the Army National Guard in 2002 after September 11. They called us the September 11 babies. I joined for the college too, but you know September 11 had a big impact on a lot of people in my generation. A lot of us were seventeen or eighteen when it happened and it had a big impact on me and that was the main reason I joined.

In 2004, we got the word that we were going to mobilize and deploy to Iraq. I was twenty-one at the time. My unit didn't actually mobilize, we were actually deployed as an attachment to backfill people that were being deployed so we actually deployed with a different unit. There were twenty of us and we were out of the artillery unit. We joined another artillery unit, but I was a medic. I had a lot of responsibility because I was the only medic called up.

We were sent to Fort Dix in New Jersey in the middle of October for training. It snowed and was really cold the whole time we were there. I qualified on the M-16, M-9, the M-2, which is a fifty-caliber machine gun, and the 249 which is a submachine gun. I also qualified with the M-40 grenade launcher. Although you are there for training it is more to get all the paperwork done and you can come together as a unit before you deploy. Before I got there and didn't hardly know anyone but after you train together you begin

119

to make friends. There were three other medics at the training site and they were all older than me. At that time the army was going through a transition period and were changing MOS's and doing different training and requiring more training for medics. The older medics had to go to a recert class to get recertified because they were changing the criteria and making them learn more stuff, and so toward the end of our training they got sent to Pennsylvania for six weeks' training, and in two weeks we left. I was the only medic for the entire company.

We flew to Kuwait. I turned twenty-two and was promoted to E-5 and was now a sergeant. I sat in on meetings with the first sergeant, the commander, and other platoon sergeants because they didn't have anyone else that had medical knowledge, so I was the de facto medical expert for one hundred and forty-five people. It was a little overwhelming. When you are young you're a little arrogant and you know a lot and think that you know what you're talking about, but I quickly learned you don't speak in the meetings unless you are specifically asked questions. It was a big learning experience for me. They were all nice to me but I understood the role and I got to see behind the scenes how a company actually operates between the first sergeant and the commander. I got to see the logistics of things and the administration side and how missions came down.

We were in Kuwait for two weeks and we didn't do anything but plan. We would get up at 11 A.M. and go to bed about two or three in the morning. There was just nothing to do. We were just getting acclimatized to the weather and we just waited for our flight to go up to Iraq. We finally got our flight and about three or four days [later] we were split into groups. We had three platoons and a headquarters element, which was all the admin people. We also got our missions. There were three of them. Although we were artillery we had been trained to be military police. The commander decided to split the three platoons into two platoons because our company was going to be in two different places. They cut a squad from each platoon and formed the fourth platoon. I was assigned to the second platoon because the second and third platoon were going to be in the same place and since I was the only medic they wanted me where the most people were located.

One of our missions was the PSD mission, which was to do convoy security for VIP's. We weren't sure who they were or where we would be going, but that was the first mission. The second mission was security at a prison called Camp Cropper. The third mission was we were going to provide security for convoys of semi-trucks that provided supplies.

We flew into Baghdad and we had a combat drop. The plane wasn't pressurized so it was like my head hurt really bad as we made the fast drop. We finally landed and after a few minutes I was better. The guys that we were going to replace were there to pick us up. They drove us to our FOB which was called Unit 3. It was very small, not over two hundred to two hundred fifty people that lived there. There were two security units there and also an attachment of the First Cavalry. I'm not sure what else they did, but for sure they ran the FOB. Shortly after we got to the FOB we found out that we would be providing security for the president and vice president of Iraq. Their government is organized quite different than ours. They have two presidents and two vice presidents and a prime minister so there were five executive people instead of one president and vice president. We had one president and he was Kurd — he was Kurdish and the Kurdish people are from up north by Turkey. I think he was the only Kurdish person on the executive board. The other executives were Sunni Shiites.

We were the outside security. I mean we did the convoys and the inside people who provided security where he worked and lived were Navy SEALs. We worked with SEAL Team 3 at first and then SEAL Team 7 later to provide the security. It sounds pretty cool, but it's actually pretty boring because he lives in the IZ which is the International Zone in Baghdad which is pretty secure. We would go and pick him up, take him to work which was four minutes away, sit there for twelve hours, and then take him home. Once in a while he would want to go somewhere out of the city and so we would run the convoy security out of the city. It was pretty boring too. The Navy SEALs were really nice to us. I didn't think they would be because usually when we ran into Special Forces groups they kind of looked down on guardsmen, but the SEALs were actually really nice to us. They were actually pretty cool guys and they probably hated being on that mission worse than we did because they are trained to do a lot more than that, but it was neat to be with them for a while.

About three months later our missions changed. Our principal, as we referred to the Kurdish president, decided that he wanted to have his people provide security for him. At that point we begin training the Kurdish Police in security measures. We were trying to turn the responsibility over to the locals as much as we could. At the same time they were doing a massive realignment with our company and our battalion. Our battalion was so spread out and they decided that they wanted to pull us all together to one central location and run our missions from that central location. That was during June and for the entire month we didn't have a particular mission, all we did was regroup.

On June 6 there was a convoy from our fourth platoon. They were going from Abu Ghraib prison to Anaconda, which is about two hours north of Baghdad. You could only enter and leave Anaconda during the dark. They had to leave really early in the morning and then have to leave that night.

When the convoy left there was another convoy in front of them. Normally when we were on the road we would drive as fast as we could. The roads were pretty nice, like interstates, and we could drive sixty or sixty-five miles an hour. We would go as fast as we could go safely because the faster we went the harder it was for the insurgents to time their IED's. Their timing would be off. The convoy in front wasn't my platoon, but they were from my company. Normally you can pass a route patrol because they just go about five miles an hour checking out bridges and looking for IED's, but this convoy in front was driving about forty miles an hour the whole time. Our fourth platoon wanted to pass, but they wouldn't let them. The convoy in front didn't want them to pass them. There was a turnpike that you had to go to and turn on to get back to Baghdad. When they got on the turnpike I don't know if it was the lead vehicle or the second vehicle got hit by an EFMP which is like an IED. It has like a copper shell on the front of it and when it goes off it somehow magnetizes and it liquefies and magnetizes the copper so that when it goes into the armor it is so hot that it peels the armor and goes right through the armor into the vehicle. My friend Brian was driving the Humvee that got hit and Brian was hit in the head and killed instantly. Another friend of mine, Spurlock, who was actually the gunner, got hit by shrapnel in the leg and had a big shrapnel cut in his neck. The guy that was the truck commander got minimal damage from the shrapnel. The blast didn't go all the way through the radio and there was a radio mount between the driver and him.

We learned that night that there was a fatality, but we didn't know at the time who it was. Our platoon sergeant was really very upset and we realized that it was probably someone who had been in our platoon. Come to find out he was right. That was the turning point of our deployment. Before that incident it wasn't that bad, but after that everything got real.

I went to work at the combat support hospital in Baghdad. I worked in the emergency room for a month there, which was a good learning experience for me. I saw burn victims, gunshot wounds, blast injuries, amputees. Every type of injury came through there and I learned a lot of medical skills and gained a lot of medical knowledge.

After that month we did convoy duty from Abu Ghraib prison to Anaconda, which was very scary because that is where we had the fatality. We ran twelve-hour shifts every day until January of 2006 when we came home. During those convoys my truck got hit by three IED's, but we had no fatalities or real injuries out of it. The IED's were small and they went off either before we got to them or after we passed them so we were very lucky with that. During our deployment we had lots of incidents of IED's, a lot of explosions, and a couple of snipers. We were lucky we came home with only one fatality.

Afghanistan is a different place. The people are different. They are just poor with little education and it's a different kind of culture. They are Muslim in Afghanistan. I worked with the police. It was a police mentoring program there and I was the medical support for our team. We had thirteen police districts in and around Kabul. We would just go out every day and talk to the police and help them get their paperwork together and their finances in order and we also built things for them. We also got them the equipment they needed.

The police districts there kind of reminded me of the American police districts of the early 1900s. The captain was boss of his area and the other officers did as he instructed. They would shake down vendors for money that would be in their area so they were not very advanced. We did our best to get them to do their jobs correctly and a lot of them tried hard to do it. It was just hard for them to understand our culture.

The IED's in Afghanistan aren't as good as Iraq. They are not very advanced and so they would just try to use more explosives to get a large explosion. They also were not very good at hiding their IED's or at building them. Most of the danger in Afghanistan was from small arms fire, so in Iraq our big worry was IED's and in Afghanistan small arms fire. I never got fired at in Iraq, but there were three incidents in Afghanistan that we were in firefights and fired back. There was a fourth day that we had on Election Day. We were at the police station and we were staying there for the four days of the election to help them with security. While we were at the police station, which was a little compound, we were attacked by about six individuals with small arms fire. They attacked the base and the firefight lasted for about two hours. Luckily we only had minor injuries on our side and we took all of the insurgents out.

The firefights would last for an hour or two because it was hard to pin down their positions. I received my combat action badge in Iraq, but in Afghanistan I treated seven or eight NATO soldiers under direct fire and received my combat medical badge there.

We were in Afghanistan for only ten months. The Iraq deployment was long. We had one year in country and two months in training and two weeks in Kuwait plus leave. I was on active duty for sixteen months for Iraq, but they wanted to cut the deployment to a year so we went to training and then were only in country for about ten months.

Afghanistan was rough on our unit because we lost five soldiers there. I wasn't close to any of them like I was with Brian, who died in Iraq. I met Brian in Iraq and I was really close to him. We were the same age and he was from Anna, Illinois, and we joined up pretty much together in the guard at the same time. Sergeant Melton, whenever he died, and he was in Iraq with us, died in Afghanistan. Lieutenant Southworth was a good friend of mine and he died in Afghanistan too. We actually had a medic die in Afghanistan. Specialist Talbert died from an IED. It was a tough deployment for the unit in particular.

I think that some guys that have problems when they come home, have a hard time letting go of what they see, and I think some people that are in America have a disconnect of what is going on because they may not know people who have been deployed and they see it on the news and they think that it's different, but you know it's tough to see what people do to each other. It's hard to see war and put it into perspective. I think a lot of the guys can't put it in perspective, the things they saw and the things they did, and separate it from their lives now at home. A lot of them have difficulty finding help to help them out. You are pushed so hard and you're trained to be tough and it's hard to ask for help whenever you are supposed to be tough. I have been fortunate because I have been able to process that information personally and have had the ability to deal with the stuff that I saw and process the information a lot better than some people have been able to. Maybe it's my medical background. I will say I am proud of my service and wouldn't take anything for the things I have experienced.

CHAPTER 21

====

Private First Class Nicholas Jennings

1st Cavalry, HSB-1-92

BAGHDAD, IRAQ • 2004–2005

We were in Kuwait and were going to convoy to Baghdad. A lot of the convoys coming in from Iraq had been getting hit with IED's so we had to armor our vehicles the night before we left. I got the short straw and didn't get a quarter-inch steel on my side of the vehicle so when we left for Iraq I had no real protection. I drove with one hand and had my M-16 in my lap on the way up. Going through southern Iraq at that time was a bad deal. We were pretty much open anywhere we were located.

I ended up with Charlie Battery. I was an artillery surveyor and so they assigned me to them in the convoy. We got split from the convoy and got lost so we were stuck in some village circling around, split from the convoy. We were pretty scared. We finally ran across a British unit and they told us to get the hell out of there. We were in a hot spot and they were getting ready to clear out a group of insurgents in the area. We left and found a checkpoint. We went from checkpoint to checkpoint and finally found the convoy. We made it into Baghdad and the first thing I noticed was the foul smell. It was like seven different smells and all of them were foul-smelling. That's when I saw my first Iraqis. We had always been told that they were slender and feminine. I saw a couple right off the bat that looked like body builders. I knew we were going to be facing something other than what we had been told.

We stayed right outside Sadr City at the north end of Baghdad, which was a hot spot. We were going to be stationed there for a week before we were going to Camp Cuervo, which was a farming community in the southeastern part of Baghdad. Our first night there we was at War Eagle which was a run-down FOB. We slept on top of our Humvees or next to them. We heard some gunfire and some Arabic taunts toward the United States, but that was all. We didn't have any mortar attacks that night but we were all expecting them and waiting on them. There just wasn't much sleep that night. We did our job there for a week.

We left a day before my birthday, April 3. We set up at Cuervo and I was part of the information group for my commander, Captain Bennett. On April 4, my birthday, was the first big push against the 1st Cavalry at Sadr City. The enemy wanted to test our limitations and how we would respond in a firefight. That's when we lost our first two soldiers. I knew both of them, but was really friends with Sheehan. We had trained together and we talked a lot when we were in California together. We got the call around three in the morning and just had a temporary hospital set up. That is when it all hits home, when they start bringing in the wounded and killed in action. You realize this is the real thing and that everybody isn't going to make it back home. It hits you real hard.

Then it wasn't long after that we had our first rocket attack on the FOB. The first sergeant of Alpha Company was killed in the attack. We had what we called monster crews of Iraqis that were coming in the base to do labor work and we figured they had paced off the area for targets for the rocket attack. We had to change our policies after that on screening the Iraqis and how we allowed the Iraqis on the base. It really tore up Alpha Battery. It tore all of us up. It was our first sergeant and everyone really liked him. Everyone felt unsafe after that and no one wanted to live in the barracks after that. When you walked past the barracks on the way to the mess hall you could see the holes in the concrete walls of the barrack where the rocket had hit. It changed our whole perspective of things.

The longer we were there the more the mortar and rocket attacks intensified. One day I was escorting a monster crew onto the FOB from the back gate. We were following a small track vehicle. All at once we got hit with a mortar attack and about one hundred meters in front of us a mortar hit and exploded. The monster crew all dropped to the ground, and I was still standing there kind of in shock and started looking for a close bunker because we had bunkers all over the FOB. None of the shrapnel made it to us because most of it was deflected. We made it to a bunker until the attack, which lasted for about ten minutes, was over. I had to get them inside and keep an eye on them until the attack ended because you didn't know who you could trust. I had my rifle but we were in condition yellow which is having a magazine in the weapon but not locked and loaded. Then when the attack was over we had to run out and help look for anyone that had been hit by the attack. You are doing that and looking over your shoulder at the Iraqis at the same time because you are not sure some of them might not be insurgents and try to pull something during the attack. It makes things very tense during those situations.

We had a helipad at the FOB for helicopters to come in and out of the FOB. It made our area a good target for mortar and rocket attacks by the Iraqis. Mortar and rocket attacks were in our conversations daily and we had to be in full Battle Rattle all the time. We had to wear Kevlar flak jackets and we were always concerned about going out to the shower or the shitter and some dumb Iraqi lobbing a mortar in on you and killing you.

We started to do missions. At the War Eagle FOB, where we had stayed for a week when we first got there, was asking for more artillery survey because they were getting hit so hard by mortar and rocket attacks. We sent a radar crew to help them out. The very first time the radar crew tried to go over to War Eagle they got hit. They had to drop all their radar equipment and return to our base. The radar equipment is real sensitive equipment and tracks mortars and rockets and just about anything else and will trace locations where all this stuff is being fired from.

The next time they went I went with them. We retrieved all the equipment on the way, but this time when we went we were escorted with two tanks, and two Apache helicopters for air support. Going through Baghdad with two tanks rolling down the street and air support drew a crowd. We were moving slow and really had to keep a heads-up because of the crowd and the concern for being hit. Then going into Sadr City is always a scary situation because it was a hot spot. We finally made it into War Eagle without getting hit.

About a week later one of our convoys got hit by an IED and a friend of mine by the name of Johnson was killed. I was beginning to learn not to get too close to guys. It hurt to see or hear of any of the guys getting killed, but it really hurt when someone that you were close to got killed. I had videotaped his memorial at the FOB they had for him. It was fitting for the guy. He was a really nice guy and I felt sorry for his family. It was really hard on them.

In March we started being able to draw leave. I was one of the first ones to draw leave and I was going to get to go home on the 4th of July. The night before I was to leave I volunteered for an OP mission. We wanted to find out where these mortars and rockets were coming from. We had to go to the water treatment facility which was east of the FOB. We had to climb this water tower and sit up there in shifts throughout the night with night vision. We thought we had some insurgents but it turned out they were normal Iraqis. They were doing a lot of stopping and watching. They would pull their car up and stop and get out and walk around like they were looking around and then get in their car, go about one hundred meters and stop and do it again. They could have been involved in the attacks but we weren't sure. They didn't have any weapons so we couldn't detain them. That morning I drew the last shift, and it was supposed to end at 6 A.M. but I was still there at 7 A.M. and we spotted some Iraqis sleeping on top of a building nearby. We detained them and questioned them, but they didn't appear to know anything so we weren't sure if they were involved in the attacks or not. Once again they had no weapons so we had to let them go.

Then while I was on leave they caught some Iraqis that were involved in the mortaring. They had improvised mortars out of PVC pipe. That is regular plumbing pipe and they used diesel fuel to pour in them to get a longer range with the mortars. It backfired on them several times and the fuel would catch on fire and blow them up.

My job in field artillery surveying was pretty cut and dry. I had a secret clearance and that's why I ended up in information operations. When I got back off of leave we started a new program where we were going to push propaganda approved by First Brigade and First Cavalry. We took over the FOB Cuervo which was the Revolutionary Guards base. We took over the hospital there as well and lived in the hospital. On the third floor we set up operations and that is where we set up a radio station. I had to use a monster crew for that. We used them on the radio to push the propaganda. They did all the talking on the air. We never talked on the air. I had to run the equipment, but I never talked on the radio. There were several lives saved by the use of the radio. We called it Peace FM. Civilians begin to call in and give tips and we would send out patrols to squash the incident or detain whoever was caching weapons. It really helped save a lot of civilian lives.

I learned a lot with the program about the culture and kind of became fond of the things they had done or were capable of doing. I was around a bunch of musicians and artists. They would entertain people, they didn't care who you were. What I learned from the whole experience was that you didn't have hatred towards a whole group of people or a whole country, it was just the ones shooting at you or the ones throwing mortars or rockets at you.

I was outside one day and getting ready to go on a convoy to War Eagle. A car bomb hit a nearby gas station. It sounded like a mortar dropped next to me it was so loud. It was down the street from us but the explosion was so loud and we could feel the concussion from the blast we were all checking our bodies to see if we had been hit by something. Then we started on our convoy. The orders from the First Cavalry were that if you got cut off from the convoys or your vehicle broke down you were left. The convoy wouldn't stop. The convoy was a scary situation that day. The convoy was moving fast. I don't know why but we couldn't get them on the radio. We were playing chicken with the Iraqis. We were passing vehicles, in the wrong lane too long and I ran an Iraqi vehicle off the road. My co-driver turned white as a sheet once because he thought we were going to have a head-on collision and he started complaining and bitching about my driving. I told him, "Do you want to be cut off from the convoy or do you want to make it in with them?" and he shut up. We made it into the FOB with the rest of the convoy. It was a scary and stressful drive.

While I was there I pulled a lot of double duty. The max time I slept was four hours. The max time I went without sleep at all was seventy-two hours. That really messes with your head. I would work all night, usually doing reports and listening to whatever we had to push out over the radio, [then had] to get up and do convoys and not get any sleep. I guess you don't need to sleep in those situations as much as you would think with all that went on.

The times that I was the most scared was when I was either out in the street and didn't know what was going or when the mortar rocket attacks took place. You just never knew when you were going to get hit or with what you were going to get hit. It keeps you on guard all the time. The green zone was tricky too at the international airport. It is more open than in the FOBs and Iraqis can come in the green zone and back out of the green zone pretty much unchecked. We were always getting some kind of shit going in the green zone.

As I think of the experience today there many mixed emotions. One is the movies they have coming out about the Iraq War. They are more bogus than they are anything else and they offend those veterans that were there because they don't portray what we really experienced. I won't even watch them. The older I get the more I think of the friends I lost over there. Drake, who was shot by a sniper. He was a gunner and a sniper killed him while he was in an intersection. Me and Drake were really good friends. He had a wife and a kid at the time and you know you always worried about your friends. One of the things you got cussed at was telling your buddies who were going out on a convoy to be safe. We would always get a big fuck you from them when you told them that. "It's a learning experience," you would like to say, but it is more than that. You get home and see how trivial some people make life. They want to sit and whine and complain about nothing and complain about how they are getting screwed at their jobs and just the smallest thing will ruin their day. You try to explain to them what you have been through and you say, "You know, if I had worried about stuff like that I would have never come out of my room." It still doesn't get through to them. They want to say that it is your deal or you got post traumatic stress disorder. The first couple of years after I came home I tried to explain to my family and my friends about the experience over there, but you just can't talk to them about it. I just keep close to veterans because if I have something going on in my head I can talk to them and they understand what I am talking about.

How I dealt with being over there is that I put it out of my mind. If you worried about mortars and rockets and all the other stuff all the time you didn't perform your job the way you were supposed to, so you just kept it out of your mind and did your job. We were all scared to death, but if you think about it all the time you are just not going to perform. It was like a secret pact between us all. We all understood the situation we were in but we just didn't think about it. We turned our daily lives into doing what it was we were supposed to be doing. We would go on convoys or do other duties and until you heard a shot fired or you had someone try to hit your vehicle or something like that, you carried on and when you needed to respond with a situation you responded. There is no telling how many people we ran off the road over there. Then we had this Iraqi at the front gate and he was in a car and we thought he was going to bomb the front gate. What happened was he just couldn't read the road signs and drove down the road the wrong way. They turned his car into Swiss cheese. They opened up on him with fifty-calibers and M-16s. When the car stopped we went over to it and it had so many holes in it there was no way the driver couldn't not have been killed. The Iraqi got out of the car and walked away without a scratch. I just could not believe it and wouldn't have if I hadn't seen it with my own eyes.

While we were there they were constantly testing us. They would see how close they could get with a car or try throwing things and hitting us to see what our reaction would be. We had an Arab family that got mad at us, I guess from some attack in their neighborhood, and threw their dead child out near the front gate. We all got to see that. It was odd to see an infant thrown in the street and just left there. Just to send us a message.

The longer we were there the more advanced we were getting in a lot of drones. My buddy John Hurst got to go back to Kuwait to learn how to fly a radio flier to help scan outside the FOB, but he had to be on top of the hospital to fly it. It was a neat little deal. You had to throw it off the roof and then guide it with a control.

It was isolated there. You couldn't talk to anyone about what was going on in your head at the time. I am sure I could go to the VA and they would tell me that I had post-traumatic stress disorder, but in my opinion you can get PTSD from life. What happened over there was life, but it was something different. Isolation is what I called it and it took me a while to get over it because I was away from all my friends over there that I went through all the experiences with, and you come home and you try to tell your family and friends about it and they don't get it. It was like I was trying to explain to one of my friends, "Imagine getting up and going to brush your teeth and use the restroom and some dumb Iraqi dirt famer lobs a damn mortar on your FOB and hits right where you are at and you're either wounded or dead." Now there is nothing honorable about that and you try to explain that and it doesn't even register when you try to tell it, it doesn't even register with them. The experience over there changes you inside and it makes you more callous. It makes you more cold in certain situations. Life here is trivial. People here complain and whine and talk about things that are bad to them. I have told several people quit doing what you are doing it will help you out. Quit doing what hurts you. Don't force yourself into things that hurt you. I didn't force myself to be in my situation over there. I signed a contract and knew if the time came what I would have to do and I went there and did it. You can't help getting shot at. You can't help seeing dead people, but you learn to deal with it and then come back home and listen to whining and bitching about nothing.

On occasion I see one of my buddies that I was in Iraq with and we get together and talk about the experiences we had, and you are with someone that understands and gets what you were feeling and how you feel now. And then there are other war veterans that you can talk to and they understand what you have gone through and how you feel and what you are thinking. When I first got out I stuck around Austin where I was discharged because some of my buddies were there and I could see them all the time. I knew if I came home things wouldn't be the same. Finally I did come back home and I guess the things that stick in my head more than anything is the guys that I lost. A couple of them died on April the fourth. One was shot and the round penetrated his helmet and the round caused his brain to swell and he died in Germany. The other guy was shot in the face and he died instantly from a sniper. I was one of those that went out and never got shot at. It almost makes you feel like you didn't get tested. It almost feels like you weren't there because even though you were risking your life going out you weren't shot. It works on my mind and I don't understand it.

The night that we flew out we were supposed to fly out on the Chinook Helicopter. Thank God we didn't because those things like to fall out of the sky. We took Blackhawks out of Baghdad at night and that was a pretty interesting situation. We were very lucky we didn't have any attacks because the Iraqis like to shoot at the Blackhawks, but we made it back to Kuwait without incident.

I believe what we did was worth it. I don't regret it. I do have memories over there that's so chaotic and it's like I am bouncing around in my thoughts.

I miss my friends I lost over there but I still believe it was worth what we done. We not only saved a lot of lives, we changed a lot of minds and we turned some people who would have potentially been our enemies into our friends and we always need our allies, especially in the Middle East. I am proud of my service over there regardless of what I come home to. The closest friends I have ever had in my life were the friends I had in Iraq. They always watched my back and I always watched theirs. That is true friendship.

CHAPTER 22

Private First Class
Joseph Underhile

234th Signal Battalion

BAGHDAD INTERNATIONAL AIRPORT, IRAQ •
2003–2004

It started in March of 2003. I got a phone call from Sergeant Rogers saying we got activated. We didn't know anything else, I just had to be there Monday morning to find out what we were going to do. On Monday morning I checked in and they told us we were going to Mareilles on the 15th of March to go start getting shots. When we got there they wouldn't tell us anything about where we were going. I was scared shitless. Twenty years old, there's a war going on in Afghanistan and one in Iraq. You don't know where you are going to be at and you got a bunch of teenagers that haven't done anything and a leader that has been nowhere. We always heard, "Oh, no, we aren't going anywhere," but now we are here in line getting shots. They started pulling out anthrax vaccinations and that kind of told me that we were going somewhere because once they start giving malaria shots and anthrax shots they don't do that for no reason.

When we got back we traveled between our unit and another local unit near us for a couple of weeks and then we got orders to go to Fort Riley to hook up with a couple different signal battalions. My unit was the 133rd Signal Battalion and I was a Bravo Heavy Diesel mechanic for them. We had guys from Iowa, some from Michigan, and some from a unit up by Chicago along with us and we formed the 234th Signal Battalion.

PFC Joseph Underhile on R&R leave in Qatar, Iraq, in 2004 (Joseph Underhile).

We shipped out to Fort Riley at the end of March or the beginning of April and we stayed there till June. Then we got our orders to go to Iraq. We got everything loaded and got everything prepared and we shipped out for Iraq on June 13. We arrived in Kuwait on June 14 and stayed there until July 2 to get acclimated to the weather. Being a mechanic we had to make sure all our vehicles were ready because we were going to convoy from Kuwait to Baghdad. That was a scary thought because we didn't have armored vehicles. All we had were old ragtops and no specialized stuff to stop the IED's. All we had was sand bags in the bottom of the floorboard. Luckily when we left and went to Baghdad we didn't get hit by any IED's. We were really lucky on that aspect because we went through some hot shit and real slow. I mean we weren't driving the right convoy speed and just doing stupid stuff and getting separated from people and a couple of trucks broke down and [we] had to tow the trucks that broke down.

We arrived in Baghdad on July 2, 2003. Our chain of command was all messed up. We had a fuel point we stopped at, and instead of doing a zigzag formation so we would be more safe they had us pull in a half circle around this curb in the middle of Baghdad. Then in addition our standard operating procedure was that we were supposed to be in Condition Red. Condition Red was that we weren't to allow any locals to come within one hundred meters of us. If they did you were supposed to fire a warning shot and then shoot them if they kept coming. Instead our chain of command put us in Condition Amber which is to load a magazine, but you can't lock and load. We were backwards the very first day that we arrived in Iraq.

The first day I was in Iraq I had some local come up to me acting all weird and sporadic and he jumped in my Humvee. We got into an altercation and he's no longer with us. After I killed him I threw him out of my Humvee. The people he was with drug him off. In Iraq there were dead bodies everywhere. They never picked them up. They just let them lay there and rot. The people will only pick them up if they have something important on them so when they drug him off I knew he had a bomb or something on him to hurt me. My friend from high school was with me. He was my co-driver and he thought it was pretty cool what I did. Another girl I went to high school with was there and she came up to me and said, "You killed him!" I said, "What did you expect me to do? He came at me and wouldn't stop." I told him to *holt*. That's the word in Arabic for halt. He just kept coming with me having my weapon pointed at him. This is war.

We got to the international airport that night. We had set down and we were all really tired. We had the old fashioned MRE's with the bricks in 'em to heat the food up. Me being the redneck that I am and my friend Brandon took the brick and put it in a two-liter water bottle and made an MRE bomb out of it. We weren't thinking, we were just trying to relieve the tension of what we were doing. It went off and we scared the shit out of everyone. We had a few sergeants came running out in their underwear and boots with their M-16's looking around and asking, "What the hell was that?" We hid the evidence. Being twenty-year-old kids, we just kinda kicked it under a truck and acted like we didn't know what the hell it was. I don't know if anyone ever figured it out, except those of us that did it.

The next morning we got up and had a little makeshift area to work. The first thing I had to work on was a trailer that needed to go to Camp Anaconda. We didn't have anything to fix it with. The axle was broken. I had a couple other guys helping me. We had dug out a hole under this old trailer that we had that wasn't going to be used for a while. I suggested that we take the axle off of it and put it on the trailer with the broken axle because the old trailer wasn't going to be used for a while. That was the first day I ever heard mortar fire. I had taken the axle off the old trailer and had crawled under the other trailer to put the axle on. They started walking in mortars. They got about two hundred yards away and I don't think I touched the ground coming out from under that trailer. I remember I said, "What the fuck is that?" It really scared me, but as time went on any type of rocket fire or mortars, or even gunfire, you just got used to it. You get used to stuff like that going off. It just becomes part of your everyday life, just like getting up in the morning and driving to work. You just don't think about it because if a mortar hits on top of you, you are not going to feel anything, you are going to be blown to pieces.

About a week or so after we got there we got all set up and we stayed at the My House which was part of Saddam Hussein's resort. He had a little zoo set up for all his generals. We stayed in his houses and there were three walls, but they had been broken down a little bit and on the outside of the walls there was a little farmhouse. That was the first time we had ever got shot at by AK-47 fire. It was about ten or eleven o'clock at night. We had just gotten into bed because we had a long day doing mechanic work and woke up to AK-47 fire and tracers coming in and hitting the top of our roof. They never did come over the wall. We got up and put all our gear on and set up a perimeter. It was just specialists and privates. Me and my friend Brandon Spradling were the ones that did everything. We helped set up the perimeter. The kids we had were all eighteen or nineteen years old, fresh out of high school, and they didn't know their ass from a hole in the ground. They were just sitting there and we told them where to go and what to do. There were no sergeants there and they didn't show up until all the firing stopped. Then Sergeant Sharrard got the credit for setting up the perimeter and got a Bronze Star out of it before we left deployment. That was a disgrace to the military, but that is another story.

We started working fourteen hours a day, six days a week, working on trucks because the sand and heat just tore up every CV boot and wheel hub just traveling from Kuwait to Iraq. The trucks just weren't made for that much heat. It would be 130 degrees by ten o'clock in the morning and the sand would melt the rubber and would melt the boot leather off your feet.

Then they started making us do PT. About two months into it I tore my left knee up. I twisted it somehow doing a run one morning and I started having to go to sick call for that and had a medical officer that wanted to send me to Germany to have my knee scoped. Instead he had to put me on convalescent leave because my commanding officer wouldn't approve me going to Germany. That was for those who were wounded only, according to him. The medical officer tried to make him send me, but it didn't happen. I got kicked out of the motor pool for a month or so and they tried to make me do some supply work. That didn't go over very well with my personality at the time because I was pissed off because my knee was all swollen up and I had to keep flying around from doctor to doctor getting my knee drained. I had to see so many helicopter rides and saw so many doctors it was unbeliev-

The house located just outside of Baghdad that Joseph Underhile lived in during the second half of his tour in Iraq in 2004 (Joseph Underhile)

able. I remember one helicopter ride and we were coming up on this little village. In combat the helicopter pilots would fly low and fast. They didn't want to get too high and didn't want to get too low. The lower they were the better they could maneuver. I don't fully understand that but we come around this little village and you could see it. We were 100 meters or so off the ground. You could fly that low because there isn't any electricity in that country and there are no telephone poles or any big structures to run into. We saw this little white truck and I remember the pilot saying, "Look at that." The kids down there were playing soccer and other games and this little white truck drove up and it blew up. It blew up the village and the flea market they were having there. The ball of fire went higher than the helicopter, but was to the left of us. A few more feet and we would have been right in the middle of the fire. We got the hell out of there. I understood it was the Shiites and the Sunnis just fighting each other. There were no military personnel there. It was a terrible sight. Little kids running around on fire, and that was the first time I had ever saw anything like that. That has been eight years ago and I can still see them running around on fire.

We landed up north of the airport about thirty minutes later and I went up and stayed with Sergeant Dobbs and Sergeant Cruz. They had been there for a few months. It was the first time I had been up there, and the place was right on the Tigris River. The first night the Iraqis on the other side of the river started firing AK-47 rounds across the river at us. I had one round hit right in front of my foot. They did it every night and it didn't seem to bother Sergeant Dobbs and Sergeant Cruz. They had been there for three or four months and they were used to bullets hitting all around them and going through their tent, but it freaked me out. There wasn't anything you could do about it though. We had a boat crew with a fifty-caliber machine gun and a Mark 19, which is a fully automatic grenade launcher. If the firing got to be too much you would hear them fire up the boat motor and they would go fire the machine gun and Mark 19 several times and then the firing would stop. They either were killed or stopped and went home, I don't know which because I didn't want to go out and look. It wasn't worth getting killed for.

The next day after getting my knee drained I went back to my unit. They put me back in supply for another three or four weeks. By that time my master sergeant, Jack Claire, had got back to Iraq. He was sent home because of a heart condition and fought and fought to get back to his unit and finally made it back. When he saw that one of his best mechanics was sitting in supply on a computer it pissed him off. The first sergeant called me a broke-dick and that pissed me off. I told him, "I will show you a broke-dick, you motherfucker," and threatened to beat his ass. That didn't go over very well, but luckily my master sergeant who had been in for twenty years got that swept under the rug so I didn't get into trouble. The master sergeant told the first sergeant that he was being disrespectful too, calling me a broke-dick in front of me. He told him if he wanted to make fun of his soldiers he should do it somewhere where the soldiers couldn't hear him.

What they didn't know was that I was still fixing the Humvees even though I was assigned to supply. My fellow mechanics would still call me on the phone system we had and asked questions and drive the Humvees up to me and I would walk out there and look at them and start fixing them, and after the argument with the first sergeant I ended up back at the motor pool and doing what I was supposed to do, which made me so much happier. I was back with my friends and fellow mechanics.

I still had the knee problem, but being in the army, you know, you just drive on. You don't think about the pain you are in or your knee swelling up. I would just go to the doctor and they would drain it and I would go back to work. I didn't do any more running or squats, just did some push-ups and weight training. When the medical doctor that had tried to get me sent to Germany came back from leave he was trying to figure out why I was still in country. I told him and he signed off on a profile that allowed me to do mechanic work, but no running or any exercise that affected my knee.

We worked ten- to fourteen-hour days and then at night there would be two mechanics on call. We only had three actual generator mechanics so one of them guys was always on call. It would be one mechanic and then another one and then me. I was able to work on generators too because my father was a master AFC certified mechanic and when I was a kid he started me working on cars when I was four years old. I was able to fix whatever they needed me to fix and they liked that. They put me in the rotation a little bit more and if there was something one of the eighteen- or nineteen-year-old kids couldn't fix they would wake me up and I would fix it. It was usually a generator that would go down because we had the main body of the signal battalion at the airport and the generators were used a lot. The generators ran their signal trucks so that people could call into to them on the radio or they could communicate with them. The generators ran twenty-four/seven. Usually they let them run out of fuel. We would have to go out there and crack the system and bleed the air out of the system. It was because they were so retarded, they were too busy watching movies and bitching because they were hot because their air conditioners went out, when all my mechanics were working out in 130-degree to 140-degree weather all day long. We had no air conditioning at all, but anybody who is in mechanics knows you are going to get called for all the shitty jobs. It went on like that all the time.

They told us originally that we were going to be there six months. Six months came and they told us we were going to be there seven months. Seven months came and they told us we were going to be there eight months. By then it was February and they asked me if I wanted to go home on leave. I took two weeks leave to come back home to see my friends and family. It was good to see them, but that second goodbye going back to Iraq was harder because the two weeks I was home I was still in combat mode. I'm used to being shot at, rocketed and mortared, and I wasn't normal the two weeks that I was home. I just stayed secluded and basically stayed drunk for two weeks because I knew when I was sober I wasn't normal around my friends or family. I just stayed drunk for two weeks. If I could do it again I wouldn't have went home. I would have just went to Germany or some place I could have went sightseeing or something like that so I didn't have to tell anyone goodbye again.

I got back to Iraq and started back to work on the trucks. Then the stupid chain of command came down with a new rule that we had to salute the officers. You weren't supposed to salute the officers because if a sniper is in the area that is who they are going to shoot because they want to take out officers first. Then my father called a congressman and complained to them about my knee and told the congressman that I was crawling around on my knees working on trucks. When my commanding officer found out it pissed him off. I was called in and chewed out and told that we weren't allowed to do that. I got in an argument with my executive officer who was a lieutenant. He stuck his finger in my face and started screaming at me and I told him I would break his damn finger if he didn't get it out of my face. I am outspoken and I don't like stupid people on trivial bullshit and that's what I told him. There were other people in the office and he said, "You can't talk to me like that," and I laughed and said, "I just did." He just stormed out of the room.

Then we found out that we were going to be in country until April or May 2004. They had just passed a rule that all army units had to stay for twelve months. We had a Humvee Bravo 37 that we basically robbed of parts so we could fix other vehicles. Specialist Patterson, who had been in the army for fifteen years, just started putting the vehicle back together. He knew we needed it. In Baghdad it is hard to get parts. If you ordered them it might take two or three months to get them. He just went around to different units picking up a part here and there until he had enough to put it back together. Then we began scrounging for parts on other vehicles too. We would just take parts from other units because they weren't using them and we needed them to keep vehicles running.

There were some FBI agents and Special Forces down the road from us. I'm not sure what they did because some of them looked like Chuck Norris and carried double 1911's and they didn't have any dog tags, no wallets, no nothing. We had been in country about six or seven months and they got satellite cell phones to where we didn't need any card or anything to call home. Since we were working on their vehicles and fixing them for them they allowed us to use their telephones to call home. It was much better because it was a straight up satellite phone and you didn't have to dial nothing special. [With] the old military phones you had to call Hawaii and they hopped an operator to somewhere in California and they would hop an operator home. It was all static and you would be in the middle of a conversation and then get cut off because some emergency came up so we mechanics had it a little bit better to be able to call home.

The FBI and Special Forces unit would have a party every Friday night. They would drink beer and cook out and we had orders that we couldn't drink, but they would invite us to it and we went anyway because of all the stress we were under we needed something to calm us down. We had all the mechanical problems we had to deal with and then we had to deal with the chain of command all the time. You can't do this and you can't do that, don't lock and load when you leave, or we had Battalion CQ, which is where you go to headquarters and sit there and you got a list of who can go through the first set of double doors and if they are not on the list you have to call the battalion commander and see if they're okay to come in. The shift I was on was three to midnight. After I would get off they didn't want to take me back to my living area and they started just leaving me there and I would have to walk two miles back to my area. I was in the airport area, but there were big holes in the walls from mortars and wild hyenas and no telling what else running around. I tried talking to them about it, but nothing was done about it. I had to walk back every night. Me being a mechanic, I started taking some of their supply vehicles and just disabling them in front of the headquarters because they didn't know how to re-enable them and my fellow mechanics wouldn't fix the vehicles for them. They didn't have the part to do it anyway because I had it in my pocket. I'd disable the computer brain. I would take the cord off or pull out a couple of fuses and put them in my pocket. Then they would ask me to fix the vehicle and I would so that I had a ride back to my area when I got off. It was super dangerous putting a soldier out in the middle of Baghdad at night even if we were on our own base.

The United States government was trying to make the Iraqis like us so they let them come in and work in our areas. This started right after we got into Iraq. When they came in we would have to go out to the main gate and physically search them and any equipment they had for weapons or explosives. We had this sergeant that nobody liked, Sergeant Glade. He became friends with them and started taking gifts from them and one day I noticed he wasn't searching this one guy he had become friends with. I was on that duty one day and we went out to the main gate to search them. The sergeant started yelling at me and saying he was good to go we didn't have to search him. Anyone knew in a combat situation that you have to search all of these people. They are coming from Baghdad and they deal with the highest bidder. You don't know if the bad people have their family or are threatening to kill them or their family. I went to some MP's and told them that we hadn't searched this Iraqi when he came through the gate and that caused a big uproar. I made the battalion commander look bad because he had an E-7 sergeant not searching people and that didn't go over very well. People got mad at me for telling, but you know it was the right thing to do because if he had came in with a bomb or AK-47 with a hundred-round drum he could have killed a lot of soldiers. That would have looked even worse on their record. The sergeant got a slap on the wrist and they didn't do anything to me.

A few weeks later I got stuck back on guard duty at a bazaar which is like a big flea market. It was me and Sergeant Glade and about fifty Iraqis. I turned around and noticed that Sergeant Glade didn't have his weapon. This was in March 2004, and I asked him where his weapon was at. He said it was inside. I asked him what he meant, it was inside, there was only Iraqis in there. His weapon and 60 rounds of ammo was in there. He said, "Well, one of [my] friends was watching it for [me]." The next thing I know a Iraqi comes out of the building with Sergeant Glade's weapon in his hand. I drew down on him and was about to shoot him and he threw the weapon, yelling, "No, No, No!" Then Sergeant Glade tried to step in front of me to tell me not to do that and I ended up beating an E-7's ass. We got into a fistfight and I kicked the shit out of him and took his weapon away from him. Then I called my commanding officer and told him what the situation had been and what I had done. Later that evening they called me into headquarters and were going to try to punish me for hitting the sergeant. I told them to go ahead because I was going to go to the base commander of the airport and tell him about all the things that had been going on. Like the black sergeant that tried to rape a female soldier. He tried to pull her in his room. They transferred him to Kuwait just to get him away from everyone and promoted the female soldier so she wouldn't talk about it. And [I would] tell them about all the medals being given out to guys for nothing. And then I was going to tell them about all the sleeping around that was going on between soldiers. Then they just told me to have a nice day and they left me alone after that. Sergeant Glade ended up kicked off duty for giving the rifle to the Iraqi, which no one heard about.

There is one other story I like to tell. I went to Babylon on a convoy once. There was another convoy that wasn't attached to us, but they got ambushed a few miles in front of us. They weren't attached to us but they were fellow soldiers. They came over the radio and asked for help. The captain refused. We pulled over and waited for the fight to end. They kept asking for help and that bothers me to this day. We sat there for a couple of hours before we left and when we finally went through the area you could tell they had been hit pretty hard. I don't know if anyone was killed but they were fellow soldiers and we should have helped them. No one wants to be in a firefight, but if a fellow soldier needs your help you go help them. That captain has to live with that today.

One night not too long before our deployment was over I had to pull an all-night shift at battalion headquarters. I was actually talking online to my father through a video chat. He can vouch for this because he heard the explosion and saw all the dust go around but it was late past midnight when the explosion went off. I had to wait there because I was at battalion head-quarters but it woke everyone up. It was about a thousand pounds of explosives that had been brought on base through the holes in the wall, and what had happened was a tank ran over it and exploded. It killed two soldiers in the tank. The next morning I got debriefed on what they said happened, or what they were going to tell everyone that had happened. They said that EOD

[Explosive Ordinance Detection] had blown up stuff. They had set it off at the wrong time by accident. That was bullshit. EOD don't blow up anything in the middle of night. It is too dangerous, and I had already heard the reports of the tank getting opened up like a can opener and the two patrol soldiers that were driving it getting killed. They had already covered the hole up with bulldozers and all the engineers got rid of the evidence of their screw-up. That would make people look bad if they knew they had brought in a thousand pounds of explosives on the base and planted it without us knowing. That was the first time I really realized that the military can do some shady shit. I wonder what they told the families of those that were killed because they didn't want nobody to know that a big bomb went off on base. An IED, that was the biggest explosion I ever felt. I mean I had rockets and mortars blow up fifty feet away from me but a thousand pounds of explosives hit a few hundred away. It knocked me out of my chair and even my dad could see the dust coming off the building in the video chat and that scared the hell out of him because I told him I had to go, had to go to work, and he could see dust swirling everywhere. It really bothered me that we had all these retards in charge of us.

We finished all the maintenance on the Humvees to get them ready to go because we were going to head back to Kuwait. We had a debriefing before we left. By this time Iraqis were using little girls. They would strap explosives on them and put them in the middle of the road and Americans were stopping and they would blow the little girl up and then ambush the convoy. They wanted to know what our thoughts were on that. They asked me what I would do if I saw a kid in the road and I told them I would honk my horn and speed up and go on past them because we couldn't stop. You don't want to get blown up. They told me that wasn't allowed, to drive back because they weren't going to allow soldiers to run over people or to run over kids. Luckily it never happened because I would have hated to see what happened. We would have [been] ambushed or something. They basically put me on security and mechanic duty.

We finally got to leave and head back to Kuwait. It takes two days to drive to Kuwait. On the first day of the convoy we had a trailer to break down. We had two types of trailers, A-1s and A-2s. The A-2 took a smaller tire like the Humvee and I'd saw which trailer broke down was a A-2. I knew we didn't have a tire that fit the trailer. They had gotten a tire to take back to fix the broken-down trailer. I was on security and I kept trying to radio back and tell them that it was the wrong tire, but they wouldn't listen. They ended up getting a tire off a Humvee and threw it on my truck and said, "That's the tire." It was signal people and they didn't know their ass from a hole in the ground when it came to mechanics. I kept trying to tell them but they told the driver of the Humvee I was in to go back to the trailer, which was thirty minutes behind the convoy, to go take the tire. We drove back the thirty minutes. When we got there a sergeant came up and grabbed the tire out of the truck. I told him, "That's the wrong tire." Besides that, we had broken convoy — there are not supposed to be less than three trucks in a convoy — and we had spent thirty minutes on our own with this tire that was the wrong tire. When my buddy Brandon saw the tire he said, "That is the wrong tire, you morons, and my guy's been telling you for the past forty minutes that it wasn't the right one."

Well, a convoy that was coming in behind where the trailer was broke down had a wrecker. They were going to tow it. We didn't have a radio or anything in our Humvee and instead of staying there with that convoy till the wrecker arrived we ended up driving back to the other convoy alone. No radio or anything for about forty-five minutes by ourselves. We broke all the rules of the SOP and it was the dumbest thing I had ever saw in my life.

I'm not religious or anything but God must have been with us that day because we had locals driving all over the place and looking at us and probably calling people and telling them to get over to where we were, but no one ever got hurt and we never got shot at one time that day. We got back to the convoy and made it to our destination for the night.

The next morning we were going on one of the more deadlier parts of the convoy because it was nothing but gravel. The road had been blown away back in the first Gulf War and it had never been rebuilt. We had to get in the gravel off the road to get back to Kuwait. When we started in the gravel, instead of driving a decent speed the commander drove at ten miles an hour on a thirty- or forty-mile stretch. We didn't get hit, luckily, but the convoy behind us got hit because we were driving so slow. The convoy returned fifty-caliber fire and it ended up that no one was hurt. We finally got into Kuwait and it was one of the best feelings because we all got back alive. We had two people that did get Purple Hearts from mortar fire. One guy got a piece of shrapnel in the chest and a girl got a piece of glass from the blast. They were minor wounds as compared to many that people received. I got in trouble for smoking a cigar in my Humvee. It was a celebration. This sergeant saw me and told me I couldn't smoke in a military vehicle. I wouldn't put it out. I was so happy to be in a friendly country.

We stayed in Kuwait for a couple of weeks, then we flew home. They didn't really have much help for us because we were National Guard. We were at Fort Riley for five days and then they took us home and dumped us back into civilian life. I spent a few years in a bottle after that because I didn't know anything else to do. I stayed drunk for a couple of years and then I met a woman named Jessica. We hit it off. We got married in 2007 and my master sergeant that had been with me in Iraq came to the wedding. He noticed I was casing my wedding and had problems and he pulled me aside and demanded that I go get counseling. He told me not to wait thirty years like he did because he had been in Vietnam. He said, "You're going to get help. You have a wife and a baby on the way," so I decided to go to counseling in 2007. I was diagnosed with post-traumatic stress disorder and it's now 2012. I still have troubles with people and it is hard to get work as a veteran right now. I'm eighty percent disabled through the military but a lot of people tell me thank you for your service. I am raising my family and thankful to be alive.

Afghanistan: U.S. Combat Chronology

2001

Oct. 7: Air Campaign Begins against Al Qaeda and Taliban camps and bases. This included strikes from aircraft carriers in the Arabian Sea and B-2 bombers based at Whiteman AFB, Missouri. Crews from the 500th Bomb Wing fly 44 consecutive hours — the longest mission in U.S. military history.

Oct. 15: 2 AC-130H Specter gunships of the air force's 16th Special Operations Squadron attack 12 targets.

Oct. 19: Team 555 (12 men) is the first Special Forces A-team infiltrated into Afghanistan, at Bagram Air Base.

Oct. 20: Parachute Drops. 200 men of the 75th Ranger Regiment and special operators make a nighttime drop on Kandahar airstrip.

Nov. 16–Dec. 16: Tora Bora. U.S. bombs mountain strong hold of Al Qaeda. Afghan allies fight on ground. Some three dozen U.S. special operators guide strikes. Arabs escape into Pakistan.

Nov. 18: Battle of Tarin Kot: U.S. fighter jets directed by U.S. Special Forces on the ground break the back of the Taliban. Over 6–8 hours, 1,000 Taliban are decimated.

Nov. 25: First U.S. Conventional Forces on the Ground. 500 marines of the 15th MEU arrive at Kandahar. They set up at Camp Rhino from which to conduct offensive operations.

Nov. 25: First U.S. Death to Enemy Action. CIA Special Activities Division officer Johnny M. Spann is the first American killed. He is murdered by Taliban during a riot at Qala Jangi Fortress prison in Mazare-Sharif. 16 special ops troops fight 500 POWs for 72 hours. Air and gunship strikes kill most of the rioting Taliban by Nov. 27.

Dec. 5: 3 members of Op. Det. A, 3rd Bn., 5th SFG, are killed and 19 wounded by "friendly fire" near Kandahar.

2002

Jan. 4: First U.S. Military KIA. Sgt. 1st Class Nathan R. Chapman of 3rd Bn., 1st SFG, is killed at a checkpoint in Khost.

Jan. 9: A Marine KC-130 tanker of Aerial Refueler Transport Squadron 352 crashes in Pakistan, killing 7 marines.

Mar. 1–16: Operation Anaconda. 1700 U.S. troops (3 infantry battalions from the 10th MD and 101st Airborne, plus special ops units) scour the Shahi-Kot Valley near Gardez for Taliban and Al Qaeda. Intense fighting occurs at Objective Ginger. U.S. suffers 23 WIA in initial assault.

Mar. 4: Battle of Takur Ghar (Robert Ridge). In the Shahi-Kot Valley, 7 members of special operations units (75th Ranger Regt., 24th STS, 38th Rescue Sqdn., 160th SOAR, SEAL Team 2) are KIA in a 17-hour firefight during Operation Anaconda.

Apr. 15: 4 soldiers are killed clearing explosives in Kandahar: 3 of the 710th Explosive Ordnance Detection, and 1 from the 19th SFG.

May 19: 1 Green Beret is KIA during a firefight in Shkin.

Jun. 12: Accidental crash of an air force transport near Bande Sardeh dam claims 2 airmen and 1 Green Beret.

Jul. 27: 5 special ops soldiers are WIA (1 mortally) in a firefight with Arabs at Ab Khail, near Khost. The 4-hour firefight also includes 82nd Airborne Division elements.

Dec. 2: 1 U.S. soldier is KIA in an ambush in Shkin.

2003

Jan. 27–28: Battle of Spin Boldak. Heaviest fighting in 9 months. Rapid reaction force of 82nd Airborne Division participates in the 12-hour firefight on Adi Ghar Mountain with 80 enemy, 18 of whom are KIA (mostly airstrikes).

Jan. 30: MH-60l. Black Hawk crashes near Bagram Air Base during a training mission — 4 men of 1st Bn., 160th SOAR, die in the accident.

Mar. 14: Special Forces convoy is ambushed between Gardez and Khost — 5 enemy are KIA.

Mar. 20–25: Operation Valiant Strike. In the largest operation since March 2002, Special Forces (200) and 1st Bn., 504th PIR, 82nd Abn. Div (800) men, clash with the enemy in the Sami Ghat Mountains in the Kandahar area. 10 enemy fighters are KIA.

Mar. 23: Air force HH-60 helicopter crashes during a medical evacuation mission near Ghazni — 6 members of the 38th and 41st Rescue Squadrons die in the accident.

Mar. 29: 2 U.S. special ops troops are KIA in Helmand Province; 15 Taliban are killed in a convoy ambush.

Apr. 2: 45 Special Forces clash with Taliban in Tor Ghar Mountains near Spin Boldak.

Apr. 25: 35 special ops and 82nd GIs engage 20 Taliban at Shkin. 2 U.S. KIA and 4 WIA.

Jun. 3: 500 GIs launch a large-scale operation in the Shahi Kot Mountains.

Jun. 25: 1 SEAL DOW after a firefight near Gardez.

Jun. 26: 1 special ops soldier is KIA and 2 are WIA near Gardez.

Jul. 20: Convoy/patrol of 12 special operations troops is ambushed near Spin Boldak by 100 Taliban troops, and helicopters kill 22 Taliban in the firefight.

Aug. 21: 1 SEAL DOW from a firefight near Orgun.

Aug. 26: Operation Mountain Viper is launched. Fighting centers in the Dai Chupan area of southern Zabul Province.

Aug. 31: 2 U.S. soldiers are KIA in a firefight near Shkin.

Sep. 1: During Operation Mountain Viper, special operations troops and 10th MD soldiers sustain 2 KIA in a 90-minute firefight in Paktika Province.

Sep. 4: Operation Mountain Viper: A 9-day siege in the Dai Chupan District ends with 124 Taliban KIA.

Sep. 29: A Co., 1st Bn., 87th IR, 10th MD, engage a large Al Qaeda force east of Shkin firebase, losing 1 KIA and 3 WIA.

Oct. 25: 2 CIA operatives are KIA near Shkin.

Oct. 30: 1 Green Beret is KIA near Shkin.

Nov. 14: 1 Ranger is KIA by an IED in Asadabad.

Nov. 23: 5 Americans — 4 special ops airmen and 1 soldier — die in a MH-53M helicopter crash near Bagram.

2004

Jan. 29: 8 soldiers (4 from the 10th MD and 4 army reservists) are killed near Ghazni in a weapons cache explosion.

Mar. 18: 2 GIs are KIA in a firefight in Deh Rawood.

May 7: 2nd Marine Light Armored Recon Battalion is ambushed near Tirin Kot, losing 1 KIA — the first marine combat death in Afghanistan.

May 29: 4 U.S. — 3 soldiers (2 from 1st Bn., 3rd SFG, and 1 from the 329th Psychological Ops. Co., Army Reserve) and 1 SEAL — are KIA in Kandahar by an IED.

Jun. 2–3: 1st Bn., 6th Marines, engages Taliban, killing 25 in the Dai Chupan District of Zabul Province.

Jun. 24: 2 marines are KIA by an IED near Deh Rawood.

Aug. 7: 2 GIs are KIA by an IED in Ghazikel.

Sep. 20: 2 Green Berets are KIA in an ambush in Shkin. 1 GI is KIA by small-arms fire in Naka.

Oct. 14: 2 GIs are KIA by a roadside bomb in Miam Do.

Oct. 20: 1 GI is KIA by an IED in Naka.

Nov. 1: 1 GI is KIA by an RPG in Sharan.

Nov. 24: 2 GIs are KIA by an IED in Deh Rawood.

Nov. 27: 3 soldiers from the 3rd Sqdn., 4th Cav, 25th ID, are killed in Bamian in an accidental aircraft crash.

2005

Jan. 1: 1 Green Beret is KIA in a firefight in Shindand.

Jan. 3: 1 Green Beret is KIA by an IED in Asadabad.

Feb. 11: Combat Action Badge created by army for non-infantrymen who engage the enemy.

Mar. 15: 1 GI is KIA by an IED near Shindand.

Mar. 26: 4 GIs from the Indiana National Guard's 76th Inf. Bde. (Sep.) are KIA by an IED in Kabul.

Apr. 6: Deadly Helicopter Crash. 14 soldiers (5 from the 159th Avn. Regt., 3 from the 508th IR, 2 from the 25th ID, 2 National Guardsmen, 1 from Southeast European TF, 1 army reservist) and 1 marine (4th MAW), plus 3 civilians are killed in a CH-47 Chinook helicopter crash due to weather in Ghazni.

Apr. 8: Afghanistan Campaign Medal rules released. Presidential Executive Order 13363 (Nov. 29, 2004) establishes it retroactive to Oct. 24, 2001 (later to Sep. 11).

May 3: Battle of Arghandab Valley. Soldiers of Headquarters and Headquarters Company, 2nd Bn., 503rd Inf., 173rd Abn., battle 30 Taliban, killing 17. 6 U.S. WIA: 3 Silver Stars.

May 21: 1 GI is KIA by an IED on June 16.

Jun. 3: 2 Green Berets are KIA by an IED at FOB Orgun-E. 1 DOW

Jun. 8: 2 GIs are KIA by small-arms fire in Shkin.

Jun. 10: 2nd Bn., 504th Inf., 82nd Abn. Div., and Special Forces fight a 9-hour battle with the Taliban along the Pakistan border. U.S. 1 KIA.

Jun. 28: War's Second Deadliest U.S. Battle: 19 KIA. During Operation Red Wing, 3 SEALs are KIA in a firefight in Kunar Province with 25 to 50 Taliban. 8 SEALs (Team 10 and Delivery Vehicle Team 2) and 8 soldiers from the 160th SOAR are KIA when their CH-47 Chinook helicopter is shot down by an RPG near Asadabad in a rescue attempt. 3 Team 10 SEALs receive the Navy Cross (2 posthumously). The SEAL lieutenant is awarded (posthumously) the Medal of Honor on Oct. 22, 2007.

Jul. 14: Taliban attack a U.S. outpost in Khost Province: 24 enemy die in the fighting.

Jul. 23: Firefight at Qal'eh-ye Gaz. Members of the 1st Bn., 3rd SFG, are attacked by 15 enemy, engaging them in a 7-hour gun battle. U.S.: 1 KIA, 1 WIA.

Jul. 25: 1 GI is KIA by gunfire in Oruzgan.

Jul. 25–26: Firefight at Sayhcow. U.S. Special Forces drive enemy from town, losing 1 KIA.

Aug. 4: 1 marine is KIA by an IED near Gardez.

Aug. 7–9: Battle of Mari Ghar. During a 54-hour series of running firefights, 12 members of an A team of 1st Bn., 3rd SFG, and 16 Afghans engage 200 Taliban, killing 65. "The Spartans" lose 1 KIA.

Aug. 8: 1 Green Beret is KIA by small-arms fire in Deh Afghan.

Aug. 9: 1 GI is KIA by an IED in Ghazni.

Aug. 11: 1 engineer is killed by ordinance at Orgun-E.

Aug. 18: 1 marine is KIA by small-arms fire near Taleban.

Aug. 18: 2 engineers are KIA by an IED in Kandahar.

Aug. 21: 4 soldiers from 2nd Bn., 503rd Inf., 173rd Abn. Bde., are KIA near Baylough by an IED.

Aug. 26: 1 paratrooper is KIA by an IED in Khayr Kot.

Sep. 25: 5 crewmen —1 of the 7th Bn., 159th Avn. Regt., and 4 from the Nevada National Guard's D Co., 113th Avn. Regt — die when their CH-47 Chinook helicopter is shot down near the Dai Chupan District.

Sep. 26: 1 marine is KIA by mortar fire in Camp Blessing. 1 paratrooper is KIA by small-arms fire near Kandahar.

Sep. 30: 1 paratrooper is KIA by an RPG in Shah Wali Kot.

Oct. 7: 1 paratrooper is KIA by an IED in Helmand.

Oct. 9: 1 GI is KIA by a grenade; 3 WIA at Qalat.

Oct. 29: 1 paratrooper is KIA in an ambush at Lwara.

Nov. 15: 1 Green Beret is KIA by an IED at Orgun-E.

Nov. 22: 1 paratrooper is KIA by an IED in Shah Wali Kot.

Dec. 15: 1 paratrooper is KIA in Shah Wali Kot.

Dec. 28: 1 Army reservist is KIA by an IED in Asadabad.

2006

Jan. 25: 1 marine is KIA by an IED.

Feb. 6: 1 GI is KIA in a firefight near Mehtar Lam.

Feb. 13: 4 GIs of the 3rd Bn. and Grp. Support Bn., 7th SFG, and 321st Civil Affairs Bn., are KIA by an IED near Deh Rawood.

Feb. 28: 1 Green Beret of the 3rd Bn., 7th SFG, is KIA by an IED in Tarin Kowt.

Mar. 12: 4 engineers of the Army Reserves' 391st Eng. Bn. are KIA by an IED near Asadabad.

Mar. 25: 1 Green Beret of the 2nd Bn., 20th SFG (Missouri ARNG), is KIA in the Sangin District.

Mar. 28: 1 GI of the 15th Civil Support Team (Vermont ARNG) is killed by "friendly fire" in a firefight in Lashkagar. A U.S.-led retaliation kills 32 Taliban.

Apr. 20: 1 National Guardsman of the 149th Armor Bde. (Kentucky ARNG), 35th ID, is KIA in a firefight in the Deh Rawood District.

May 5: Deadly Helicopter Crash. CH-47 Chinook crashes, killing 10 soldiers — 6 of the 3rd Bn., 10th Avn, Regt., and 4 of the 71st Cav Regt., 10th MD — near Abad.

May 19: 1 Green Beret of the 3rd Bn., 7th SFG, is KIA in a firefight in Oruzgan Province, 6 other Americans are WIA in the convoy ambush.

Jun. 6: 2 National Guardsmen of the 1st Bn., 188th Air Defense Arty (North Dakota ARNG), are KIA by an antitank mine in Khogyani.

Jun. 11: 1 GI of the 303rd Military Intelligence Bn., 504th MI Bde., is KIA in a firefight in Ghanzi.

Jun. 13: 1 GI of C Co., 1st Bn., 1R, 3rd BCT, 10th MD, is KIA in a firefight in Korengal.

Jun. 14: 1 GI of B Co., Special Troops Bn., 10th MD, is KIA in the Pech River Valley by an IED.

Jun. 21: 1 GI of the 3rd Sqdn., 71st Cav Regt., 3rd BCT, 10th MD, is KIA in a firefight in Naray. Another GI, of the 159th Air Ambulance Medical Evac. Co., 421st Med. Bn., accidentally dies attempting to retrieve his body.

Jun. 23–24: Operation Kaika. 18 Green Berets of A Co., 2nd Bn.,7th SFG, and 48 Afghan soldiers fight 200 Taliban for a total of 17 hours in several firefights. 125 Taliban are killed. 2 Americans and 3 Afghan interpreters are killed. 1 Green Beret is awarded the Distinguished Service Cross; four the Silver Star.

Jun. 24: 1 Green Beret of the 2nd Bn., 7th SFG, is KIA in a firefight near Ghecko. 1 National Guardsman of HQ Co., 53rd Inf. Bde. (Florida ARNG), is KIA in an ambush in the Panjaway District.

Jun. 25: 1 GI of the 1st Bn., 32nd IR, 3rd BCT, 10th MD, is KIA at the Korengal Outpost.

Jun. 28: 1 GI of the 2nd Bn., 87th IR, 3rd BCT, 10th MD, is KIA by an IED in Helmand.

Aug. 11: 3 GIs of B Co., 1st Bn., 32nd IR, 3rd BCT, 10th MD, are KIA in a firefight in Nangalam.

Aug. 19: 3 GIs (2 of the 710th Combat Spt. Bn.) of 3rd BCT, 10th MD, are KIA by an IED in Kunar. 1 airman of the 23rd STS is KIA in an ambush in Oruzgan Province.

Sep. 8: 2 Army reservists of the 405th Civil Affairs Bn. are KIA by a bomb in Kabul.

Sep. 11–14: Battle of Sperwan Ghar. Three Operational Detachment Alpha teams of the 3rd SFG (Task Force 31) and 123 men from the 10th MD kill 500 Taliban south of the Arghandab River during Operation Medusa in the Panjwayi Valley. 1 GI is killed.

Oct. 2: 2 GIs of A Co., 1st Bn., 32nd IR, 3rd BCT, 10th MD, are KIA in a firefight in Korengal.

Oct. 5: NATO assumes full command of military.

Oct. 31: 3 GIs — 2 from B Co., 1st Bn., 32nd IR, and 1 from A Co., 3rd Bde., Spec Troops Bn, 3rd BCT, 10th MD — are KIA by an IED in the Wygal Valley.

Nov. 28: 2 MPs of the 230th MP Co., 95th MP Bn., 18th MP Bde., are KIA by an IED in Logar.

Dec. 15: 1 GI of the 1st Bn., 102nd IR (Connecticut ARNG), is KIA by an IED in Mehtar Lam.

2007

Jan. 10: Margah Outpost. U.S. forces kill 130 Taliban in their attempted attack on the outpost near the Pakistan border manned by elements of the 10th MD. Combined air and artillery strikes took them out before they ever got close.

Feb. 18: 8 GIs—5 of the 2nd Bn., 160th SOAR; 2 of the 3rd Bn., 75th Ranger Regt.; and 1 of the 24th STS—die in a helicopter crash due to a mechanical malfunction in Zabol Province.

Apr. 12: 2 paratroopers of the 2nd Bn., 508th IR, 82nd Abn. Div., are KIA by an IED in Miri.

Apr. 22: Firefight at Shudergay. Three members of 2nd Plt., C Co., 1st Bn., 32nd Inf. Regt., 10th MD, earn the Silver Star during a 17-hour engagement in Kunar Province.

Apr. 27, 29: U.S. Special Forces call in airstrikes in the Zerkoh Valley near the Iranian border 30 miles south of Herat, killing 49 Taliban in the first strike and 87 in the second 14-hour battle/strike.

May 30: 5 GIs of the 3rd General Support Avn. Bn., 82nd BCT, 82nd Abn. Div., are KIA in Upper Sangin Valley when their helicopter is shot down. Troops sent to the site are ambushed by the Taliban.

Jun. 17: 3 GIs—2 of the 1st Bde., 1st ID, and one of the 3rd Bn., 156th IR (Louisiana ARNG)—are KIA in Panjway by an IED.

Jul. 5: 2 soldiers of the 2nd Bn., 503rd Inf., 173rd Abn. BCT, are KIA in a firefight in the Watapor Valley.

Jul. 23: 5 paratroopers of the 1st Bn., 503rd IR, 173rd Abn. Bde., are KIA by an IED in the Sarobi District.

Jul. 27: 2 paratroopers of the 1st Sqdn., 91st Cav Regt., 173rd Anb, BCT, are KIA in a firefight near Kamu.

Aug. 8: Taliban attack Firebase Anaconda, losing 20 dead, mostly to airstrikes.

Aug. 9: Raid on Kamdesh. 3rd Bn., 71st IR, 10th MD, repels Hezbe-Isami attack, killing 19 while sustaining only 2 WIA.

Aug. 12: 3 Green Berets of the 2nd Bn., 7th SFG, and 2nd Ops. Grp. are KIA by an IED in Nangarhar Province.

Aug. 27: 3 soldiers—2 of the 55th Bde. (Pennsylvania ARNG), and 1 of the 1st Bde., 1st ID—are KIA in an attack in Jalalabad.

Sep. 25: U.S. airstrikes and artillery repel two large assaults on Musa Qala and Deh Rawood, killing 165 Taliban.

Oct. 25: 2 GIs of 2nd Bn., 503rd IR, 173rd Abn. Bde, are KIA in a firefight in the Korengal Valley.

Oct. 27: U.S.-led Afghan forces kill 80 Taliban in a six-hour battle near Musa Qala.

Nov. 9: Ambush at Aranus. 5 soldiers of 2nd Bn., 503rd Abn. IR, 173rd Abn. BCT, and 1 marine are KIA by direct enemy fire.

Nov. 12: 2 GIs of 1st Sqdn., 91st Cav Regt., 173rd Abn. Bde., are KIA by an IED in Bermel.

Dec. 12: 2 GIs of 1st Bn., 503rd IR, 173rd Abn. Bde., are KIA by an IED at FOB Curry.

2008

Jan.7: 2 GIs are KIA by an IED in Laghar Juy.

Mar. 3: 2 paratroopers of the 1st Bn., 508th IR, 82nd Abn. Div., are KIA in the Sabari District.

Apr. 6: Day of the Silver Star. Green Berets of C Co., 3rd Bn., 3rd SFG, earn 10 Silver Stars in a cliffside firefight in the Shok Valley. Nearly 200 enemy troops are KIA. No U.S. KIA. An air force combat controller is awarded the Air Force Cross.

Apr. 15: 2 marines of Combat Logistics Bn. 24, 24th MEU, are KIA by an IED outside Kandahar.

May 1: 32,500 U.S. troops are deployed to Afghanistan.

May 7: 2 GIs of 4th BCT, 101st Abn., are KIA by an IED in the Sabari District.

May 31: 2 GIs of 173rd Special Troops Bn., 173rd Abn. BCT, are KIA by an IED in Jalalabad.

Jun. 3: 2 GIs—1 of 451st Civil Affairs Bn. And 1 of 228th Bde. Support Bn.— are KIA by an IED in Zormat.

Jun. 14: 4 marines of 2nd Bn., 7th Marines, 1st Marine Div., are KIA by an IED in Farah Province.

Jun. 18: 2 sailors of Provincial Recon Team Sharana are KIA in a rocket attack in northern Paktika Province.

Jun. 19: 2 marines of 2nd Bn., 7th Marines, 1st Marine Div., are KIA in a rocket attack in Farah Province.

Jun. 21: 4 GIs—3 of 2nd Sqdn., 101st Cav, and 1 of MTT, 1st Bde., 1st ID— are KIA by small-arms fire in Kandahar City.

Jun. 26: 3 GIs—2 of 2nd Sqdn., 101st Cav Regt., and of 425th IR (Co F, Michigan ARNG)—are KIA in a firefight near FOB Shank.

Jun. 29: 3 SF of 1st Bn., 7th SFG, are killed when their vehicle rolls into a canal in Khosrow-E Sofla.

Jul. 10: 2 GIs of 1st Bn., 294th IR (Guam ARNG), are KIA by an IED in Babo Kheyl.

Jul. 13: Assault on Wanat — Deadliest Single Firefight of U.S. War. 9 GIs of 2nd PLT., C Co., 2nd Bn., 503rd IR (Abn.), 173rd Abn. BCT, are KIA in an attack at Vehicle Patrol Base Kalder and OP Top Side near Wanat. 11 Silver Stars are awarded.

Aug. 1: 4 GIs of 3rd BCT, 1st ID-3 of Special Troops Bn. and 1 of 6th Sqdn., 4th Cav Regt—are KIA by an IED in Chowkay Valley.

Aug. 8: Battle at Shewan. In an all-day firefight, Force Recon Plt, attached to G Co., 2nd Bn., 7th Marine Regt., while outnumbered 8:1, kills some 50 Taliban. One marine receives the Navy Cross.

Aug. 14: 2 marines of 2nd Bn., 7th Marine Regt., 1st Marine Div., are KIA in Helmand.

Aug. 15: 2 GIs of 1st Bn., 506th IR, 4th BCT, 101st Abn. Div., are KIA by an IED in Wardak Province.

Sep. 17: 4 GIs from three units are KIA by an IED in Gerdia Seria.

Sep. 20: 2 GIs of 1st Bn, 26th IR, 3rd BCT, 1st ID, are KIA by an IED in the Korengal Valley.

Sep. 29: 3 Green Berets of 1st Bn., 7th SFG, are KIA by an IED in Yakehal.

Oct. 14: 3 GIs of 1st Bn., 26th IR, 3rd BCT, 1st ID, are KIA by an IED in Qazi Bandch.

Oct. 22: 2 marines of 7th Marine Regt., 1st Marine Div., are KIA in Helmand Province.

Oct. 27: 2 GIs —1 Green Beret and 1 Illinois National Guardsman — are KIA by a suicide bomber in Baghan.

2009

Jan. 8: 2 GIs of 2nd Bn., 2nd Inf., 1st ID, are KIA by an IED in Maywand.

Jan. 9: 3 GIs of 1st Bn., 178th IR, 33rd IBCT (Ill. ARNG), are KIA by an IED in Jaldak.

Feb. 8: 2 GIs of the Illinois National Guard are KIA by an IED in Kabul.

Feb. 10: 2 GIs of the 2nd Bn., 506th Inf., 101st Abn. Div., are KIA by an IED at Salerno.

Feb. 20: 2 GIs of 3rd SFG and 720th STG are KIA by an IED in Khordi.

Feb. 24: 4 GIs are KIA by an IED in Kandahar.

Mar. 21: 2 marines of 3rd Bn., 8th Marines Regt., 2nd Marine Div., are KIA in Helmand Province.

May 1: 3 GIs of the 1st and 3rd BCTs, 1st ID, are KIA in a firefight in Nishagam.

Jun. 1: 3 GIs of 2nd Bn., 87th IR, 10th MD, are KIA by an IED in Nerkh.

Jun. 4: 3 GIs of 108th RSTA Sqdn., 48th BCT (Georgia ARNG), are KIA by an IED and small-arms fire near Kapisa.

Jul. 6: 4 GIs of the 48th BCT (Georgia ARNG) are KIA by an IED in Konduz.

Jul. 20: 4 GIs of 4th Bn., 25th FA, 10th MD, are KIA by an IED in Wardak Province.

Aug. 1: 3 GIs of the 1st Bn., 12th IR, 4th ID, are KIA by IEDs and RPGs in Mushan village.

Aug. 2: 3 Green Berets of 2nd Bn., 20th SFG (Mississippi ARNG), are KIA by an IED in Qole Gerdsar.

Aug. 6: 4 marines of 2nd Bn., 3rd Regt., 3rd Marine Div., are KIA by an IED in Farah Province.

Aug. 25: 4 GIs of 1st Bn., 17th IR, 2nd ID, are KIA by an IED in southern Afghanistan.

Sep. 8: Battle of Ganijgal. 5 U.S. — 3 marines and 1 Navy corpsman of Marine Embedded Training Team 2-8, and 1 soldier DOW — are KIA in a 6-hour firefight in Kunar Province. 2 marines receive Navy Crosses. 1 marine receives Medal of Honor for carrying 12 wounded to safety, covering the withdrawal of 24 and retrieving the bodies of 4 Americans. 1 soldier is recommended for the Medal of Honor.

Sep. 16: 3 Green Berets of 3rd Bn., 7th SFG, are KIA by an IED in Helmand Province.

Sep. 24: 3 GIs of 4th Bn., 23rd IR, 2nd ID, are KIA by an IED in Omar Zai.

Oct. 3: Second Deadliest U.S. Firefight. 8 GIs of 3rd Sqdn., 61st Cav. Regt., 4th BCT, 4th ID, are KIA in the assault on Combat Outpost Keating in Kamdesh.

Oct. 15: 4 GIs of 569th Mobility Augmentation Co., 4th Eng. Bn., are KIA by an IED in Kandahar Province.

Oct. 26: 11 soldiers and marines, as well as 3 DEA agents, die in two separate helicopter incidents, 5 members of the 3rd Bn., 160th SOAR along with 2 soldiers from the 3rd Bn, 7th SFG die in a MH-47 helicopter crash at Darreh-ye Bum. 4 marines of MAG-39, 3rd MAW, die in midair collision over Helmand Province.

Oct. 27: War's Single Deadliest IED Attack on GIs. 7 GIs of C Co., 1st Bn., 17th IR, 5th Styker Bde., 2nd ID, are KIA by an IED in the Arghandab Valley.

2010

Jan. 3: 3 soldiers of 1st Bn., 12th IR, 4th BCT, 4th ID, are KIA by IEDs and small-arms fire in Ashoque.

Jan. 11: 3 marines of 3rd Recon Bn., 3rd Marine Div., are KIA in Helmand Province.

Feb. 3: 3 soldiers — 2 of 95th Civil Affairs Bde. (Abn.), and 1 of 4th Psy Ops. Grp. (Abn.) — are KIA by an IED in Pakistan.

Feb. 13: 3 soldiers of the 1st Bn., 12th IR, 4th BCT, 4th ID, are KIA by an IED in the Zhari District.

May 18: 5 soldiers from 3 different units are KIA by a roadside bomb in Kabul.

Jun. 6: 3 marines of 3rd Bn., 1st Marine Regt., 1st Marine Div., are KIA in Helmand Province.

Jun. 7: 4 soldiers of 2nd Bn., 327th IR, 1st BCT, 101st Abn. Div., are KIA by a roadside bomb in Konar. Another is KIA by an RPG/small-arms fire.

Jun. 9: 4 Air force pararescuemen — 2 of 48th, 1 of 58th, and 1 of the 66th Rescue Squadrons — are KIA when their helicopter is shot down by an RPG near FOB Jackson in Sangin District.

Jul. 6: 3 soldiers of 1st Bn., 4th IR, are KIA by a roadside bombing in Qalat.

Jul. 13: 3 soldiers of the 4th BCT, 82nd Abn Div. — 2 of 1st Bn., 508th Parachute IR, and 1 of the 782nd Bde., Support Bn — are KIA in a firefight in Kandahar City.

Jul. 14: 4 soldiers of the 27th Eng. Bn., 20th Eng. Bde (Combat), are KIA by a roadside bomb in Zabul Province.

Jul. 24: 5 soldiers of the 5th Bn., 3rd FA Regt., 17th Fires Bde., are KIA by a roadside bomb in Qalat.

Aug. 30: 5 soldiers — 4 of 1st BCT, 4th ID, and 1 of 71st EOD Grp — are KIA by an IED in the Aeghandab River Valley.

Aug. 31: 4 soldiers of 173rd Bde, Support Bn., Abn, BCT, are KIA by a roadside bombing in Logar Province.

Sep. 21: 9 Americans—4 Navy SEALs and 5 101st Abn Div. soldiers—are killed in an accidental helicopter crash in Dalat.

Oct. 13: 4 marines of the 3rd Bn., 5th Marine Regt., 1st Marine Div., are KIA in Helmand Province.

Oct. 14: 3 soldiers of the 7th Sqdn., 10th Cav. Regt., 1st BCT, 4th ID, are KIA by an IED between Moqur and Darreh-Ye-Bum.

Nov. 13: 3 soldiers of the 2nd Bn., 502 IR, 2nd BCT, 101st Abn. Div. are KIA by a suicide bomber in Kandahar Province.

Nov. 14: 5 soldiers of A Co., 1st Bn., 327th IR, 1st BCT, 101st Abn Div., are KIA by small-arms fire during a six-hour firefight in the Watapur Valley.

Nov. 29: 6 soldiers of 1st Sqdn., 61st Cav Regt., 4th BCT, 101 Abn. Div., are murdered by an Afghan border policeman near Jalalabad.

Dec. 12: 6 soldiers of B Co., 2nd Bn., 502nd IR, 2nd BCT, 101 Abn. Div., are KIA by a minibus loaded with 1,000 pounds of explosives in Zahari.

2011

Jan. 12: 3 soldiers of the 7th Eng. Bn., 101st Sustainment Bde., 10th Mountain Div., are KIA by an IED in Ghazini Province.

Mar. 29: 6 soldiers of C Co., 2nd Bn., 327th IR, 1st BCT, 101st Abn. Div. (Air Assault), are KIA by small-arms fire during a five-hour firefight in Baraqolo Kaway and Sarowbay.

Apr. 16: 5 soldiers—4 of 101st Special Troops Bn., 101st Sustainment Bde.,101 Abn. Div., and 1 from the 17th Combat Sustainment Support Bn., 3rd Maneuver Enhancement Bde.—are KIA when an Afghan National Army soldier attacks them with grenades at FOB Gamberi.

Apr. 27: 8 airmen from different units are KIA by gunfire from an Afghan air officer during a meeting in an operations room at Kabul International Airport.

May 2: Eradication of Osama bin Laden. SEAL Team 6 and the 160th Special Operations Aviation Regiment kill the Al Qaeda leader in a daring raid on his compound in Abbottabad, Pakistan, earning the Presidential Unit Citation.

May 16: 4 soldiers—1 of Fires Sqdn., 2nd Stryker Cav Regt., and 3 of Bde. Troops Bn., 1st Stryker BCT, 25th ID—are KIA by an IED in Zabul Province.

May 23: 4 soldiers of 2nd Bn., 27th IR, 3rd BCT, 25th ID, are KIA by an IED in Kunar Province.

May 26: 8 Americans—6 soldiers of 4th Bn., 101st Avn. Regt., 159th CAB, and 2 airmen (1 of the 52nd Civil Eng. Sqdn., and one of the 775th Civil Eng. Sqdn.)—are KIA by roadside bombs in the Shorabak District.

May 29: 3 soldiers of the 3rd Special Forces Grp. are KIA by an IED in Wardak Province.

Jun. 4: 4 soldiers of the 793rd MP Bn. are KIA by an IED in Laghman Province.

Jun. 18: 4 soldiers of the 4th Bn.,70th Armor Regt., 170th IBCT, die in a vehicle rollover in Uruzgan Province.

Jul. 5: 3 soldiers of the 21st Theater Sustainment Command are KIA by an IED in Paktia Province.

Jul. 18: 3 soldiers of the 131st Transportation Company (Pennsylvania ANG) are KIA by an IED in Ghazini Province.

Aug. 6: Deadliest Single Hostile U.S. Loss in War. 30 Americans are KIA when their helicopter is shot down by an RPG over the Tangi Valley.

Aug. 11: 5 soldiers of the 1st Bn., 32nd Inf. Regt., 10th MD, are KIA by an IED in Kandahar.

Sep. 9: 3 Guardsmen of the 1st Bn., 279th IR, 45th BCT (Oklahoma ARNG), are KIA in a firefight in Paktika.

Sep. 28: 3 engineers of the 5th Eng. Bn. are KIA by an IED in Ghazni Province.

Oct. 7: 4 U.S. FOBs near the Pakistan border are attacked simultaneously by the Taliban.

Oct. 13: 1 marine 1st Bn. 6th Marine Reg., 2nd Marine Div. and 1 soldier 2nd Bn. 27th Infantry Reg. 3rd Brigade, 25th Infantry div. KIA in IED attacks in Helmand and Kandahar. 2 soldiers 3rd Bn. 82 Combat Aviation Brigade Airborne and 3rd Squadron 71st Cavalry Reg. 3rd Brigade Combat Team, 10th Mountain Div. were KIA by small arms fire Kunar.

Oct. 14: I soldier 1st Bn, 26th Inf. Reg., 3rd Brigade Combat team, 1st Infantry Div. is KIA by small arms fire in Khowst.

Oct. 19: 1 National Guardsman from the New Jersey national Guard is KIA by an IED attack in Paktika.

Oct. 22: 4 soldiers 2 from 230th Brigade Support Bn. 30th Heavy Brigade combat team and 2 from 2nd Bn. 75th Ranger Regiment are KIA by IED attacks in Kandahar.

Oct. 23: 1 marine 3rd Bn. 7th Marine Reg., 1st Marine Expeditionary Force is KIA by an IED attack in Helmand.

Oct. 24: 1 marine 3rd Bn.7th Marine Reg., 1st Marine Expeditionary Force is KIA by small arms fire in Helmand.

Oct. 26: 1 marine 3rd Bn. 7th Marine Reg., 1st Marine Expeditionary Force is KIA by small arms fire in Helmand.

Oct. 28: 1 marine 3rd Bn. 7th Marine Reg., 1st Marine Expeditionary Force is KIA by an IED in Helmand.

Oct. 29: 4 soldiers 1 from 756th Trans. Co. 224th Sustainment Reg., California National Guard, 1 from the 101st Finance Co., 101st Spe. Troops Bn., 101st Sustainment Reg. 101st. Airborne, 1 from Medical Co. A, and 1 from Uniformed Services University of Health Science are KIA by suicide car bomb in Kabul.

Oct. 30: 1 National Guardsman 3rd Brigade Spe. Troops Bn., 3rd Brigade Combat Team, 1oth Mountain Div. is KIA by an RPG attack in Kandahar.

Nov. 1: 2 soldiers from the 700th Brg. Support Bn.45th Inf. Reg. Combat Teat are KIA by an IED attack in Paktia.

Nov. 3: 1 soldier 2nd Bn. 34th Armor Reg. 1st Brig. Combat Team, 1st Inf. Div. is KIA by an IED in Kandahar.

Nov. 4: 1 marine 3rd Combat Engineer Bn. 1st Mar. Div. is KIA by small arms fire in Helmand.

Nov. 9: 1 soldier 2nd Bn. 34th Armor Reg. 1st Heavy Brig. Combat Team is KIA by small arms fire in Kandahar.

Nov. 11: 1 soldier 3rd Sqd., 71st Cavalry Reg., 3rd Brig Combat Team 10th Mountain Division is KIA by an IED in Kandahar.

Nov. 13: 2 soldiers 1st Bn. 5th Inf. Reg. 1st Stryker Brg. 25th Inf. Div. are KIA by an IED in Kandahar.

Nov. 16: 2 soldiers 1st Bn. 5th Inf. Reg., 1st Stryker Brig. Combat Team 25th Inf. Div., are KIA by an

Nov. 18: 1 marine 3rd Bn. 7th Marine Reg. 1st Marine. Expend. Force is KIA by small arms fire in Helmand and 1 soldier 8th Engineer Bn. 36th Eng. Brig., is KIA by an IED in Kandahar.

Nov. 21: 1 marine 3rd Bn. 7th Marine Reg., 1st Marine Div. in Helmand is KIA from an IED and 1 soldier from 3rd Sqd. 71st Cal. Reg., 3rd Brig Combat team, 10th Mountain Div is KIA from small arms fire and 1 soldier from 2nd Bn. 34th Army Reg., 1st Brigade Combat Team, 1st Inf. Div by an IED both in Kandahar.

Nov. 26: 1 marine 3rd Recon Bn., 3rd Marine Div. is KIA by small arms fire in Helmand.

Nov. 30: 1 marine 2nd Bn. 11th Mar Reg. 1st Marine Div. is KIA by an IED in Helmand.

Dec. 3: 3 soldiers from 2nd Bn. 5th Inf. Reg., 3rd Brig Combat Team are KIA By an IED attack in Wardak.

Dec. 10: 1 marine from 1st Bn. 6th Marine Reg., 2nd Marine Div., II Marine Exped. Force is KIA by small arms fire in Helmand.

Dec. 11: 1 soldier from 3rd Brg. Spe. Troops Bn., 3rd Brig, Combat Team, 25th Infantry Div is KIA by IED in Kunar.

Dec. 13: 1 soldier 3rd Brg. Combat team, 25th Inf. Div. is KIA by IED in Kunar.

Dec. 14: 1 marine 4th Air Naval Gunfire Liaison Co., Marine Force Reserves is KIA by small arms fire in Helmand.

Dec. 21: 1 soldier 201st Brg. Support Bn., 3rd Brg. Combat Team, 1st Inf. Div. is KIA by small arms fire in Khowst.

Dec. 25: 1 soldier 2nd Bn. 27th Inf. Reg., 3rd Brg. Combat Team, 25th Inf. Div. is KIA by small arms fire in Kunar.

Dec. 27: 3 MP's 720th MP Bn., 84th MP Reg. are KIA by an IED in Paktika.

2012

Jan. 2: 1 Petty Officer 1st Class Marine Special Ops Co., Bravo Explosive Ord., Disposal Unit 3 is KIA by an IED in Helmand.

Jan. 5: 1 soldier 90th Civil Engineer Squad and 1 airman 2nd Civil Engineer Squad is KIA by an IED in Helmand.

Jan. 6: 1 Airman 21st Civil Engineer Squad is KIA by small arms fire in Helmand. 4 soldiers from the 81st Troop Command Indiana National Guard are KIA by small arms fire in Kandahar.

Jan. 8: 1 soldier 1st Bn. 24th Inf. Reg. 1st Stryker Brig. Combat Team 25th Inf. Div. is KIA by small arms fire in Zabul.

Jan. 15: 1 marine 2nd Bn. 4th Mar. Reg. 1st Marine Div., 1 Marine Expeditionary Force is KIA by small arms fire in Helmand and 1 seaman 3rd Bn. 1st. Special Forces Group is KIA by small arms fire in Balkh.

Jan. 18: 1 marine 1st Bn. 6th Mar Reg. 2nd Mar Div. II Marine Expeditionary Force is KIA by small arms fire in Helmand.

Jan. 20: 6 marines Marine Heavy Helicopter Squad 363, Mar. Air Grp., 24 1st Marine Air Wing III Expeditionary Force are killed in Helicopter crash.

Jan. 21: 1 marine 3rd Combat Eng. Bn. 1st Mar. Div. 1 Marine Expeditionary Force is KIA by small arms fire in Helmand.

Jan. 25: 1 soldier 5th Bn. 25th Inf. Reg. 3rd Stryker Reg. Combat team 2nd Div. is KIA by an IED in Kandahar.

Jan. 31: 1 marine 2nd Bn. 4th Mar. Reg. 1st Mar. Div. 1st Marine Expeditionary Force is KIA by small arms fire in Helmand.

Feb. 1: 1 marine 2nd Bn., 9th Marine Reg., 2nd Marine Div., 11 Marine Expeditionary Force is KIA by small arms fire in Helmand.

Feb. 10: 1 marine 2nd Bn., 6th Marine Reg., 2nd Marine Div., 11 Marine Expeditionary Force is KIA by small arms fire in Helmand.

Feb. 17: 1 First class Petty Officer USS *Carl Vinson* (CVN 70) is KIA by small arms fire in Dubal.

Feb. 18: 3 Air force officers and 1 senior airman 319th Special Ops. Squadron are KIA by small arms fire at Camp Lemon.

Feb. 23: 2 soldiers from the 385th MP Bn., 16th MP Brigade, XVIII Airborne Corp are KIA at by small arms fire at Nangarhar.

Feb. 25: 1 Air force officer 866th Air Expeditionary Squadron and 1 Army National Guard officer 1st Bn., 29th Inf. Div. Security Partnering Team of Maryland Army National Guard is KIA by small arms fire at Kabul.

Mar. 1: 2 soldiers 2nd Bn., 508 Parachute Inf. Reg. 4th Brigade Combat Team, 82nd Airborne Division are KIA by small arms fire at Kandahar and 1 marine 2nd Bn. 11th Marine Reg. 1st MarDiv., 1st Mar. Expeditionary Force is KIA by small arms fire in Southern Afghanistan.

Mar. 5: 1 soldier 2nd Bn., 5th Inf. Reg., 3rd Brigade Combat Team 1st Armored Division is KIA by an IED in Wardak.

Mar. 15: 1 Army officer 2nd Bn., 35th Inf. Reg., 3rd Brigade Combat Team 25th Inf. Div., is KIA in Kunar.

Mar. 21: 1 soldier 4th Sqd., 4th Cavalry Reg., 1st Heavy Brigade Combat Team 1st Inf. Div., is KIA by small arms fire at Kandahar.

Mar. 24: 1 soldier 2nd Bn., 8th Inf. Reg., 2nd Brigade Combat Team, 4th Inf. Div. is KIA by an IED in Kandahar.

Mar. 26: 1 soldier 2nd Bn., 23rd Inf. Reg., 172 Inf. Brigade is KIA by small arms fire in Paktika.

Mar. 27: 1 marine 8th Eng. Support Bn., 2nd Marine Logistics Grp, 11 Marine Expend., Force is KIA in Helmand.

Mar. 29: 1 soldier 2nd Bn., 508 Parachute Inf. Reg., 4th Brigade Combat Team, 82nd Airborne is KIA by small arms fire in Kandahar and 1 Marine HO Bn., 3rd Marine Div., III Marine Expend. Force is KIA by an IED in Helmand.

Mar. 30: 1 marine 1st Light Armored Recon. Bn., 1st Marine Div., 1 Marine Expend. Force is KIA by an IED in Helmand.

Apr. 3: 1 marine 1st Bn. 6th Marine Regiment, 2nd Marine Div., II Expeditionary Force is KIA by small arms fire in Helmand. 1 Soldier 2nd Bn., 12 Inf. Reg., 4th Brigade combat Team, 9th Inf. Div. is KIA by an IED in Kunar. 1 soldier 2nd Bn., 508th Parachute Inf. Reg., 4th Brigade Combat Team 82nd Airborne Div. is KIA by an IED in Kandahar. 1 Soldier 1st Bn. (Airborne) 501st Inf. Reg. 4th Brigade Combat Team, 25th Inf. Div. is KIA by an IED in Khost.

Apr. 4: 3 soldiers 1st Bn. 148th Inf. Reg. 37th Inf. Brigade Combat Team Ohio National Guard are KIA by a suicide bomber in Faryeb.

Apr. 6: 1 soldier 1st Brigade Special Troops Bn, 1st Brigade Combat Team 82nd Airborne is KIA by small arms fire in Ghazni.

Apr. 11: 1 marine 1st Light Armored Recon. Bn., 1st Marine Div., 1 Marine Expeditionary Force is KIA by an IED in Helmand and 1 soldier 1st Bn. 23rd Inf. Reg. 3rd Stryker Brigade Combat Team 2nd Inf. Div. is KIA by small arms fire in Kandahar.

Apr. 12: 1 marine 2nd Bn. 9th Marine Reg., 2nd Marine Div. 2 marine Expeditionary Force is KIA by IED in Helmand.

Apr. 14: 1 soldier 1st Bn. 75th Ranger Reg. is KIA by small arms fire in Logar.

Apr. 15: 1 soldier 2nd Bn. 12th Inf. Reg. 4th Brigade Combat Team 6th Inf. Div. is KIA by IED in Kunar and 1 marine 2nd Bn. 9th Marine Reg., 2nd Marine Div. 2 Marine Expeditionary Force is KIA by small arms fire in Helmand.

Apr. 19: 4 soldiers 2nd Bn. 25th Aviation Reg., 25th Combat Aviation Brg., 25th Inf. Div are KIA in a Helicopter crash in Helmand.

Apr. 22: 2 soldiers 2nd Bn, 504th Inf., 1st Brigade Combat Team, 82nd Airborne are KIA by IED attack in Paktia and 1 marine 7th Eng. Support Bn., 1st Marine Logistics Grp., 1 Marine Expeditionary force is KIA by an IED in Helmand.

Apr. 25: 1 soldier 1st Bn. 508th Parachute Inf. Reg., 4th Brigade Combat Team, 82nd Airborne and 1 marine 2nd Bn., 7th Special Forces Group are KIA by IED and small arms fire in Kandahar.

Apr. 26: 2 soldiers 4th Bn. 3rd Special Forces Group and 95th Military Police Bn., 18th Police Brigade and 1 sailor Navy explosive Ordnance Disposal unit are KIA by an IED in Ghazni. 1 soldier 1st Sqd., 13th Cavalry Reg. 3rd Brg. Combat Team,1st Armored Div is KIA by small arms fire in Laghman.

Apr. 28: 1 soldier 1st Bn., 504th Parachute Inf. Reg. 1st Brig. Combat Team, 82nd Airborne is KIA by an IED in Kandahar and 1 marine 1 Marine Expeditionary Force HQ Group, 1 Marine Expeditionary HQ is KIA by an IED in Helmand.

Apr. 29: 1 soldier 5th Bn., 20th Inf. Reg. 3rd Stryker Brg. Combat Team, 2nd Inf. Div. is KIA by small arms fire in Kandahar.

Apr. 30: 1 Army officer A Company, Troop Command is KIA by small arms fire in Helmand.

May 2: 2 soldiers 7th Eng. Bn., 10th Sustainment Brg., 10 Mountain Div. is KIA by IED attack in Logar.

May 6: 1 marine 7th Eng. Support Bn., 1st Marine Logistics Group, 1 Marine Expeditionary Force is KIA by small arms fire in Helmand and 1 soldier 3rd Bn. (Airborne) 509th Inf. Reg., 4th Brigade Combat Team, 25th Inf. Div is KIA by an IED in Paktia.

May 7: 3 soldiers 3rd Squadron, 73rd Cavalry Reg, 1st Brigade Combat Team, 82nd Airborne is KIA by an IED attack in Ghazni.

May 11: 1 marine 5th Marine Reg., 1st Mar Div., 1 Marine Expeditionary Force is KIA by small arms fire in Helmand and 1 soldier 1st Bn., 12th Inf. Reg. 4th Brigade Combat Team, 4th Inf. Div is KIA by small arms fire in Parwan.

May 12: 1 soldier 741st Ordnance Co., 84th Ordnance Bn, 71st Ordnance Grp. is KIA by an IED in Kandahar.

May 13: 2 soldiers 425th Brg., Special Trp Bn., 4th Brigade Combat Team (Airborne), 25th Inf. Div are KIA by an IED attack in Khost.

May 18: 2 soldiers 1st Bn. (Air Assault) 377th Field Artillery Reg., 17th Fires Brg. are KIA by indirect fire in Kunar.

May 19: 1 soldier 1st Bn. 508 parachute Inf. Reg. 4th Brigade Combat Team, 82nd Airborne is KIA by an IED in Kandahar.

May 20: 2 Army officers 168th Brigade Support Bn., 214th Fires Brg. are KIA by IED attack in Oruzgan.

May 21: 1 soldier 81st Troop Command is KIA by an RPG attack in Nangahar.

May 23: 1 Army officer 5th Bn. 20th Inf. Reg., 3rd Stryker Brg. Combat Team, 2nd Inf. Div is KIA by an IED in Kandahar.

May 24: 1 marine 1st Law Enf. Bn., 1st Marine HQ Group, 1 Marine Expeditionary Force is KIA by small arms fire in Helmand and 1 soldier 4th Bn., 23rd Inf. Reg., 2nd Stryker Reg., Combat Team, 2nd Inf. Div. is KIA by IED in Kandahar.

May 25: 1 soldier 1st Bn., 41st Inf. Reg., 3rd Brigade combat Team, 1st Armored Div. is KIA by indirect fire in Logar.

May 26: 1 sailor 1st Bn., 8th Marine Reg., Regimental Combat Team 6, 1st Mar Div, I Marine Expeditionary Force is KIA by an IED in Helmand and 1 soldier 4th Bn., 23rd Inf. Reg., 2nd Stryker Brg. Combat Team, 2nd Inf. Div. is KIA by small arms fire in Kandahar.

May 27: 1 soldier 3rd Sqd. 61st Cavalry Reg., 4th Brg. Combat Team, 4th Inf. Div. is KIA by an IED in Kandahar. 1 marine 1st Bn. 8th Marine Reg., 2nd Mar. Div., 2 Marine Expeditionary Force is KIA by small arms fire in Helmand. 2 soldiers 125th Brg. Support Bn., 3rd Brigade Combat Team, 1st Armored Div. are KIA by small arms fire in Wardak.

May 28: 2 Army officers 12th Combat Aviation Brg. are KIA in Helicopter crash in Kabul and 1 Marine 5th Air Naval Gunfire Liaison Company, III Marine Expeditionary Force is KIA in Helmand.

May 30: 1 soldier 4th Sqd., 73rd Cal. Reg. 4th Brg. Combat Team, 82nd Airborne is KIA by an IED in Kandahar. 1 sailor Naval Base Kitsap Security Detach. is KIA by small arms fire in Kandahar and 1 marine 2nd Bn. 5th Marine Reg., 1st Marine Div. I Marine expeditionary Force is KIA by small arms fire in Helmand.

May 31: 1 marine unit not reported is KIA in South Afghanistan by small arms fire and 1 soldier 14th Eng. Bn., 555th Eng. Brigade is KIA by an IED in Kandahar.

Jun. 2: 1 soldier 4th Bn. 23rd Inf. Reg., 2nd Stryker Brg. Combat Team, 2nd inf. Div. is KIA by small arms fire in Kandahar.

Jun. 4: 1 soldier 1st Sqd. 4oth Cavalry Reg. 4th Airborne Combat Team, 25th Inf. Div. is KIA by Small arms fire in Khowst.

Jun. 6: 2 Army officers 1st Sqd. 17th Cavalry Reg. 82nd Combat Aviation Brigade, 82nd Airborne are KIA in Helicopter crash in Ghazni.

Jun. 7: 1 soldier 4th Sqd., 73rd Cavalry Reg., 4th Brigade Combat Team, 82nd Airborne Div. is KIA by an IED in Kandahar.

Jun. 8: 1 marine 2nd Bn., 5th Marine Reg., 1st Mar. Div., I Marine Expeditionary Force is KIA by small arms fire in Helmand.

Jun. 9: 1 soldier 1st Bn., (Airborne) 501st Inf. Reg. 4th Brigade Combat Team (Airborne), 25th Inf. Div. is KIA by an IED in Khowst.

Jun. 10: 1 soldier 1st Bn. 64th Armor Reg., 2nd Brigade Combat Team, 3rd Inf. Div. is KIA by small arms fire in Kandahar.

Jun. 12: 2 soldiers 562nd Engineer Co., 2nd Stryker Brg. Combat Team, 2nd Inf. Div. and 18th Engineer Co., 1st Bn. 37th Field Art. Reg. 3rd Stryker Brg. Combat Team 2nd Inf. Div. are KIA by an IED attack in Kandahar.

Jun. 14 1 soldier 8th Engineer Co. 1st Bn., 37th Field Art. 3rd Stryker Brig. Combat Team, 2nd Inf. Div. is KIA by an IED in Kandahar.

Jun. 15: 1 soldier 1st Bn. 504th Parachute Inf. Reg., 1st Brg. Combat Team, 82nd is KIA by small arms fire in Kunar.

Jun. 18: 1 soldier 1st Bn., 508 Parachute Inf. Reg., 4th Brg. Combat Team, 82nd Airborne is KIA by small arms fire in Kandahar.

Jun. 19: 1 soldier 4th Bn. 23rd Inf. Reg. 2nd Stryker Brg. Combat Team, 2nd Inf. Div. is KIA by small arms fire in Kandahar.

Jun. 20: 3 MPs 133rd MP Company, 51st MP Bn., are KIA by small arms fire and IED attack in Khost.

Jun. 22: 2 marines 1st bn. 8th Marine Reg. 2nd Mar. Div. II Marine Expeditionary Force and 1st Combat Eng. Bn. 1st Marine Div., I Marine Expeditionary Force are KIA by small arms fire in Helmand.

Jun. 23: 2 marines 1st Bn. 8th Marines, 1st Marine Div., I Marine Expeditionary Force and 1st Bn. 7th Marines 2nd Marine Div. II Marine Expeditionary Force are KIA small arms and IED attack in Helmand.

Jun. 27: 3 soldiers 4th Bn. 319th Airborne Field Art. Reg. 173rd Airborne and 4th Bn. 1st Field Art. Reg. 3rd Reg. Combat Team 1st Armored Div. are KIA by an IED attack in Wardak.

Jul. 3: 1 soldier 1st Bn. Inf. Reg. 4th Inf. Brig Combat Team, 1st Inf. Div. is KIA by small arms fire in Gayan Alwara Mandi.

Jul. 4: 1 soldier 502nd Military Intelligence Bn., 201st Battlefield Sur. Brg. is KIA by small arms fire in Kandahar.

Jul. 7: 1 soldier 1st Bn. 23rd Inf. Reg. 3rd Stryker Brigade Combat Team, 2nd Inf. Div. is KIA by a IED in Kandahar.

Jul. 8: 1 soldier 2nd Bn. 326th Airborne Field Art. Reg., 4th Brg. Combat Team, 82nd Airborne small arms fire in Kandahar and 6 MPs 978th M.P. Co., 93rd Military Police Bn. Are KIA by a IED attack in Wardak.

Jul. 11: 1 soldier 5th Bn. 20th Inf. Reg. 3rd Stryker Brg. Combat Team, 2nd Inf. Div is KIA by small arms fire in Kandahar.

Jul. 13: 1 soldier 5th Bn. 20th Inf. Reg. 3rd Stryker Brg. Combat Team, 2nd Inf. Div. is KIA by an IED in Zabul.

Jul. 14: 1 soldier 1st Bn. 501st Inf. Reg., 4th Airborne Brg. Combat Team, 25th Inf. Div. is KIA by small arms fire in Khowst.

Jul. 16: 2 soldiers 81st Troop Command are KIA by an RPG attack in Kandahar.

Jul. 17: 1 soldier 1st Bn. 508 Parachute Inf. Reg., 4th Brg. Combat Team, 82nd Airborne is KIA indirect fire in Kandahar.

Jul. 18: 2 soldiers 110th Tran. Co. 548th Combat Sus. Support Bn. 10th Sus. Brg. are KIA by a IED attack in Ghanzi.

Jul. 19: 1 marine and 2 soldiers 54th Eng. Bn., 18th Eng. Brg. 21st. Theater Sus. Command, the 2nd Law Enforcement Bn, II Marine Expeditionary Force, and 20th Eng. Bn., 36th Eng. Brigade are KIA by a IED attack in Kandahar, Helmand, and Ghanzi.

Jul. 21: 1 soldier 4th Bn, 3rd Special Forces Grp is KIA by small arms fire in Ghanzi and 1 soldier Navy Region Southwest Security Detachment is KIA while defusing a IED in Kandahar.

Jul. 22: 1 airman and 1 soldier 1st Bn. 503rd Inf. Reg. 173rd Airborne are KIA by small arms fire and a IED in Logar. 2 soldiers 508th Special Troop Bn, 4th Brg. Combat Team, 82nd Airborne are KIA by a IED attack in Kandahar.

Jul. 23: 1 soldier 3rd Bn., 82nd Combat Aviation Brg., 82nd Airborne is KIA by small arms fire in Logar.

Jul. 24: 1 marine 2nd Marine Special Ops. Bn. is KIA by small arms fire in

Badghis and 1 soldier 2nd Bn. Special Inf. Reg. 173rd Airborne is KIA by small arms fire in Wardak.

Jul. 26: 2 soldiers 2nd Bn., 17th Field Art. Reg., 2nd Stryker Brg. Combat Team, 2nd Inf. Div. is KIA by a IED attack in Kandahar.

Jul. 27: 1 soldier 1st Bn., 503rd Inf. Reg., 173rd Airborne is KIA by small arms fire in Logar.

Jul. 28: 2 soldiers 630th Eng. Co., 7th Eng. Bn., 10th Sus. Brg. are KIA by small arms fire in Wardak.

Jul. 29: 2 marines 1st Marine Special OPs Bn. And 2 Marine Special OPs Bn. Are KIA by small arms fire in Badghis and 1 soldier Georgia Army National Guard is KIA by small arms fire in Helmand.

Aug. 1: 1 marine 1st Bn. 7th Marine Reg., 1st Marine Div., I Marine Expeditionary Force is KIA in Helmand. 1 Soldier 143 3rd Eng. Co., 507th Eng. Bn., 177th MP Brigade is KIA in Kandahar. 2 soldiers 1st Bn. 28th Inf. Reg., 4th Inf. Brg. Combat Team, 1st Inf. Div are KIA in Paltika. All by IED attack.

Aug. 2: 2 soldiers 1st Bn. 508th Parachute Inf. Reg., 4th Brigade Combat Team, 82nd Airborne are KIA by a IED attack in Kandahar.

Aug. 6: 1 marine 2nd Tank Bn, 2nd Marine Div., II Marine Expeditionary Force is KIA by small arms fire in Helmand.

Aug. 7: 1 sailor 1st Bn. 1st Marine Reg. Combat Team 6, 1st Marine Div., I Marine Expeditionary Force is KIA by an IED attack in Helmand and 1 soldier 1st Bn. 40th Cavalry Reg., 4th Brg. Combat Team (Airborne) 2nd Inf. Div. is KIA by small arms fire in Khost.

Aug. 8: 1 soldier 4th Bn. 3rd Special Forces Grp. (Airborne) is KIA by small arms fire in Bethesda. 3 soldiers 13th Air support Ops. Sqd. and HQ and HQ co. 4th Brg. Combat Team, 4th Inf. Div. are KIA by a suicide bomber in Kunar.

Aug. 10: 6 marines 1st Marine Special Ops Bn. And 3rd Bn. 8th Marine Reg., 2nd Marine Div., II Marine Expeditionary Force are KIA by small arms fire green on blue in Helmand.

Aug. 15: 1 soldier 2nd Bn. 25th Aviation Reg. 25th Combat Aviation Brg. 25 Inf. Div. is KIA by a IED in Ghazni.

Aug. 16: 8 soldiers explosive ordinance disposal mobile unit, Naval Special Warfare Unit, and 1st Bn. 23rd Inf. Reg. 3rd Stryker Brg. Combat Team are KIA in a helicopter crash.

Aug. 17: 1 marine and 1 Navy Corpsman 3rd Marine Special Ops. Bn. are KIA by small arms fire in Farah and 1 soldier 192nd Ordinance Bn., 52nd Ord. Grp., 20th Special Com. is KIA by small arms fire in Wardak.

Aug. 18: 1 soldier 351st. Inf. Reg, 158th Brg., 1st Army Div. East is KIA by small arms fire in Kandahar.

Aug. 22: 1 soldier 2nd Bn. 3rd Inf. Reg. 3rd Stryker Brg. Combat Team is KIA by a IED in Kandahar.

Aug. 27: 2 soldiers 4th Special Troops, 4th Brg. Combat Team, 4th Inf. Div. are KIA by small arms fire blue on green in Kalagush.

Aug. 28: 1 soldier 1st Bn. 503rd Inf. Reg. 173rd Airborne Combat Team is KIA by shrapnel in Eastern Afghanistan.

Sep. 1: 2 soldiers 192nd Ordinance Bn., 52nd Ordinance Grp., 20 support Command and 1st Bn., 1st Special Forces Group are KIA by small arms fire in Ghazni.

Sep. 3: 1 marine 1st Combat Eng. Bn., 1st Marine Div., I Marine Expeditionary Force is KIA by a IED in Helmand.

Sep. 5: 2 soldiers 1st Sqd. 17th Cavalry Reg. 82nd Combat Aviation Brg., 82nd Airborne are KIA in helicopter crash in Logar.

Sep. 13: 1 soldier 1st Bn. 503rd Infantry Reg. is KIA by small arms fire in Eastern Afghanistan.

Sep. 15: 2 marines Marine Aviation Log. Sqd. 13, Marine Aircraft Grp 13, 3rd Marine Air Wing, I Marine Expeditionary Force and Marine Attack Sqd. 211, Marine Aircraft Grp. 13, 3rd Marine Air Wing I Marine Expeditionary Force are KIA by small arms fire green on blue in Helmand.

Sep. 16: 4 soldiers 1st Bn. 23rd Inf. Reg. 3rd Stryker Brg. Combat Team, 2nd Inf. Div., 52nd Inf. Reg. 3rd Stryker Brg. Combat Team, 2nd Inf. Div., 202nd Military Intelligence Bn. 513th Inf. Brg., and 2nd Bn. 3rd. Inf. Reg. 3rd Stryker Brg. Combat Team, 2nd Inf. Div. are KIA by small arms fire in Zabul.

Sep. 20: 1 soldier 1st Bn. 64th Armor Reg., 2nd Heavy Brg. Combat Team, 3rd Inf. Div. is KIA by small arms fire in Kandahar.

Sep. 26: 2 soldiers 1st Sqd. 91st Cavalry Reg. 173rd Airborne are KIA by a suicide bomber in Logar.

Sep. 28: 1 soldier 1st Bn. 3rd Special Forces Group is KIA by small arms fire in Wardak.

Sep. 29: 1 soldier 2nd Bn., 503rd Inf. Reg. 173rd Airborne Brigade Combat Team is KIA by small arms fire green on blue in Wardak.

Oct. 1: 3 MPs 514th MP Company, 60th troop command are KIA by a suicide bomber in Khost.

Oct. 2: 1 soldier 2nd Bn. 5th Special Forces Grp. Airborne is KIA by a IED in Southern Afghanistan.

Oct. 6: 2 soldiers 1st Bn. Special Forces Bn. 3rd Special Forces Grp. Airborne are KIA by small arms fire in Wardak.

Oct. 12: 1 soldier 2nd Bn. 75th Ranger Reg. U.S. Army Special OPs Command is KIA by small arms fire in Ghazni.

Oct. 13: 2 soldiers 5th Bn. 20th Infantry Reg., 3rd Stryker Brg. Combat Team, 2nd Inf. Div. and 572nd. Military Intelligence Co. 2nd. Stryker Brg. Combat Team, 2nd Inf. Div. are KIA by a IED attack in Kandahar, and 1 soldier HQ and HQ Co. U.S. Army Special OPS Command is KIA by small arms fire in Kunduz.

Oct. 23: 1 soldier 1st Bn. 3rd Special Forces Grp. Is KIA by small arms fire in Wardak.

Oct. 25: 2 soldiers 9th Military Information Support Bn. Airborne, 8th Military Information Support Grp. and 95th Civil Affairs Bn. Airborne, 95th Civil Affairs Brg. Airborne are KIA by small arms fire green on blue in Uruzgan.

Nov. 1: 1 sailor Naval Special Warfare Unit is KIA by small arms fire in Zabul.

Nov. 3: 3 soldiers 178th Engineer Bn. 412 Theater Brg. Command are KIA by a IED attack in Paktika.

Nov. 9: 1 soldier 2nd Bn.16th Inf. Reg. 4th Brig. Combat Team. 1st Inf. Div is KIA by small arms fire in Ghazni.

Nov. 10: 1 soldier 53rd Ordnance Co., 3rd Ordnance Bn. is KIA by a IED in Kandahar.

Nov. 12: 1 soldier 1st Bn. 28th Inf. Reg. 4th Brg. Combat Team 1st Inf. Div. is KIA by small arms fire in Paktika.

Nov. 13: 1 soldier 38th Eng. Co. 4th Stryker Brg. Combat Team, 2nd Inf. Div. is KIA by hostile fire and explosion in Kandahar.

Nov. 16: 2 soldiers 1st Bn. 28th Infantry Brg., 4th Brg. Combat Team,1st Inf., Div. is KIA by an IED attack on Paktika.

Nov. 18: 1 marine Combat Logistics Bn. 2. Combat Logistics Reg. 2, 2nd Marine Logistics Grp. II Marine Expeditionary Force is KIA by a IED in Helmand.

Nov. 24: 1 sailor Naval Special Warfare Unit is KIA by hostile fire in Uruzgan.

Nov. 26: 1 marine Combat Logistics Bn. 2nd Combat Logistics Reg. 2, 2nd Marine Logistics Group, II Marine Expeditionary Force is KIA by a IED in Helmand.

Dec. 2: 1 marine 3rd Bn. 9th Marines, 2nd Marine Div., II Marine Expeditionary Force is KIA by small arms fire in Helmand.

Dec. 3: 2 soldiers 818th Engineer Co. 164th Eng Bn. are KIA by a IED attack in Helmand.

Dec. 9: 1st Class Petty officer SEAL Team 6 is KIA by small arms fire Kabul.

Dec. 10: 1 soldier 1st Bn. 38th Inf. Reg. 4th Stryker Brigade Combat Team, 2nd Inf. Div. is KIA by a IED in Kandahar.

Dec. 14: 1 soldier 56th Inf. Brigade Combat Team is IED attack in Kandahar and 1 soldier Headquarters and Headquarters Company 173rd Airborne Brigade Combat Team is KIA by small arms fire in Logar.

Dec. 24: 1 soldier Headquarters and Headquarters Detachment 173rd Special Troops Bn., 173rd Airborne Brigade is KIA in Logar.

Dec. 29: 1 soldier 38th Engineer Co., 4th Stryker Brigade Combat Team, 2nd Infantry Div. is KIA by a IED attack in Kandahar.

Dec. 30: 1 soldier Georgia National Guard is KIA from small arms in Helmand.

Iraq: U.S. Combat Chronology

2003

Mar. 19: Operation Iraqi Freedom is launched to overthrow the regime of Saddam Hussein. The initial invasion force involves 150, 000 U.S. troops.

Mar. 19: 5 teams of 20 SEALs each are inserted at the Faw oil refineries to prevent their destruction. 40 Iraqis are killed. No Americans are lost.

Mar. 21: First U.S. KIA. 2nd Lt. Therrel Shane Childers of 2nd Plt., A Co, 1st Bn, 5th Marines, 1st MD, is shot in the stomach while securing Pumping Station No. 2 at the Rumaylah oil field in southern Iraq.

Mar. 23–27: Battle of Nasiriyah. 11 army personnel, including members of the 507th Maintenance Company, are KIA during a 90-minute attack. 18 marines of C Co., 1st Bn, 2nd Marines are killed — 10 due to friendly fire from the air force A-10 and 8 solely to enemy fire. The battle rages until March 27, claiming the lives of 29 marines and soldiers.

Mar. 26: Airborne Assault in North. 1,000 paratroopers of the 173rd Abn. Bde. parachute at night to secure Harir Airfield near Bashur. Most troops are members of the 2nd Bn., 503rd PIR, and 1st Bn., 508th PIR. They go on to protect the oil fields around Mosul and Kirkuk. The 173rd suffers only 1 accidental death in the operation.

Mar. 29: War's First Fatal Suicide Bombing. 4 soldiers of the 2nd Bn., 7th IR, 3rd ID, are KIA by a car bomb at a checkpoint in central Iraq.

Mar. 31–Apr. 6: Battle of Karbala. 101st Airborne Div. and 2nd Bn., 70th Armd. Regt., 1st AD, clear the city.

Apr. 2: An army UH-60 Black Hawk helicopter is shot down in Karbala, killing 6 soldiers of the 2nd Bn., 3rd Avn. Regt.

Apr. 3–9: Battle of Baghdad. The 3rd ID and the 1st MD capture the city after several hard days of fighting. In the 3-week advance on Iraq's capital, the 3rd ID loses 34 KIA and the 1st MD sustains 24 KIAs.

Apr. 6: Battle of Debecka Pass. 2 Special Forces A-Teams (Operational Detachment Alpha 391 and 392) comprising 26 Green Berets, 3 air force combat controllers and 2 intel operators, fight a reinforced Iraqi rifle company. At the Alamo between Irbil and Makhmur, they kill up to 50 Iraqis. No U.S. casualties.

May 19: A marine CH-46 helicopter of Sqdn. 364, MAG 39, 3rd MAW, crashes into the Shat al-Hillah canal. 4 die in crash, 1 in a rescue attempt.

Sep. 29: Firefight in Khaldiyah. Enemy ambushes 2 U.S. convoys, provoking an 8-hour firefight. 82nd Airborne sustains 1 KIA.

Nov. 2: 13 KIA in Helicopter Shoot-Down. CH-47 Chinook helicopter is shot down by an SA-7 missile near Fallujah, killing 13 soldiers from 5 units.

Nov. 7: UH-60 Black Hawk helicopter is shot down by an RPG near Tikrit, killing 6 soldiers of various units.

Nov. 15: 17 KIA in Helicopter Shoot-Down. 2 Black Hawk helicopters collide in midair and crash near Mosul, killing 17 and wounding 5 soldiers of the 101st Abn. Div. 1 of the helicopters had been hit by an RPG or SA-7.

Nov. 30: Firefight in Samarra. 1st Bn., 66th Armd. Regt., 1st AD, fights a 4-hour battle with 100 enemy, killing 54. U.S. sustains 5 WIA.

Dec. 13: Operation Red Dawn. Task Force 121— CIA paramilitary forces, 40 special ops troops and 600 GIs from the 1st Bde., 4th ID —captures Saddam Hussein in Adwar, 10 miles south of Tikrit.

2004

Jan. 8: Rocket downs a UH-60 Black Hawk helicopter south of Fallujah, killing 9 members of various units.

Mar. 31: Roadside bombs kill 5 soldiers of the 1st Eng. Bn., 1st Bde., 1st ID, in Habbaniyah.

Apr. 1: 1,200 men of 2nd Bn., 1st Regt., 1st MD, assault Fallujah. Some 21 marines are killed around the city during the month and 25 more over the next 6 months.

Apr. 4: Firefight in Baghdad kills 8 soldiers—7 from 1st CD (5 in 2nd Bn., 5th Cav) and 1 from the 1st AD.

Apr. 6: Ambush in Ramadi: 11 marines are KIA—10 from E. Co., 2nd Bn., 4th Regt., 1st MD—and 30 WIA. 3rd Platoon alone loses 6 KIA (including a navy corpsman). Over 3 days, the marines kill 250 of the enemy. During the entire 5-day battle of Ramadi, the 2nd Bn. sustains 16 KIA and 100 WIA.

Apr. 9: A convoy of the 724th Trans Co. (Illinois Reserve) is attacked outside Balad, killing 8 and wounding 17 Americans. 2 soldiers and 6 civilian truck drivers are killed. Sgt. Keith M. Maupin is captured; missing for four years, his body is found in March 2008.

Apr. 10: E Co., 2nd Bn., 7th Marines, engages in a 4-hour firefight in the Sofia District of Fallujah. 4 attached snipers kill 15 enemy personnel.

Apr. 13: Firefight in Karma. 3rd Bn., 4th Marines, kills 100 Iraqis during 14 hours of fighting.

Apr. 17: Firefight at Husaybah. 4 marines of 3rd Bn., 7th Regt., 1st MD, are KIA in a day-long combat.

Apr. 24: Suicide boat (*dhow*) explosion kills 2 sailors and 1 Coast Guardsman aboard the patrol coastal boat *Firebolt* in the Arabian Gulf near the Iraqi Khawr Al Amaya oil terminal. The Coast Guardsman is the first such KIA since the Vietnam War.

Apr. 24: Mortar rounds kill 4 soldiers of the 39th Support Bn., 39th BCT (Arkansas ARNG) at their camp in Taji.

Apr. 29: Car bomb kills 8 GIs and wounds 4 of the 4th Bn., 27th FA, 1st AD, at Mahmoudiya.

May 2: Mortar attack near Ramadi kills 5 Reserve Seabees of Naval Mobile Construction Battalion 14.

Jun. 4: Roadside bombs and RPGs kill soldiers of the 2nd Bn., 162nd IR (Oregon ARNG),in Baghdad.

Jun. 17: F Trp., 4th Cav, 3rd BCT, 1st ID, engages in a 12-hour firefight near Baqubah.

Jun. 24: Battle of Baqubah. 3rd Bde., 1st ID, and A Co., 1st Bn, 120th IR, 30th Separate Bde. (North Carolina ARNG), fights a pitched 8-hour battle in city streets, killing 60 of the enemy. The 30th sustains 2 KIA and 6 WIA.

Jul. 8: Mortar attack on the Iraqi National Guard HQ in Samarra kills 5 soldiers of the 1st Bn., 26th IR, 1st ID.

Aug. 5–27: Battle of Najaf. 1st Bn., 4th Marines and three battalions from the 5th Cav, 7th Cab and 227th Avn. Regts., 1st Cav Div., evict the Mahadi Army of Muqtada al-Sadr from the "City of the Dead." Total U.S. casualties number 13 KIA and 100 WIA.

Sep. 6: Suicide bomber kills 7 marines of F Co., 2nd Bn., 1st Marines, 1st MD, traveling in a convoy near Fallujah.

Oct. 30: Car-suicide bomber hits a convoy near Fallujah, killing 8 marines of B Co., 1st Bn, 3rd Marines, 3rd MD.

Nov. 8–16: Battle for Mosul. 1st Bn., 24th Inf; 3rd Bn., 21st Inf; and 1st Bn., 5th Inf., clear city.

Nov. 8–25: Battle of Fallujah. Operation Phantom Fury involves 10,000 U.S. troops from 5 marine battalions and 2 army battalions. It is most intense urban combat for GIs since Hue in 1968. Perhaps 1,500 enemy fighters are killed in the 17-day battle. U.S. 63 KIA and 535 WIA.

Nov. 20: Battle at the Adhamiya Police Station. 3rd Plt. (26 men), C Co., 3rd Bn., 153rd Inf. Regt. (Arkansas ARNG) engage 75 insurgents at a Baghdad police post, killing at least 30. Platoon leader earns Silver Star.

Nov. 29: Executive Order 13363 establishes Iraq Campaign Medal.

Dec. 21: 14 KIA. Suicide bomber hits a mess tent at FOB Marez in Mosul, killing 13 U.S. soldiers (6 from the 25th ID) and 1 Seabee, as well as 5 civilian contractors. 42 GIs are WIA.

2005

Jan. 6: Roadside bomb in Baghdad kills 7 GIs —1 of the 69th IR (New York ARNCO and 6 from C Co., 2nd Bn., 156th IR, 256th BCT (Louisiana ARNG).

Jan. 24: 5 soldiers of the 1st ID die in a road accident when their vehicle rolls into a canal near Khan Bani Saad.

Jan. 26: War's Deadliest Single U.S. Loss. 30 marines and a navy corpsman die in an accidental CH-53E Sea Stallion helicopter crash during a sandstorm new Rurbah. 27 men are from the 1st Bn., 3rd Regt., 3rd MD, and the flight crew is from Sqdn. 361, MAG 16, 3rd MAW.

Feb. 11: . Army creates Combat Action Badge for non-infantry MOS soldiers.

Mar. 4: Roadside bomb kills 4 soldiers of the 1st Bn., 9th IR, 2nd ID, in Ramadi.

Mar. 20: A 10-soldier squad of the 617th MP Co (Kentucky ARNG) kills 27 enemy in a 25-minute firefight after their convoy is ambushed near Salman Pak.

Apr. 4: First Medal of Honor: President Bush presents Medal of Honor to the widow of Army Sgt. 1st Class Paul R. Smith for saving 100 American lives by killing 50 Iraqis on April 4, 2003. Smith belonged to B Co., 11th Eng Bn., 1st BCT, 3rd ID.

Apr. 8: Iraq Campaign Medal rules are released. It is awarded for the first time on June 29.

Apr. 26: Marines engage in a fierce house-to-house fight in the Jolan cemetery area of Fallujah.

Apr. 28: Roadside bomb kills 4 soldiers of the 25th ID and 3rd ACR in Tal Afar.

May 11: Roadside bomb kills 4 marines and wounds 10 of the 1st Plt, L Co., 3rd Bn., 25th Regt., 4th MD (MCR), in Haban on the Syrian border.

May 18–Sep. 18: Battle for Tal Afar. 3rd Armored Cavalry Regiment clears the city in a classic counterinsurgency campaign, sustaining 39 KIA.

May 23: Roadside bomb in Haswa kills 4 soldiers of C Co., 1st Bn., 155th IR (Mississippi ARNG).

Jun. 9: Roadside bomb in Haqlaniya kills 5 marines —1 of the 1st Tank Bn., 1 of 4th Tank Bn., and 3 from the 3rd Bn., 25th Marines, 4th MD (MCR Ohio).

Jun. 15: Roadside bomb near Ramadi Kills 5 marines of 1st Bn., 5th Marines, 1st MD.

Jun. 23: Suicide car bombing Fallujah kills 5 Americans —4 marines and 1 sailor.

Jul. 24: Roadside bomb in Baghdad kills 4 soldiers of 3rd Sqdn., 3rd ACR.

Jul. 24: Roadside bomb in Baghdad kills 4 soldiers of 2nd Bn., 121st IR, 48th BCT (Georgia ARNG).

Jul. 30: Roadside bomb in Baghdad kills 4 soldiers of 2nd Bn., 121st IR, 48th BCT (Georgia ARNG).

Aug. 1: 6 snipers of H&S Co., 3rd Bn., 25th Marines, 4th MD (MCR Ohio), are KIA in a firefight in Haditha.

Aug. 3: 14 KIA. Roadside bomb hits an APC in Haditha, killing 14 marines —
9 from 1st Squad., 3rd Plt., L. Co., 3rd Bn., 25 marines, 4th MD (MCR Ohio) alone.

Aug. 9: Mine and small arms in Bayji kill 4 soldiers of the 1st Bn., 111th IR,
28th ID (Pennsylvania ARNG).

Aug. 18: Roadside bomb in Samarra kills 4 soldiers of the 3rd Bn., 69th Armor,
1st BCT, 3rd ID.

Aug. 25: Roadside bomb in Husaybab kills 4 soldiers —1 Ranger and 3 Special
Forces personnel.

Sep. 19: Roadside bomb in Ramadi kills 4 soldiers —1 of the 42nd ID (New
York ARNG) and 3 of the 28th ID (Pennsylvania ARNG).

Sep. 28: Roadside bomb/ambush near Ramadi kills 5 soldiers of the 1st Bn.,
109th IR, 28th ID (Pennsylvania ARNG).

Oct. 6: Roadside bomb near Al Karmah kills 4 marines of the 2nd Bn., 2nd
Regt., 2nd MD.

Oct. 15: Roadside bomb in Ramadi kills 5 soldiers of the 2nd Bn., 69th Armor
Regt., 3rd Bde., 3rd ID.

Oct. 17: Roadside bomb in Samarra kills 6 soldiers of the 1st Bn., 15th IR, 3rd
Bde., 3rd ID.

Oct. 28: U.S. Troop Strength: 161,000.

Oct. 31: Roadside bomb in Mahmudiyah kills 4 soldiers of 2nd Bn., 502nd
IR, 2nd BCT, 101st Abn. Div.

Nov. 5–22: Euphrates Valley Campaign. Operation Steel Curtain seeks to
clear the Syrian border of foreign terrorists. It involves 2,500 U.S. troops.

Nov. 7: Car bomb in Baghdad kills 4 soldiers of the 3rd ACR.

Nov. 15: Roadside bomb in Taji kills 4 soldiers of the 1st Bn., 320th F A Regt.,
101st Abn. Div.

Nov. 15: Car bomb explodes in Ramadi, killing 5 men of the 2nd MD.

Nov. 16: Firefight at a farmhouse in Ubaydi results in 4 marines KIA and 11
WIA from 2nd Bn., 1st Marines, 13th MEU.

Nov. 19: Roadside bomb in Bayji kills 4 soldiers of the 1st Bn., 187th IR, 3rd
BCT, 101st Abn Div.

Dec. 1: Massive Booby-Trap in Fallujah. 10 marines are KIA and 11 WIA by
booby-trapped artillery shells at an abandoned flour mill after attending a pro-
motion ceremony. They belonged to 2nd Bn., 7th Marine Regt., 1st MD.

Dec. 13: Roadside bomb in Taji kills 4 soldiers of 2nd Bn., 70th Armor, 3rd
BCT, 1st ID.

2006

Jan. 5: Roadside bomb in Najaf kills 5 soldiers of the 3rd Bn., 16th FA Regt.,
2nd BCT, 4th ID.

Jan. 7: UH-60 Black Hawk helicopter accidentally crashes near Tal Afar, killing
8 soldiers of the 3rd ACR and 1st Bn., 207th Avn. Regt (Alaska ARNG). 4 U.S.
civilians also die.

Jan. 20: Roadside bomb in Huwijah kills 4 soldiers of the 1st BCT, 101st Abn. Div.—3 in the 1st Bn. 327th IR, and 1 in 1st Special Troops Battalion.

Feb. 1: Roadside bomb in Baghdad kills 3 soldiers of the 1st Bn., 327th IR, 1st BCT, 101st Abn Div.

Feb. 22: Roadside bomb near in Al Hawijah kills 4 soldiers of the 1st Bn., 8th IR, 3rd BCT, 4th ID.

Apr. 2: 6 marines — 5 of the 1st Marine Logistics Group and 1 of 3rd Marines — die in an accident when their truck rolls over in a flash flood near Al Asad.

Apr. 2: 3 marines and 1 corpsman of the 3rd Bn., 8th Marines, 2nd MD are KIA in Anbar Province.

Apr. 11: Roadside bomb in Taji kills 3 soldiers of the 7th Sqdn., 10th Cav. Regt., 1st BCT, 4th ID.

Apr. 15: Roadside bomb in Al Anbar Province kills 4 marines — 3 of the 2nd Tank Bn., MD, and 1 of the 3rd Bn., 8th Marines, 2nd MD.

Apr. 22: Roadside bomb in Baghdad kills 4 soldiers of the 1st bn., 67th Armed Regt., 2nd BCT, 4th ID.

Apr. 23: Roadside bomb in Taji kills 3 soldiers of the 7th Sqdn., 10th Can. Regt., 1st BCT, 4th MD.

May 5: Roadside bomb in Baghdad kills 3 army reservists (civil affairs) attached to the 2nd BCT, 4th ID.

May 14–15: Battle of Yusufiyah. A series of ferocious firefights kills 40 Sunni Arabs. 4 U.S. KIA — 2 of the 160th SOAR.

May 18: Roadside bomb in Baghdad kills 4 soldiers — 3 of the 2nd bn., 22nd Inf., 1st BCT, 10th MD, and 1 from the 353nd Civil Affairs Command.

Jun. 16: An ambush at a checkpoint in Yusufiyah kills 3 soldiers of the 1st Bn., 502nd Inf. Regt., 101st Abn Div. They had been abducted first.

Jun. 20: 4 marines — 2 of the 1st Bn., 1st Marines, 1st MD and 1 from the 5th Air Naval Gunfire Liaison Co — are KIA in Anbar Province.

Jul. 8: Roadside bomb in Ramadi kills 3 soldiers of the 54th Eng. Bn., 103th Eng. Bde.

Jul. 27: 4 marines — 3 of the 3rd Bn., 8th Marines, 2nd MD, and 1 of the 1st Bn., 1st Marines, 1st MD — are KIA in Anbar Province.

Aug. 6: Roadside bomb in Baghdad kills 3 soldiers of the 2nd Bde. Special Troops Bn., 2nd BCT, 101st Abr. Div.

Aug. 27: Roadside bomb in Taji kills 4 soldiers of the 1st Bn., 66th Armor, 1st Bde., 4th MD.

Sep. 14: Roadside bomb in Baghdad kills 3 soldiers — 2 of the 4th Support Bn., 1st Bde., and 1 of the 4th Bn., 27th FA, 4th ID.

Oct. 2: Roadside bomb in Taji kills 4 soldiers of the 7th Sqdn., 10th Cav, 1st Bde., 4th ID.

Oct. 8: 3 marines — 2 of the 2nd Bn., 3rd Marines, and 1 of the 3rd Bn., 12th Marines, 3rd MD — are KIA in Anbar Province.

Oct. 9: 3 marines of the 1st Bn., 6th Marines, 2nd MD, are KIA in Anbar Province.

Oct. 14: Roadside bomb in Baghdad kills 3 soldiers of the 1st Bn., 67th Armor, 2nd Bde., 4th ID.

Oct. 17: Roadside bomb in Baghdad kills 3 soldiers of the 1st Bn, 68th Armor, 3rd BCT, 4th ID.

Oct. 18: Roadside bomb in Baghdad kills 4 soldiers of the 1st Bn., 22nd Inf. Regt., 1st Bde, 4th ID.

Oct. 21: 4 marines — 3 of the 1st Bn., 6th Marines, and 1 of the 2nd Tank Bn., 2nd MD — are KIA in Anbar Province.

Nov. 2: Roadside bomb in Baghdad kills 3 soldiers — 2 of the 1st Bn., 506th IR, 4th BCT, 101st Abn. Div., and 1 of the 2nd BCT, 2nd ID.

Nov. 11: Roadside bomb in Ramadi kills 3 soldiers of the 16th Eng. Bn., 1st Bde., 1st AD.

Nov. 12–Jan. 14, 2007: Campaign in the Turki Bowl. 5th Sqdn., 73rd Cav Regt., 82nd Abn. Div., crushes the Wahabist "The Council" along the Iranian border, sustaining 22 KIA and 95 WIA and earning the Presidential Unit Citation.

Nov. 14: 3 marines of 2nd Bn., 3rd Regt., 3rd MD, are KIA in Anbar Province.

Nov. 26: Roadside bomb in Baghdad kills 3 soldiers — 2 of the 3rd Bn., 67th Armor, 4th Bde., 4th ID and 1 of 1st Bn., 8th Cav, 2nd Bde., 1st CD.

Dec. 6: Roadside bomb in Hawijah kills 5 soldiers — 4 of 2nd Bn., 27th Inf., 3rdBCT, and 1 of the 3rd Bde. Special Troops Bn., 25th ID.

Dec. 10: Roadside bomb in Baghdad kills 3 soldiers of 3rd Bn., 509th Inf., 4th BCT, 101st Abn. Div., attached to 25th Div.

Dec. 11: 3 marines of Sqdn 373, Support Grp. 37, 3rd MAW, are killed in Anbar Province.

Dec. 16: Roadside bomb in Taji kills 3 soldiers of the 1st Sqdn., 7th Cav., 1st Bde., 1st CD.

Dec. 23: Roadside bomb in Salman Pak kills 3 National Guardsmen of 1st Bn., 125th IR (Michigan NG).

Dec. 25: Roadside bomb in Baghdad kills 3 engineers of 9th Eng. Bn., 2nd BCT, 1st ID.

Dec. 28: 3 marines of 24th Regt., 4th MD (Reserve), are KIA in Anbar Province.

2007

Jan: Troop Surge. Will ultimately lead to completion of U.S. military mission in Iraq.

Jan. 15: Roadside bomb in Mosul kills 4 soldiers of the 2nd Sqdn., 7th Cav. Regt., 4th BCT, 1st CD.

Jan. 20: Roadside bomb in Karma kills 4 soldiers of the 3rd Bn., 509th Inf. Abn. Regt., 4th BCT, 25th ID.

Jan. 20: Patrol ambushed while conducting dismounted operations in Karala, killing 4 soldiers of the 2nd Bn., 377th Parachute FA Regt., 4th BCT, 25th ID.

Jan. 28–29: Battle of Zarqa. In an apocalyptic 24-hour battle at a nearby compound with 800 members of the radical cult called "Soldiers of Heaven," U.S. forces kill 256, nearly half with gunships. Participating units include Special Forces Operational Detachment Alpha 566, 512 and 513; combat controllers of the 21st Special Tactics Sqdn; Military Transition Team 0810 of the 4th BCT, 25th ID; Cos B and C of the 3rd IR, 2nd ID, 4th Bn., 227th Avn. Regt., 1st CD.; and the 352nd and 510th Expeditionary Fighter Sqdns. 2 American helicopter pilots are KIA.

Feb. 7: 5 marines of Squadron 364 and Squadron 262 are killed in a helicopter crash in Anbar Province.

Feb. 19: Battle of Tarmiyah. 2 platoons (38 men) of D Co., 2nd Bn., 8th Cav, 1st Cav Div., sustain 2 KIA and 28 WIA in a firefight in which they are outnumbered 3 to 1.

Mar. 5: Roadside bomb in Samarra kills 6 soldiers of the 2nd Bn., 505th PIR, 3rd BCT, 82nd Abn. Div.

Mar. 15: IED in Baghdad kills 4 soldiers of the 1st Sqdn., 8th Cav. Regt., 2nd BCT, 1st CD.

Mar. 17: Roadside bomb in Baghdad kills 4 soldiers of the 2nd Bn., 12th Cav. Regt., 4th BCT, 1st CD.

Mar. 25: Roadside bomb in Baghdad kills 4 soldiers of the 5th Sqdn., 73rd Cav. Regt., 3rd BCT, 82nd Abn. Div.

Apr. 1: Roadside bomb in Baghdad kills 4 GIs of 2nd Bde. Special Troops Bn., 2nd BCT, 10th Mtn. Div.

Apr. 7: IED in Zaganiyah kills 4 soldiers of the 5th Sqdn., 73rd Cav. Regt., 3rd BCT. 82nd Abn. Div.

Apr. 23: Suicide truck bombing in Sadah kills 9 soldiers of the 5th Sqdn, 73rd Cav. Regt., 3rd BCT, 82nd Abn. Div.

May 6: Roadside bomb in Baghdad kills 6 soldiers of the 5th Bn., 20th IR, 3rd Bde., 2nd ID.

May 19: Roadside bomb in Baghdad kills 6 soldiers of the 1st Bn., 5th Cav. Regt., 2nd BCT, 1st CD.

May 28: Roadside bomb in Abu Sayda kills 5 soldiers of the 6th Sqdn., 9th Cav. Regt., 3rd BCT, 1st CD.

May 30: Helicopter crash due to enemy fire in Upper Sangin Valley kills 5 soldiers of the 3rd General Support Avn. Bn., 82nd BCT, 82nd Abn. Div.

Jun. 3: Roadside bomb in Thania kills 4 soldiers of the 1st Bn., 37th FA Regt., 3rd Bde., 2nd ID.

Jun. 20: Roadside bomb in Baghdad kills 4 soldiers of the 1st Bn., 64th Armor Regt., 2nd BCT, 3rd ID.

Jun. 21: Roadside bomb in Baghdad kills 5 soldiers of the 1st Bn., 26th IR, 2nd BCT, 1st CD.

Jun. 23: Roadside bomb in Taji kills 4 soldiers of the 2nd Bn., 8th Cav. Regt., 1st BCT, 1st CD.

Jun. 28: Firefight in Baghdad kills 5 soldiers of the 2nd Bn., 12th IR, 2nd BCT, 2nd ID.

Jun. 30: Battle of Donkey Island. In an all-night fight near the village of Tash, 9 men of C Co., 1st Bn., 77th Armor Regt., kill 32 Al Qaeda out of a force of 70 at the cost of 2 U.S. KIA and 11 WIA. This firefight stops a suicide attack on Ramadi.

Jul. 6: IED in Baghdad kills 3 SEALs.

Jul. 18: Roadside bomb/small-arms fire in Adhamiya kills 4 soldiers of the 1st Bn., 26th Inf., 2nd BCT, 1st ID.

Aug. 6: IED in Baqubah kills 4 soldiers of the 1st Bn., 23rd IR, 3rd Bde., 2nd ID.

Aug. 11: IED in Arab Jabour kills 5 soldiers of the 1st Bn., 30th IR, 2nd BCT, 3rd ID.

Aug. 14: Helicopter crash in Al Taqqadum kills 5 soldiers of 1st Bn., 52nd Avn. Regt.

Aug. 22: Helicopter crash in Multaka kills 14 soldiers of the 4th Sqdn., 6th Air Cav Regt. and 2nd Bn., 35th IR, 3rd Inf. BCT, 25th ID.

Sep. 6: Roadside bomb in Anbar Province kills 4 marines of 3rd Assault Amphibian Bn., 1st MD.

Sep. 10: Vehicle rollover in Baghdad kills 7 soldiers of the 1st Sqdn., 73rd Cav Regt., 2nd BCT, 82nd Abn. Div.

Sep. 14: Roadside bomb in Mugdadiyah kills 4 soldiers of 6th Sqdn.,9th Cav., 3rd BCT, 1st CD.

October: Peak of U.S. Troop Strength: 166,000

Nov. 1: Roadside bomb in Baad kills 3 airmen of Air Force Office of Special Investigations.

Nov. 5: Roadside bomb in Tal Al-Dahab kills 4 soldiers of the 1st BCT, 10th Mtn. Div.

Dec. 25: Christmas Raid. On Christmas Day in Mosul, 18 Rangers engage in a 17-hour battle with Al Qaeda. Without losing a man, the 75th Ranger Regiment eradicates the 10-man terrorist cell, heralding an offensive against the group in northern Iraq.

2008

Jan. 9: IED in Sinsil kills 6 soldiers of the 3rd Sqdn., 2nd Cav Regt., 1st AD.

Jan. 28: Roadside bomb in Mosul kills 5 soldiers of the 1st Bn., 8th IR, 3rd BCT, 4th ID.

Feb. 5: Roadside bomb in Taji kills 4 soldiers of the 2nd BCT, 25th ID.

Mar. 10: IED in Baghdad kills 5 soldiers of the 1st Bn., 64th Armor Regt., 2nd BCT, 3rd ID.

Mar. 23: Roadside bomb in Baghdad kills 4 soldiers of the 4th Bn., 64th Armor regt., 4th BCT, 3rd ID.

May 2: Roadside bomb in Anbar Province kills 4 marines of Combat Logistics Battalion 1.

Sep. 18: Ch-47 helicopter crashes near Tallil, killing 7 Oklahoma and Texas National Guard soldiers of the 2nd Bn., 149th Avn., 36th Combat Bde.

2009

Jan. 26: OH-58D Kiowa Warrior helicopter crash in Kirkuk, killing 4 soldiers of the 6th Sqdn., 6th Cav Regt., 10th Combat Avn. Bde., 10th Mtn. Div.

Feb. 9: Roadside bomb kills 4 soldiers of 3rd Bn., 8th Cav Regt., 3rd BCT, 1st CD in Mosul.

Feb. 23: Insurgent attack in Balad kills 3 soldiers of 5th Sqdn., 1st Cav Regt., 1st Stryker BCT, 25th ID.

Apr. 10: Vehicle-borne IED in Mosul kills 5 soldiers of the 1st Bn., 67th Armor., 2nd BCT, 4th ID.

Apr. 12: Suicide bomber in Mosul kills 5 soldiers of 1st Bn., 67th Armor Regt., 4th ID.

Apr. 30: Roadside bomb kills 2 marines of 1st MD and 1 sailor of EODU 12 in Anbar Province.

May 31: IED near Baghdad kills 3 soldiers of the 252nd Combined Arms Bn. (North Carolina NG) and Missouri NG.

Jun. 29: Roadside bomb in Baghdad kills 4 soldiers of the 120th Combined Arms Bn. (North Carolina ARNG).

Jul. 16: Insurgent attack in Basra kills 3 soldiers of the 34th MP Co., 34th ID (Minnesota ARNG).

Sep. 8: IED in Baji kills 3 soldiers of the 545th MP Co., Arctic MP Bn.

2010

Jan. 23: Marine role in Iraq ends with withdrawal from Anbar Province.

Aug. 18: Last U.S. conventional combat unit—4th Bn., 9th Inf. Regt., 4th Bde., 2nd ID—leaves Iraq.

2011

Jan. 6: Rocket fire kills 5 soldiers of the 1st Bn., 7th FA, 1st ID, in Baghdad.

Jan. 29: Mortar fire kills 3 soldiers of the 2nd Sqdn., 3rd ACR in Badrah.

Nov. 14: Last U.S. KIA. Spc. David E. Hickman of 2nd Plt., B Co., 2nd Bn., 325th IR, 82nd Abn. Div., is mortally wounded by an IED while convoying from Camp Taji to Joint Security Station Muthana, outside of Baghdad.

Dec. 15: Iraq War Officially Ends. Secretary of Defense officially declares the Iraq War over at a formal ceremony in Baghdad.

Dec. 18: Last U.S. Unit Departs Iraq. 110 vehicles transporting 500 soldiers of the Special Troops Bn., 3rd Bde., 1st Cav Div., cross over the border into Kuwait at Khabari Crossing at 7:45 A.M. The 218-mile journey began at Contingency Operating Base Adder near Nasiriyah.

APPENDIX C

Statistical Tables

Iraq

U.S. combat troop deaths: 4,464 U.S. troops; 98 percent male; 91 percent non-officers; 82 percent active duty; 11 percent National Guard; 74 percent Caucasian; 9 percent African American; 11 percent Latino; 19 percent killed by non-hostile causes; 54 percent of U.S. casualties were under 25 years old; 72 percent were from the U.S. Army.

—◊◊◊—

U.S. combat troops wounded: 32,226, 20 percent of which are serious brain or spinal injuries.

—◊◊◊—

U.S. combat troops returning with serious mental health problems: 30 percent of U.S. troops develop serious mental health problems within three or four months of returning home.

—◊◊◊—

U.S. non-combat troop deaths total: 316.

—◊◊◊—

U.S. military helicopters shot down in Iraq: 75 total, at least 36 by enemy fire.

—◊◊◊—

Total U.S. Troops Killed in Iraq

	Army	*Marines*	*Navy*	*Air Force*	*Total*
Combat	2,573	851	55	29	3,508
Non-combat	719	171	40	26	956
Totals	**3,292**	**1,022**	**95**	**55**	**4,464**

U.S. Troops Combat Deaths by Year in Iraq

Year	Number	Year	Number
2003	316	2008	221
2004	713	2009	74
2005	673	2010	19
2006	704	2011	34
2007	764	**Total**	**3,518**

U.S. Troops Cause of Death in Iraq

Explosive Devices	63%
Gunshot	19%
Artillery, mortar, rocket	6%
Aircraft shoot-downs	3%
Other (RPGs, etc.)	9%

U.S. Troops Deaths by Race/Ethnicity in Iraq

White	3,337	75%
Hispanic	447	10%
Black	434	10%
Asian	83	2%
Native Hawaiian/Pacific Islander	52	1%
Other (Mixed, Unidentified)	49	1%
American Indian/Alaska Native	42	1%

U.S. Unit Casualties in Iraq, 2003–2011

1st Armored Division	133	3rd Armored Cavalry Regiment	114
82nd Airborne Division	140	1st Cavalry Division	294
3rd Infantry Division	186	101st Airborne Division	204
1st Infantry Division	221	3rd Marine Division	69
172nd Brigade Combat Team	26	1st Marine Division	472
4th Infantry Division	228	173rd Airborne Brigade	8
2nd Infantry Division	115	10th Mountain Division	142
Army National Guard	501	2nd Marine Division	302
25th Infantry Division	163	Army Special Forces	107
2nd Stryker Cavalry Regiment	50	75th Ranger Regiment	19
Navy Special Warfare	12		

Single Deadliest U.S. Losses to Enemy Action in Iraq, 2003–2011

Action—KIA	Date	Cause	Unit
Fallujah—*63*	Nov. 8–25, 2004	Battle	1st, 2nd, and 3rd Marine Division; 1st Infantry and 1st Cavalry Divisions
Baghdad—*58*	Mar.–Apr. 9, 2003	Battle	3rd Infantry and 1st Marine Divisions
Nasiriyah—*19*	Mar. 23, 2003	Battle	507th Maint. Co. & C Co. 1st Bn, 2nd Marines
Mosul—*17*	Nov. 15, 2003	Helicopter shoot-down	101st Airborne Division
FOB Marez—*14* Mosul	Dec. 21, 2004	Suicide bomber	25th Infantry and 1 Seabee in mess tent
Haditha—*14*	Aug. 3, 2005	Roadside bombs hit APC	1st Sqd, 3rd Plt., I Co. 3rd Bn, 25th Marines
Fallujah—*13*	Nov. 2, 2003	Helicopter shoot-down	F Co. 106th Aviation Bn; 2nd Bn, 5th Field Artillery Regt; Air Defense Artillery Bn; 1st Squad, 3rd Armored Cavalry; 2nd Squad, 3rd Armored Cavalry Regt.
Ramadi—*11*	Apr. 6, 2004	Ambush	E Co. 2nd Bn., 4th Regt., 1st Marine Division.
Fallujah—*10*	Dec. 1, 2005	Massive booby trap	2nd Bn., 7th Regt., 1st Marine Division.
Sadah—*9*	Apr. 23, 2007	Suicide truck bombing	5th Sqdn., 73rd Cav. Regt., 82nd Abn. Division.
Fallujah—*9*	Jan. 8, 2004	Helicopter shoot-down	571st Medical Co; 603rd Transportation Co; 142nd Comps Support Bn; D Co., 82nd Support Bn; 82nd Airborne Division; B Co. 1st Bn., 9th Cavalry Regt, 1st Cavalry Division; C Co., 782nd Main Support Bn., 82nd Airborne Division; C Co. 1st Squad 17th Cavalry Regt, 82nd Airborne Division.

Afghanistan

Total U.S. Troops Killed in Afghanistan

	Army	Marines	Navy	Air Force	Totals
Hostile	994	331	67	46	1,438
Non-Hostile	249	59	29	30	367
Totals	**1,243**	**390**	**96**	**76**	**1,805**

—∿∿—

U.S. Troops Combat Deaths by Year in Afghanistan

Year	Number	Year	Number
2001	3	2007	83
2002	18	2008	132
2003	17	2009	271
2004	25	2010	437
2005	66	2011	301
2006	65	**Totals**	**1,418**

—∿∿—

U.S. Troops Killed by Component

Active Duty	1,014	351	92	72	1,529
National Guard	170	N/A	N/A	2	172
Reserve	59	19	4	2	84
Totals	**1,243**	**370**	**96**	**76**	**1,785**

—∿∿—

U.S. Troops Wounded in Action in Afghanistan

	Army	Navy	Marines	Air Force	Totals
Active Duty	8,055	263	3,826	286	12,430
National Guard	1,303	N/A	N/A	24	1,327
Reserve	352	16	210	7	585
Totals	**9,710**	**279**	**4,036**	**317**	**14,342**

—∿∿—

U.S. Unit Casualties in Afghanistan, 2001–2011

1st Infantry Division	71	75th Ranger Regiment	39
1st Marine Division	123	82nd Airborne Division	69
2nd Infantry Division	37	101st Airborne Division	150
2nd Marine Division	140	160 Special Ops Aviation	
2nd Stryker Cavalry Regiment	17	Regiment	22
3rd Marine Division	36	173rd Airborne Brigade	69
4th Infantry Division	56	Army National Guard	170
10th Mountain Division	150	Army Special Forces Groups	93
25th Infantry Division	58	Navy Special Warfare	49

—∿∿—

Single Deadliest U.S. Losses to Enemy Action in Afghanistan, 2001–2011

Action—KIA	Date	Cause	Unit
Tangi Valley—*30*	Aug. 6, 2011	Helicopter shoot-down	SEALs 24th STS, Army Aviators
Operation Red Wing—*19*	Jun. 28, 2005	Helicopter shoot-down	SEAL Team 10, Delivery Team 1, 160th Special Operations Avn, Regt.
Wanat-VPB Kahler—*9*	Jul. 13, 2008	Assault on base	2nd Plt. C. Co., 2nd Bn., 503rd IR, 173rd ABCT
COP Keating—*8*	Oct. 3, 2009	Assault on outpost	3rd Sqdn., 61st Cav Regt., 4th ID
Kabul International—*8*	Apr. 27, 2011	Murder	Airmen from various units by Afghan air officer
Shorabak District—*8*	May 26, 2011	Roadside bomb	4th Bn., 101st Avn., Regt., 159th CAB. 101st Div., and 2 Air Force EOD techs.
Takur Ghar/ Roberts Ridge—*7*	Mar. 4, 2002	Firefight	5 special operations Units
Arghandab Valley—*7*	Oct. 27, 2009	Roadside bomb	C Co., 1st Bn., 17th IR, 2nd ID
Aranus—*6*	Nov. 9, 2007	Ambush	2nd Bn., 503rd IR, 173rd Abn., Bde., & 1 Marines.
Jalalabad—*6*	Nov. 29, 2010	Murder by Afghan policeman	1st Sqdn., 61st Cav Regt., 101st Airborne
Zahari—*6*	Dec. 12, 2010	Suicide vehicle	B Co., 2nd Bn., 502nd IR, 101st Airborne.
Barawolo/Kalay/ Sarobay—*6*	Mar. 29, 2011	Firefight	2nd Bn., 327th IR, 101st Airborne

Index